T0321237

TRADITIONAL NAVAJO TEACHINGS
A TRILOGY
VOLUME III

The Earth Surface People

Robert S. McPherson and Perry Juan Robinson

Robert S. McPherson is Professor of History Emeritus at Utah State University—Blanding Campus and author of numerous books about the history and cultures of the Four Corners Region.

Perry Juan Robinson is from the highly traditional area of Piñon, Black Mesa, Arizona, with a strong family heritage of practicing medicine people. He has been a member of the Navajo Nation Medicine Men Association for over twenty years and continues to work as a hataałii.

Cover Art: Charles Yanito
Cover Design: Chris Monson
Interior Design: Chris Monson and Kerin Tate
Map Design: Erin Greb
Copyediting and Indexing: Kerin Tate

Other books of related interest by the author:
Traders, Agents, and Weavers: Developing the Northern Navajo Region
    (University of Oklahoma Press)
Both Sides of the Bullpen: Navajo Trade and Posts of the Upper Four Corners
    (University of Oklahoma Press)
Viewing the Ancestors: Perceptions of the Anaasazi, Mokwič, and Hisatsinom
    (University of Oklahoma Press)
Under the Eagle: Samuel Holiday, Navajo Code Talker
    (University of Oklahoma Press)
Dineji Na'nitin: Navajo Traditional Teachings and History
    (University Press of Colorado)
Navajo Tradition, Mormon Life: The Autobiography and Teachings of Jim Dandy
    (University of Utah Press)
Along Navajo Trails: Recollections of a Trader, 1898-1948
    (Utah State University Press)
A Navajo Legacy: The Life and Teachings of John Holiday
    (University of Oklahoma Press)
Navajo Land, Navajo Culture: The Utah Experience in the Twentieth Century
    (University of Oklahoma Press)
The Journey of Navajo Oshley: An Autobiography and Life History
    (Utah State University Press)
Sacred Land, Sacred View: Navajo Perceptions of the Four Corners Region
    (University Press of Colorado)
The Northern Navajo Frontier, 1860-1900: Expansion through Adversity
    (University of New Mexico Press)

Copyright © 2020 Robert S. McPherson
Printed in the United States of America
ISBN 9781646424917
All rights reserved.

Contents

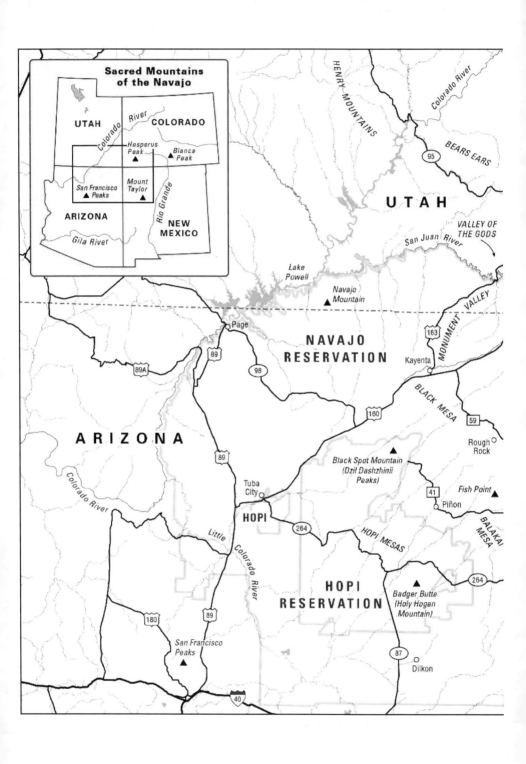

Sacred Mountains of the Navajo

UTAH

COLORADO

Colorado River

Hesperus
Peak ▲

Blanca
Peak ▲

San Francisco
▲ Peaks

Mount
Taylor ▲

Rio Grande

ARIZONA

NEW
MEXICO

Gila River

HENRY MOUNTAINS

Colorado River

BEARS EARS

95

UTAH

VALLEY OF
THE GODS

San Juan River

MONUMENT VALLEY

Lake
Powell

Navajo
▲ Mountain

Page

163

NAVAJO
RESERVATION

Kayenta

89

89A

98

BLACK MESA

160

59

ARIZONA

89

Rough
Rock

Black Spot Mountain
(Dził Dashzhinii
Peaks)

41

Fish Point

Piñon

Colorado River

Tuba
City

HOPI

264

HOPI MESAS

BALAKAI MESA

Little

Colorado River

HOPI
RESERVATION

Badger Butte
(Holy Hogan
Mountain)

264

180

89

San Francisco
Peaks
▲

87

Dilkon

40

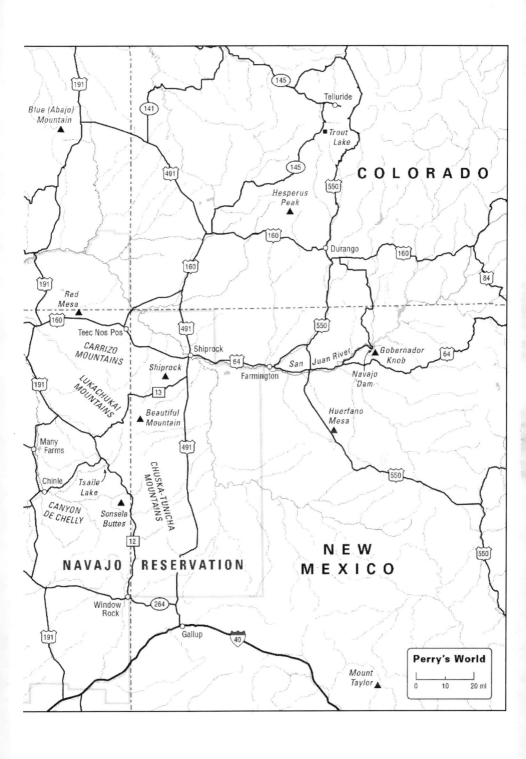

INTRODUCTION

On Being the Earth Surface People

Most of the planning and work was finished. The holy people (Diyin Dine'é) had put in motion many of the creatures, much of the physical landscape, and most of the patterns by which these beings would be known and would function. Everything operated through relationships and specified responsibilities based on respect. There was still more to do; most important, the holy beings needed to create the earth surface (nihookáá' dine'é) or five-fingered (bíla'ashdla'ii) people. White Shell Woman/Changing Woman, Talking God, and Calling God took the lead at a council of all the holy ones at Blanca Peak to decide exactly how this should take place. White Shell Woman knew what to do. Taking four white baskets and four turquoise baskets, she placed matching sets in each of the four directions—the white for the creation of males, the blue for that of females. In these containers, she placed dew from the earth, pollen from the plants, and sweet cornmeal cake, then covered the baskets and sang three songs. Next, she invited Talking God to blow upon the baskets from all four sides, moving them with his breath as he sang, after which Calling God did the same. This gave life to the contents.

Young men and young women emerged from their respective birth places and received the fine fabric and jewels White Shell Woman laid before them. She performed more songs and prayers and blessed these newly created five-fingered people before assigning them to live upon the earth's surface. She instructed: "You must continue to stay here and do your best. You will speak for us with pollen words. You will call for us with pollen words. You will not think evil about us, you will not speak evil about us, because I made you my children, I dressed you with corn pollen, because I dressed you with dews. . . . I made you, my children, so you will speak

1

wisely with pollen within your mouth. There will be blessings extending all around you." Next, she directed male and female pairs to the four directions as the holy people departed to those same locations; all was accompanied with song and prayers. Earth life for humans had begun.[1]

While there are a number of different versions about how White Shell Woman formed the Navajo, they all share three major teachings—White Shell Woman and other holy people were the creators; these earth surface beings held responsibilities placed upon them by the gods; and they were to follow a divinely inspired pattern that would bring them long life and happiness. The two previous volumes in this trilogy established the basis upon which Navajo traditional teachings are founded. The first discusses the role of the medicine man and how he connects with the holy people in assisting to heal the sick and counsel the afflicted. The second volume examines—from stars in the heavens to moles in the ground—the physical world and its relationship with the inner forms holding supernatural power. This final work looks at the divine pattern established by the holy people by which the earth surface beings are to live. As taught through a multiplicity of means, life is circumscribed with sacred responsibilities and ways to act.

Defining Traditional Navajo Values

Navajos, who follow traditional practices today, are a distinct people, a point that many take pride in. Genetic makeup, historic circumstance, and cultural teaching make this so. As mentioned previously, there are a variety of traditional activities and beliefs for practitioners, stretching in a long continuum from those who do not embrace the teachings and responsibilities outlined by the holy beings to those who are highly traditional and seek to perpetuate their cultural heritage through thought, language, and action. Not all of the 350,000-plus people identified in the Navajo Nation's 2016 Census would place themselves in the latter category.[2] When discussing group behavior or values, it does not take long before someone points out that they do not agree and that what is being described is patently false. Others will have different views that mix and match with what they consider acceptable. To meet this challenge of describing a culture's beliefs, anthropologists create a "modal personality" by which the frequency of a characteristic is mathematically measured to see how common it is within the entire group. While no statistical evaluation is offered here, it is important to note that when Perry, as a medicine man, speaks of "the Navajo" doing or saying something, he is usually referring to those oriented toward the end of the traditional spectrum. Not all Navajos follow the practices he describes.

This book is about those who do. This introduction establishes what those people consider important when following cultural practices and patterns established by the holy beings. A number of people—inside and outside of the tribe—have described what they believe to be a fair representation of a "typical" traditional Navajo personality of say the 1930s, by focusing on aspects that seem to encapsulate what it means to be an earth surface being. This includes what tribal members think and how they describe themselves. There is no definitive answer as to what comprises a "Navajo personality," but a foundational understanding of many of its important elements are offered here in preparation for what Perry discusses in ensuing chapters.

In formulating an explanation of Navajo values (ejit'į), it is important to remove as much outside influence as possible. Many interviews with Navajos revolve around discussions that are driven according to the questions of the interviewer, which may or may not reflect the concerns of the interviewee. Perhaps one of the most wide-ranging and inclusive evaluations of the Navajo personality was a four-year (1949–53) study conducted by a host of anthropologists and researchers from different disciplines in the Ramah-Zuni (pseudonym Rimrock) area of New Mexico. The goal was to study cultural values of five distinct groups—Navajo, Zunis, Spanish-Americans, Mormons (Latter-day Saints), and Texans. The various teams performing the research gathered a great deal of valuable information resulting in a host of publications, including a general summation entitled *People of Rimrock: A Study of Values in Five Cultures*, written for the nonspecialist.[3] From kinship to religion, political structure to ecology, the reports provided by different disciplines tackled what it meant to belong to a particular cultural group. Many of the findings came from the people under investigation who provided an insider view, but there was also the surface veneer of academia that sometimes covered the voice of the people and perhaps skewed some of the findings.

In 1945 Clyde Kluckhohn addressed this problem head-on. Noting that fellow anthropologists were often guilty of not letting their interviewees identify their own cultural concerns, Kluckhohn selected a previous interview in which he had remained quiet and allowed a Navajo man, Mr. Mustache (Hastiin Dághaa'), to tell his life story without interruption. The sixty-eight-year-old, at the time of the interview (1936), had recollections hearkening back to when the military released the Navajos from Fort Sumner (1868).[4] Without prompting, he summarized his life history, later reproduced without alterations in a journal article, providing for Kluckhohn what he considered the most genuine, spontaneous interview he had yet conducted as an ethnologist. Careful not to overstress the conclusions drawn from the material, the interviewer, nevertheless, felt it was an untainted glimpse into the Navajo worldview. Another source derived from a similar approach of just letting the person tell his own story without interference is that of *The Journey of Navajo Oshley*, a full-length book, which, with the exception of the last three chapters, was his own account of his life.[5] From these two works will come examples of the Navajo values under discussion.

Directing Life, Achieving Success

What then frames the Navajo worldview as organized by the holy people? What is important, how should one act, and what values dominate traditional practices? Equally significant, how does this translate into daily life? This book suggests answers to these questions based on what Navajos determine is important and how they achieve a desirable outcome. Starting with the most basic premise, "Who is a Navajo or Diné (people)?" there are two categories that quickly diverge—the holy people and the earth surface beings (humans). A second split occurs between the Navajo and the non-Navajo (ana'í) or foreigners; subsequent branches within the Navajo category are based around the sixty different clans that comprise the tribe.[6] Central to all interaction—whether human or not—is the concept of having a positive relationship (k'é). Navajo language specifies further if that relationship is between someone who is related to the speaker as a kinsman or kinswoman through descent (ak'éí) or merely by acquaintance (k'é). As Gary Witherspoon points out, "All categories of descent are discussed in terms of how one is born. A Navajo is born by and of his mother and her clan; he is born for his father's clan."[7] The importance of this link through motherhood is discussed in chapter 2.

On an individual level, a person who is self-directed down a path of spiritual discovery established by the holy people is told that "Only by strong personal motivation will one achieve an admirable life (Táá hó ájít'éehgo jiináa łeh)." In a less formal sense, this means that living in the best tradition of what the holy people established takes determination—life is not easy. The Navajo origin myth, which is a primary source of traditional teachings and behavior, is replete with examples taken from the mythic past that are reenacted in present behavior. For those wishing to pursue this further, read Katherine Spencer's *Reflection of Social Life in the Navaho Origin Myth* in which she examines twenty-three versions of the narrative—some short, others long.[8] From them she draws the patterns derived from first events such as practices in economy and division of labor, courtship and marriage, birth and puberty ceremonies, food taboos and attitudes toward animals. It is a thorough work that identifies many of the practices found in traditional

Navajo life today. Just how dependent Navajo people are on knowing the derivation of the teachings they follow is questionable, but there is no doubt that certain activities are considered the appropriate or Navajo way. The mythic source does, however, provide necessary knowledge and patterns for the medicine people and others concerned as to why a particular practice exists.

The uncensored life stories of Mustache and Oshley follow some very close parallels. While the former took approximately six pages of a journal article to describe his life and the latter about 160 pages of a book, both men spent a large majority of that time discussing their work and economic concerns. Beginning as a child and progressing through adulthood, securing a livelihood was paramount. Mustache recalled how poor his family was as he grew up: "In the old days we didn't have much food. We were often hungry. We didn't have any clothes—just rags around our bodies. We didn't have sheep. We hunted deer and other animals. We dug up wild potatoes. The women used to dig these up all day, then they'd boil them. Sometimes we even ate dirt."[9] Compare this to Oshley:

> As I remember, I did not have any shoes, and my pants were a horror to see. They had holes and were too short. The fabric in my shirt was from a flour sack, but where my relatives got it I do not know. I did not have a hat so I used a piece of rope or cloth tied together. . . . Sometimes there was little food so we would have just a few mouthfuls to eat before we went to sleep. In the morning we would drink milk and then go without food the rest of the day. . . . Life was hard when I was growing up."[10]

Little wonder that approximately two-thirds of his life history is spent chasing economic means or traveling to obtain them.

After pointing out that Mustache's autobiography started and ended with making a living, Kluckhohn suggested that his informant "never escapes very long from a realization of uneasy dependence upon the natural environment for his very existence."[11] The same is true not only for Oshley, but also Navajo women before and during this same first half of the twentieth century. A quick perusal of Tall Woman's account by Charlotte Frisbie and Kay Bennett's *Kaibah* testify to that.[12]

This becomes the jumping-off point for a study of Navajo values. In 1954 Richard Hobson, part of the Rimrock Project, published an important study called *Navajo Acquisitive Values*.[13] In it, the author identifies eight qualities of action that explain how a good Navajo person should be. They are a summation of 335 statements given by seventy-seven informants over a fifteen-year period. Their responses led Hobson to conclude, "The desire to accumulate wealth is perhaps stronger among the Navajos than among most other similar groups."[14] There will be subsequent qualifications to this statement, showing that certain aspects of this materialism take a very different form than that of Anglos; Hobson provides eight phrases that encapsulate important Navajo values.

"Make a good living" is a cardinal rule. Mustache's earliest experiences taught him what it was like to go without. As he grew and became aware of what it would mean to care for not only himself, but a family, the teachings that he received from his relatives, particularly his father, weighed heavily on his mind: "I've obeyed my father. That's why I've gotten on so well. If I hadn't minded my father and mother, I'd be without anything. I'd go broke all the time—no shoes, blankets, sheep, horses. I've told my son the same thing." Learning how to do this is an important quest in life. Knowledge—whether caring for livestock, weaving a rug, growing a garden, curing with herbs, or conducting a ceremony—provides a living that both economically and socially raises an individual and family out of poverty into a more comfortable existence. Oshley had an excellent reputation for herding and caring for sheep. He learned at a young age how to best care for the animals, and so both Anglo and Navajo livestock owners sought after him to care for their animals, often receiving higher pay than other herders. He was a trusted professional who always found work when needed. Even the traders at various posts would extend credit to him without having to pawn valuables—his word was his collateral.[15] Being accomplished at what he did provided a good living.

"Work hard and don't be lazy." Hobson is quick to point out that Navajos faced challenging personal and familial tasks necessary for survival. Consequently, there is often a deep sense of responsibility for taking care of themselves and their family members—"Look after your family." Laziness is unacceptable. Mustache, at an early age, received the responsibility of caring for the family's flocks. When it was not done right, his father spanked him and scared the boy into following the correct procedures. Stern counsel and strict behavioral guidelines were enforced as preparation for hard times in the future. "My father said not to sleep too long. Get up early and run a race. That way be stronger. If you sleep until sun-up, you'll never get anything good—sheep or horses. Be poor all the time. I had to work all of the time. My father made me. He didn't want to let me fool around. That way I'd never get lazy." Oshley had similar experiences; his life was filled with constant toil. When he was not caring for livestock, he was harvesting and storing corn for his mother, picking piñons for sale, sheering wool, building hogans, assisting in ceremonies, and traveling—often running—to places miles apart. There was nothing lazy about his lifestyle. The women he associated with were just as industrious, sitting at their looms for hours at a time, growing and preparing food, and wrangling livestock. Living on the edge left little time for play.

Three of Hobson's formulas seem to be at odds with each other: "Have lots of property," "Don't be too rich," and "Never get poor." All of these need to be qualified. Navajos often pray for wealth to come their way. This is especially true in ceremonies where frequent mention of "hard goods" and "soft goods," previously discussed, is found in the prayers, explained in the teachings, symbolized in the door structures of the hogan, replicated in the gate posts of the corral, and assigned to specific mountain ranges on the reservation. A family's reputation is often determined by the size of their herds and flocks, how well they are cared for, how a person dresses, the jewelry they have, the knowledge of their ceremonial practitioners, and the horses or cars used for travel. Public opinion was a powerful force in determining status. Mustache said his father cautioned, "Take care of yourself. Have good horses, bridles, and saddle blankets so that you can go anywhere, to a sing without being ashamed. Without good clothes, you couldn't go anywhere where there were a lot of people. Might get ashamed where they had good times." To his credit, Mustache "never got poor" and "could go anyplace."[16]

On the other end of the social spectrum, "getting poor" is followed by ostracism and loss of respect. Mustache minded his mother and father and avoided the stigma of being unwise. "I never got poor. . . . That is why I don't try to touch bad things. I never think about bad business. I don't like it. I know now my father was right. Sometime people go wrong." A prime example of what happens when one does "go wrong" is given by Oshley. Up to a certain point in life, he had been a successful person with a good horse, saddle, bridle, two fine saddle blankets, leather chaps, and a finely woven sleeping blanket given by his mother. Following a week of gambling with other Navajos in Blanding, Utah, he had lost it all. The feelings his actions generated, having "gotten poor," are instructive.

> I felt depressed because of my actions. This made me ask myself why I did this. . . . I kept thinking about it. . . . My older brother and the rest of my relatives had heard of my misfortune. They heard that I was somewhat of a hobo in Blanding and that I was living off other people. These stories about me were not good ones. . . . Some of my [relatives] were really hurt by these stories. One of my great uncles said that when they talked about one of his offspring like that, they were laughing at him. . . . I had never thought that I would be poor.[17]

Even the trader in the Mexican Water Trading Post warned that people were laughing at his misfortune. Still there were others who had compassion and eventually helped Oshley to get back on his feet and regain his good reputation.

The last two categories Hobson provides are interdependent. The first, "Don't be too rich" seems antithetical to what has just been said. Anthropologists discussing Navajo behavior often mention "leveling mechanisms" within the culture that try to maintain everyone on an even economic plain. To be too rich or too poor could lead to jealousy, accusations of witchcraft, and unfair practices, on one hand, as well as the belief that the underdog is angry and seeking revenge against that wealthy person. This is true not only of material wealth, but also of social standing—those in public office, ceremonial practitioners, and families that just seem to be "ahead" or more fortunate than others in the community. For those wishing to pursue this topic, see Clyde Kluckhohn's classic *Navaho Witchcraft*.[18]

The fact that there were some extremely wealthy Navajo men and powerful ceremonial leaders raises the question about the reality of maintaining social and financial equilibrium, which brings us to the final quality, "Help people out." In Navajo culture, generosity is an important quality for good while stinginess is maligned. Assisting family members is particularly important and expected. Kluckhohn, in his evaluation of Mustache's social standing, arrives at an interesting conclusion that balances wealth and poverty, ceremonial practices and social status. After interviewing more than fifty men and women, asking who they felt were the most highly respected Navajos in their community, the same top five or six were on everyone's list. Those who were either very wealthy or poor did not make the cut. Mr. Mustache, however, was on each one except his own. Generosity or "helping people out" was the key to being accepted. Kluckhohn points out, "The present chief and Mr. Mustache, the former chief, both fall into the lowest economic quarter. And both word and deed make it absolutely certain that their prestige is of the very highest. Of the three singers, two fell into the lowest economic quarter, one into the quarter next to the bottom. Singers receive fees which, in terms of the culture's standards, are excellent. But the cultural ideology also demands that they make many gifts and be unusually liberal in their hospitality."[19] Whereas wealth in Anglo society opens doors to power and influence, generosity with what one has is far more important in Navajo culture.

Kluckhohn raises one final issue in his article. Given that he had interviewed so many people, he was surprised that there was not nearly as much discussion about the ceremonies as he had expected. His data indicated that one in four "productive days" was spent in ritual activity, and yet little was mentioned about it. One of their primary motivations for economic wealth was to perform or participate in these frequent and often expensive gatherings. The generosity just discussed was a major reason to accumulate wealth while also easing tension from jealousy. Why not more discussion of the ceremonies? The anthropologist felt that the economic concerns were more concrete, while those associated with ceremonialism were "mainly to maintain the society's equilibrium *vis á vis* nature, by controlling the supernatural."[20] More simply put, economic concerns control activities in the physical world, while ceremonies maintain balance in the spiritual world even though both are interdependent.

In the two previous volumes, many qualities, characteristics, and teachings have already been discussed and so will be quickly referenced here. For example—the tenet that everything has a male and female part; that good and evil are derived from the same power, it is all a matter of how it is used; part of an object can represent the whole, such as a lock of hair standing for an individual; words have power to literally affect the physical and spiritual world; and respect for everything, seen or unseen, is the way that peace and health are maintained—are all part of the Navajo worldview. Other important concepts include a view of life, the seasons, and time as cyclical occurrences rather than a linear chronology; the importance of past events to produce a pattern for action rather than hope for future occurrences; the belief that harmony and peace are derived from order while evil is characterized as chaos; and the power of language to both create and destroy physically and spiritually. Many of these points are expressed within the various stages of life and ritual activities in the following chapters.

Life Is for Learning

What then, does it mean to be an earth surface being, and how does one learn the implied role of being a male or female at any given stage of life? From birth to death, an individual has cultural expectations taught by the family, peers, the community at large, and the tribe. Who is a traditional Navajo, how is this way of life learned, and why are these values taught in a particular way? As in every culture, there are underlying assumptions at work to guide an individual down a particular path. The success or failure of a person to find and stay on this track is affected by a variety of influences starting with one's inclination and personality, the effectiveness of the family, the involvement of the community, and the world at large. No one is perfect, but if an ultimate idealized goal were to be attained, it would be expressed through the oft discussed phrase of "sa'ąh naagháii bik'eh hózhǫ," glossed as "long life and happiness/harmony." This teaching is filled with significant cultural meaning and instruction. Further discussion follows in chapter 7, but for now, the question remains of how this long-term goal is taught and implemented in daily life under ideal circumstances.

The Navajo people have built in to their social mores a number of practices that encourage a harmonious approach to life. The mere acquisition and use of knowledge here are different from that of the dominant culture's use even though each places a high value on them. Obtaining it is good if it is used to help others, but if selfish motives become the reason, then the privilege of having it is abused. Maturity is important. Until one shows a real interest in learning a particular type of information, one cannot be sure how that teaching will be employed. Children have no place in asking questions or learning about things that they cannot appreciate, understand, or might misuse. Information is provided when both the giver and receiver are prepared. This is particularly true with ceremonial knowledge, since the holy people are very aware of how their teachings are shared and their power is bestowed. To learn this knowledge incorrectly or incompletely angers the gods who have shared with man a sacred trust. A classic example of this belief is found in the stories about the Anasazi (Ancestral Puebloans), who from the Navajo perspective were a gifted people endowed with great supernatural powers but abused them. Through lack of respect, greed, and profaning of the sacred, the Puebloans compromised this relationship and respect and so were destroyed.[21]

Learning through observation as opposed to intense direct instruction is another cultural expectation. Take for instance a young girl who wants to learn how to weave. Rather than bombarding her mother with endless questions from start to finish, she will spend time just watching from the sidelines. Once she is ready to try her hand—and she is the one who determines when that is—she will get some basic assistance from her mother, who then leaves her alone to learn the art. Suggestions and advice are given along the way, but the child takes on most of the responsibility for creating the end product, which may be a small rug or saddle blanket. She had waited until she understood the process and then did it slowly but correctly the first time. The same is true with boys learning tasks that they will depend on later in life. If one of the goals is to become a medicine man, then months and years of apprenticeship are often necessary before launching into the first performance. Detail in understanding both the ritual and the teaching from which it comes are equally important in getting every aspect of the ceremony right.

Educators have written extensively about Native American learning characteristics. All humans learn through either the three basic modes—visual, auditory, or physical—or the seven—adding verbal, logical, social, and solitary. Cultures, like individuals, often stress one or two of these qualities over the others. Robert W. Rhodes, an educator who has spent well over twenty years studying Navajo and Hopi learning practices, provides a lengthy list of how these people's learning differs from those promoted in Anglo society. In *Nurturing Learning in Native American Students*, he shares qualities found prominent in Navajo culture.[22] For instance, the welfare of the group is paramount over individuality and personal success. Cooperation and generosity, especially among family members, are highly desirable traits. Everyone is expected to share and support individual, family, and community efforts by lending assistance in its many forms depending upon the occasion. Refusing to do so puts a person at odds with, and sometimes outside of, the group.

Since wealth accumulation or extensive ceremonial knowledge may lay an individual open for accusations of antisocial behavior, a Navajo person may subordinate achievement and recognition in order not to appear more powerful or "better" than others. Still, each person needs to decide what is best. While a community often has a spokesman, a revered elder, or an elected official (naat'áanii—boss, chief, headman), his or her responsibility is to convince, through persuasion, what they believe the group should do. Ideally, consensus is reached, and the group enacts the plan; in reality, conflict and social pressure can force some to abandon a particular direction in favor of personal or extended family wishes. No one should be coerced, but powers—social, supernatural, or physical—may still be brought to bear to secure an outcome.

Many of the qualities and characteristics mentioned in this introduction will become apparent in the following pages. Chapter 1 takes the reader from a baby's prenatal experience through the birthing process to the naming of the child and its First Laugh ceremony. These are beginning steps taken on the path of an earth surface being. The next two chapters discuss the important spiritual, social, and economic teachings for a girl and boy upon reaching maturity (puberty) and receiving the tools they will need to prosper. Intense instruction given by respected adults ingrains traditional Navajo beliefs that will carry these youths through major events of their future life. Just as the roles of a man and woman are specified in these chapters, the division between the sexes is clearly defined in the next one, covering marriage and sexuality. Even during the wedding ceremony, the division of space in the hogan, the division of labor in daily tasks, the division of social responsibilities, and the use of gender-specific tools are discussed. Soon children will appear, and the process of enculturation begins in earnest for them, a responsibility that rests on the shoulders of the parents. But others will be involved, as discussed in chapter 5, where the role of extended family and clan members broadens the world of the nuclear family and places significant responsibilities on those kin willing to assist. Navajo culture specifies exactly what those roles look like and what should or should not be done, including discipline and instruction down to joking relationships.

The second half of the book shifts emphasis onto health and end-of-life issues. Chapter 6 examines how medicine people think about the body and how to cure its ailments. Teachings concerning the seven points of healing, the head, hands, and the types of sickness that afflict individuals provide insight into how a body functions and why different ceremonies are performed. There is often a large gap between Navajo beliefs and western medical practices, the topic of the next chapter. Today, more than ever before, new issues arise due to advances in western medicine that challenge traditional teachings about the body and its inner being. Health concerns about abortion, CPR, blood transfusions, and x-rays are placed within a Navajo context and suggest ways that these practices have affected, and are at times integrated into, cultural beliefs. Eventually, the end of the life path is reached on what is called the Old People's Road. Age has taken its toll, and whether a person has lived a full life, defined by the Navajo as 102 years old, or has been cut short, death will greet them. The spirit world, extensively described by Father Berard Haile, is added to the teachings that Perry offers for this last stage of life as an earth surface being. The concluding chapter summarizes the information discussed in this trilogy and looks at some final thoughts on contemporary illness—the hantavirus and the COVID-19 (coronavirus) pandemic—as they have played out in Navajo thought and traditional teachings.

As in all three volumes of this trilogy, each chapter has two parts. First is the chapter introduction that I have written, followed by the bulk of the chapter by Perry, which I have transcribed from interviews, organized, and edited. The change in author voice is noticeable, but we have placed a divider to visually separate the two texts. The introductory material provides supplementary information and sources for further reading. It also mentions differing views, as Navajo traditions, teachings, and stories can vary and may be at odds with information shared in other accounts.

While each book in this series is written to stand alone, having its own area of specialty—sacred narratives and their connection to ceremonies, the physical world seen through traditional eyes, the life stages of a Navajo— there are also a tremendous number of shared, interdependent values. The Navajo approach life holistically. In this final volume, one finds the culmination of the two preceding works—how the holy people designed and created a world that is helpful and accessible to those who practice traditional teachings.

CHAPTER ONE

Entering This World

From First Cry to First Laugh

E ven before first breath, entering into this world as a Navajo person is filled with cultural significance. What it means to be one of the People is emphasized in the preparation for, the arrival of, and the initial care given a newborn. Mother and father, fire (light) and water, earth and air (spirit) come together in paired duality to form the child. Male and female begin this creative bond that not only enriches the Navajo Nation, but sets in motion a series of patterns established by the holy people at the beginning of time. The conditions and teachings of what this means and the potential of what this baby may become are the topics of this chapter. Perry's insight, drawn from years of service as a medicine man, emphasizes the importance of this creative process.

Navajo women are taught at an early age that while men can take care of themselves, the mother's role in life centers on her children. One of the supreme metaphors in this culture's worldview—whether talking about Mother Earth, motherhood, livestock, the mountain soil bundle, or any other element that nurtures and brings forth life—is that of females as caregivers. Gary Witherspoon in *Navajo Kinship and Marriage* explains, "The symbols of motherhood are based on the source, reproduction, and sustenance of life, and these symbols are imbued with powerful meanings in terms of solidarity. Mother and child are bound together by the most intense, the most diffuse, and the most enduring solidarity to be found in Navajo culture."[1] A woman dedicates her life to the life she has brought forth.

This becomes apparent when looking at Tall Woman's experience (1874–1977). She grew up in a family of twelve children, had a dozen of her own, and served as a midwife for extended family and neighbors for decades. Times were harsh. Her mother, a veteran herself in midwifery and raising children, wanted her daughter to understand the responsibilities and challenges of assuming these roles. One day Tall Woman was at work in the family hogan carding wool when her mother sat beside her to spin. The now close-to-one-hundred-year-old woman recalled, "She talked to me some more about being married and raising children. She said I'd learn it was hard and that many hardships would come along. She said I would have to be very strong to bear the things that would happen to me as a married woman. She also said I should never leave my children and take off to Squaw Dances or other such places. . . . She said my duty was to take care of the home and my children. I've done that right up to the present time."[2] A strong mother in the home becomes the lodestar for the family.

Marriage and sexuality are discussed in chapter 4, but Navajo thought concerning conception and child development in the womb is important to understand now because of the external influences that affect it. A detailed study of the life stages of a Navajo woman is found in *Molded in the Image of Changing Woman* by Maureen Trudelle Schwarz.[3] In it, she discusses the traditional perspective of how the physical act of creation between a man and woman occurs through the joining of their different "waters"—the male sperm (íígąsh) comes together with male water (tó yishchíín) in the mother to create a boy or with female water (tó biyáázh) to create a girl. Navajo midwives can determine the sex of an unborn baby by where the placenta looms largest in the womb—a male if on the left side and female if on the right, much in keeping with traditional beliefs about social roles and physical makeup of the sexes. But it is the blood from the mother's body that gives growth to the child, and so the mother becomes the paramount figure in producing and later raising the child.[4]

As the fetus develops within the womb, the parents need to be circumspect about circumstances surrounding their daily life. The mother and father should speak kind words, avoid arguments, sing traditional songs, hold a Blessingway ceremony, and practice correct behavior, since the child is present and ever learning. There are also many things that have an adverse effect on the growing baby. The mother should avoid going to Enemyway, Lightningway, or other ceremonies in which sandpaintings are used. Some people believe that nothing should be made for the child before it is born or else it will die. Perry, however, teaches that during the last trimester, the infant's cradleboard should be constructed. Cutting the joints of a butchered sheep may lead to joint and bone problems; watching either an animal suffering or being killed or a snake wriggling along the ground can cause future injury; coming in contact with something left by the Anasazi can be crippling; sewing an object like a Yé'ii Bicheii mask, tying knots, or knitting may lead to a difficult birth or the umbilical cord choking the baby; viewing or walking in a cemetery or attending a funeral can cause death; and observing an eclipse will harm the baby.[5] Different families and medicine people may have beliefs that conflict with how another person has been taught, but there is no missing that this is a formative time, and caution must be taken to ensure that the child is born under the best circumstances.

The birthing process is an event that teaches procedures beneficial for mother and child. As the baby prepares to exit the womb, it continues the pattern established by the holy people. Curly Mustache, a one-hundred-year-old medicine man from Tsaile, Arizona, in 1970, shared the following account. The gods were actively discussing how the earth surface people would have their children. Some of the questions raised included who should carry the child for nine months, how should it develop in the womb, and in what way will it exit the womb—feet or head first? Many shared their ideas, but Coyote, contrary as usual, explained his plan and why it was best.

> The man will be the "holder," Coyote said. If the woman is made the holder for forming the baby, the sperm liquid will not function but just flow out without any fertilization. If the man is the "holder," he will insert the sperm into the woman. The sperm will fertilize; then an embryo will develop. "The babies should not be born with their feet first," said Coyote. "If a child is born feet first, the baby will be in the same position as the mother." The child is apparently claimed by the Creator already, because the child is in a yielding position away from the mother. When a child is facing the mother, it is ready to be received with open arms because the child is delivered in an accepted position. The holy people agreed with these remarks from Coyote. The child that is born with its head first is received with love.[6]

As the birth of the baby approaches, there are a number of precautions taken for both mother and child. In addition to the Blessingway ceremony, there may also be a Birthingway ceremony (Ch'ilíjí, or Hodoolééłji) with protection songs performed about a month before birth to avoid future problems. Pregnant women used a boiled herb called Baby's Placentaway. Greasewood, sagebrush, and Townsendia (*Townsendia aprica*) aid delivery, while there are a number of other plants that are used after delivery called awéé' biyaałáí yihéézh (literally, "that which boils the placenta").[7] John Holiday testifies that after some of this medicine is consumed, the expectant mother has no problems and "the baby might come as she is walking."[8]

More hands-on measures may also be taken. Skilled midwives are able to turn a baby positioned incorrectly to ease the child out head first. Tall Woman recalls a very difficult delivery that her daughter, Mary, had. For two days she struggled with a baby that was positioned entirely wrong with feet down. Other women had tried to reposition the infant but had succeeded only in badly bruising the mother and adding to the trauma already experienced. Finally, someone made Tall Woman aware of the problem; she went immediately to her daughter's aid. Recalling the situation, she said,

> I turned her almost upside down and started feeling her stomach, like my mother had taught me. And sure enough, I felt that her baby was turned around. Its head was facing up, not down, and that's why it wasn't getting born. I used my hands to push on her stomach and slowly turn the baby into the right position. I knew how to do this by then. . . . After I did that and told Mary the baby was ready to get born, in about an hour she had her baby. When he finally came out, I started scolding him, asking why he had given his mother so much trouble. We were joking about piercing his ears in two places, so he wouldn't be so ornery next time.[9]

Mother and baby were both fine.

A normal birth follows established practices outlined by the holy people and filled with spiritual significance. The hogan, in which it occurs, is often compared to a mother's womb—a place of peace, security, and teaching. The outside world is where danger exists. To prepare for the birthing process, an area is cleaned, a hole is scooped in the floor and then lined with a sheepskin, a sash belt or woven rope is suspended either from a beam in the roof, and a forked pole is implanted in the ground or a log is leaned at a forty-five degree angle against the wall. This is on the west side behind the fireplace. The purpose of the suspended rope is for the woman in labor to strain against during delivery, and so hand loops or knots may be tied in it for grasping. The position of the mother may be squatting or kneeling above the depression or resting propped against a backrest with a rope above to help her lift off the ground while pushing during contractions.[10] The preferred method is to have access to both the front and back of the mother.

The delivery is primarily left to women, with the medicine man providing prayers and Blessingway songs that "chase the baby out" (awéé' hanidzóód), although there may be instances in which he is asked to assist. One woman stations herself behind the mother and another in front. The one behind helps to lift up under the mother's arm during contractions while the woman in front is in charge of receiving the baby, cutting the umbilical cord, and disposing of the placenta after the baby has been initially cleaned and settled.[11] Hearing a cry from the newborn is critical; indeed, the Navajo name for a stillborn is "the infant who did not talk" (awéé'doo haa'dzíí'ii). Returning to the birth of White Shell/Changing Woman, when the holy people found her as a baby on Gobernador Knob, she had not yet received her spirit. The holy people were concerned, asking what should be done. Black Wind entered her body, first going through her right foot and exiting at the top of her head; Blue Wind went through the center spot in her hair and came out in her toes and fingers; White Wind entered into the left foot and emerged in the same place as Black Wind; and Yellow Wind went in the center spot and came out on the bottom of her right foot. With this, the baby began to cry; life was evident.[12]

Shortly after the birth, the baby is given an emetic made from tissue (phloem) found under juniper and piñon bark. This cleans the baby's system of phlegm and birth water. Both the mother and child are given a thin blue cornmeal mush (tóshchíín), the mother's abdomen may be covered with heated juniper branches that are then bound on her with a cloth, and the child is wrapped and placed a couple of feet from the fire (Long Life Fire) so that the heat and warmth will soak into its head and body.[13] The child's head is pointed toward the east to help make its mind bright. "That is the way it must be done for a child to grow right [because] the sun shines down on the heads of all things and makes them grow strong."[14] Soon a Blessingway ceremony will be held for mother and newborn.

Perry's insight concerning the handling of a miscarriage, stillborn, afterbirth, and the umbilical cord is extensive. A few additional points offered by others builds on their symbolism. If a child at birth shows no signs of life, it is still considered a whole person and so receives a traditional four-day funeral and mourning period by the family. No name is given to the infant. If there is a series of failed birthing attempts resulting in premature births, an Evilway ceremony is held for the mother to purify her of any bad influences.[15] On a different note, when the umbilical cord of the newborn is obtained by the parents, it is put in a special place that is important for the child's future growth and development, guiding its personality in a direction that will be helpful and meaningful. Schwarz adds another dimension:

> Burial of the cord in the earth anchors the child to the "belly button" of Mother Earth and establishes a lifelong connection between an individual and a place, just as the cord anchors a child to its mother in the womb and establishes a lifelong connection between mother and child. The presence of this anchoring cord is evidenced by the spirals [wind entrances and exits] on the human body. . . . The spirals at the navel and the top of the back of the head demonstrate the path of this connecting cord, which is most frequently anchored to Mother Earth.[16]

When to name a newborn is interpreted through a variety of opinions. While Perry says that "soon after a child is born" it should be named, there are others who suggest naming at either its first cry, four days after birth, the early stages of crawling, or two to three months following birth. An explanation is given for each time recommendation—crying provides immediate recognition among the earth surface people, four is the sacred number of the holy people, the crawling child is now moving upon Mother Earth on its own, or the child's chance of survival is greater with the longer period. Whatever the practice, bestowal of the name ensures a child's status among the people. In addition to the sacred or war name that Perry discusses, there are also day-to-day names provided during different stages in life, in addition to kinship terms, used to identify an individual. The bearer may or may not know what they are, depending on how they are used and who uses them. For instance, a person may have a social name that carries great prestige because it denotes a link to a respected individual; a personal peculiarity; a physical or temperamental quality; an occupation, ability, achievement, or occurrence; a characteristic of a place he or she lives; a clan relationship; or a ceremony he performs.[17] An individual may have two or three such names at any given time.

An essential item for raising a Navajo child in the traditional way is the cradleboard (awééts'áál). Not surprisingly, White Shell/Changing Woman was discovered in the first one, when First Man or Talking God, accounts vary, found her on top of Gobernador Knob. Accounts also vary as to what the cradle was made of, but many indicate that the two backboards were comprised of Mother Earth (right side) and Father Sky (left side), with an over-arching canopy of rainbow, the footrest a short rainbow, the four-to-six loops on each side being zigzag lightning, and the interlocking strap securing the baby the sun's rays. Four clouds—white, blue, yellow, and black— covered the child. When First Man brought the baby home to First Woman, they were not sure how to release the child until two holy beings arrived and announced,

> "Something great has happened, my grandchildren. This is the one we have been talking about. Hereafter her mind will be the ruling power." He put the baby on the ground in back of the fire, pulled the string, and the lacing came free in both directions. "The cradle shall be like this. Thin pieces of wood shall be placed underneath. There will be a row of loops on either side made of string. The bark of the cliffrose, shredded and rubbed fine will be used under the child for a bed."[18]

To this day, the distinctive Navajo cradleboard follows this pattern.

The Franciscan Fathers in their *Ethnologic Dictionary* and the Kluckhohns with W. W. Hill in *Navaho Material Culture* provide detailed analysis of the construction and use of the cradleboard.[19] Beyond the fact that it is very sturdy, provides excellent physical protection, and can be carried in a number of ways, there are other practical aspects found in the holy people's instruction. For instance, cliffrose (awééts'áál) bark, when shredded and rubbed fine, makes an absorbent diaper material that can be washed, dried, and reused a number of times. When coupled with the separation between the two backboards, and in the past, a few extra holes to let urine drain, a baby avoided diaper rash. The canopy served as a sunshade, a rim to drape a cloth to keep flies away, and a place to hang a squirrel tail to maintain evil at a distance. There are different teachings as to when the construction of the cradleboard should start, when a child should first be placed in it, and whether a piece of turquoise should be secured to it if used for a boy or white shell for a girl, but there is general agreement that the cradle may be used for other babies unless an infant died in it. If this occurs, the cradleboard is disassembled and left in a secluded spot to deteriorate. Whether it was made from straight cedar (preferred), yellow pine, cottonwood, oak, or even part of a wooden crate, this object highlighted traditional values and remained home for a baby during its initial year or longer.

An important rite of passage is encountered when a baby laughs for the first time, calling forth the First Laugh ceremony (awéé' ch'ídildlohgó bána'a'niih). This practice also started with White Shell/Changing Woman, when as an infant, First Woman was bathing her. The baby began laughing, alerting Coyote who showed up wanting to know what was happening. Coyote complained: "'I was told that my grandchild laughed for the first time.' [Next] A woman came saying: 'I was told that my grandchild laughed for the first time.' She was Salt Woman."[20] First Woman gave Coyote some charcoal, with which he painted his nose, and some salt to go with his meat. Satisfied, he departed. But it was Salt Woman, representing happiness and generosity, who gave the first gift of salt to First Woman, on behalf of the baby.

Today, when a baby laughs for the first time, there is reason to celebrate. Whoever prompts that reaction from the infant traditionally has to provide a sheep for a feast. Relatives and friends gather to wish happiness and success for the child and bring small gifts to model generosity. Salt crystals are placed in a wedding basket, salt is put on the food, and a small amount is planted in the baby's hand. Just as this mineral evokes the good taste of food, so will it bring out goodness and happiness in life. Wesley Thomas, professor of Navajo studies at Navajo Technical University, explained,

> The rock salt is placed in the left hand for a male child and in the right for a female child. The adult holding the child takes the hand in which the salt is held and brushes it against the right side of the child's body, starting with the soles of the feet and moving upwards. The salt is rubbed against both sides of the body. . . . The purpose of the First Laugh ceremony is to ensure that the child will be generous, not greedy, that they will be generous and productive. My mother told me it is so "wealth will seek him."[21]

With this, the child has taken an important step toward what it means to be a successful earth surface being raised in the Navajo tradition.

Identifying the People

When the holy people (Diyin Dine'é) entered into this world, they were spiritual beings. All that they did was spiritual in form, but they understood that physical elements also needed to be part of this earth experience. They set about creating tangible things to house spiritual entities. This was true for all living creatures, including human beings. Several terms that designate humans arose from the process. For instance, people can be called earth surface people (Nohokáá' dine'é) or five-fingered (Bíla'ashdla'ii) beings. Today, many Navajos assume that these terms are limited to their own race and not general humanity, but in reality, these words signify any person who walks the land, regardless of race, creed, or color. The term "earth surface people" came from the four different elements given to everyone. All of humanity lives because of the warmth of the sun, the water that comes as rain and snow, the air to breathe, and the earth to walk upon. Fire, water, wind, and soil comprise all of the basic elements of this physical life upon which all humans depend. But an individual is also considered a god or spiritual entity walking in this life because they embody these sacred components as earth surface beings. We all live on this earth in a body, knowing what and how to do things because of the divinity inside. Still, no one is perfect. We can defeat ourselves by choosing not to be a good person and not to follow the directions given us by the holy people. We are the ones responsible for what has been given to us. That is what it means to be a Navajo or T'áá Diné, meaning Men Living on Earth, shortened to Diné or "man."

The title of earth surface beings is used often in ceremonial settings or when formally addressing a group of people. It makes no difference which people are referred to in this way because we all walk the earth together and share similar experiences in this life. Whether a man or woman, Anglo, Chinese, or Black, it does not matter, and so this term is not limited to Navajos. When Navajos identify themselves solely as Diné, it technically just means man and not "The People" as some suggest. To identify specifically, a person would say Diné dóó asdzání, meaning a man or woman, Naabeehó Dine'é for Navajo people, and Bilagáana Diné for a white man. If I wish to say "we are the people," I would use "diné daniidlį," defining the group or nationality to which one belongs.

Life Begins: Protecting the Unborn

Much is understood by the value a culture places on life and how it views the development and birth of a child. Traditional Navajo society teaches a lot about the importance of bringing forth a baby into this world as a welcomed member blessed by the holy people and nurtured by its family. The initial creation of a baby is believed to be complete six months after conception. Prior to this, few people talk about the power in conceiving babies or spend a lot of time anticipating the new arrival. They will only note that a woman is pregnant and that a child is on the way. Immediate and extended family members—aunts, uncles, grandparents, brothers, and sisters—start to anticipate what this will mean to their family as the time of delivery grows closer. Once the last three months are reached, there are notable differences and actions taken to prepare.

The baby is viewed as a living, impressionable being who is influenced by things that happen both inside and outside of the womb. People begin to watch their language by sharing positive thoughts and avoiding arguments. They start to tell the expectant mother what to stay away from, where not to go, and how to prevent doing things that might harm the baby. Certain ceremonies dealing with death and illness such as the Enemyway and Evilway are avoided. The woman is strictly coached, particularly by her relatives, as to what she can and cannot do, especially if this is to be her first child. "Do not talk like this. Do not lie this way. You can't go in the sweat lodge. You cannot heat your back too much because there's a sickness called spina bifida that will affect the baby. Because of that, you should not heat your body in certain areas, so don't go in the sweat lodge." The third trimester is also when fathers and grandfathers talk about the development of the baby—its feet, head, arms, eyes, and ears. The men are just as involved as the women in enlisting spiritual aid at this critical time.

Often the family will hold a Blessingway ceremony to bring peace and protection to those involved but especially to the unborn child. Now that the baby is fully formed and growing in size, this ceremony becomes an important addition as the holy ones step in to assist with physical and spiritual development. Singing and praying for the baby now has an important impact, since by this time the child is considered old enough to receive it. This puts more responsibility on the mother to live the teachings and follow positive practices, as the holy ones provide guidance to assist the developing child. She is told to exercise through walking, greet the sun when it rises, drink a lot of water, and bless herself with the cool air of the morning. These are elements that provide the foundation of life—fire (sun), water, air, and earth. She is encouraged to understand her situation and to breathe deeply to relieve pressures on her stomach, the walls of her body, and the cramps that set in. A lot of these problems can be controlled by how she sits, turns, moves, and lies in a fetal position on the earth. By resting on her side in this way, the mother blesses herself and the baby. When she assumes the fetal position, the baby is in contact with the earth; when she shifts to her other side, the same is true, but a mother should never lie on her front. Sleeping on one's back is used very little. Watch an animal—it rarely lays on its back but only on its side often curled up. This is how first life comes into play with the baby lying sideways. Even lambs, when born, are on their side, but rarely their back or face. By doing this, the four elements are involved in caring for the mother and solving her problems. The father also receives his dos and don'ts about how he should think and act during the last three months.

At the beginning of the last three months of pregnancy, the husband also has his responsibilities to help the child into this world. One task is to select elements from a beautiful cedar tree for building a cradleboard. He will cut a wide strip that will act as the protecting band or hood above the baby's head. After thinning the wood by shaving it to a point where it can be bent, he puts it in water to soak until pliable. Next, he bends it to form and places it in the wet earth to obtain and maintain its u-shape. This process molds it into a permanent half-circle or rainbow. If the board does not break, then the man is doing a good job and has strong thoughts and prayers. He is urged to think, walk, talk, and act like a rainbow. What this means is that everything during this last three months should be positive and uplifting. Rainbows have many colors, and this is how one's mind should be. A person's thoughts and language are to be colorful, encouraging the unborn child to learn, use different languages, and understand easily things about people and places in this world. Rainbows do not give out thunderstorms and lightning, but are peaceful and kind, offering what medicine people call "The Little Rain." It comes in with small clouds and haze, is very delicate, and brings no hardship or anything harsh, but only good feelings and thoughts. There is the promise of new horizons and things getting better while trouble and sorrows are left behind. The child is going to walk through the rainbow into the new world, see new things, and experience creative ways with many colors in order to live a good life. The expecting mother and father start the child on this path even before he or she is born. There is no mention of the Evilway or Enemyway, but only the Rainbowway or Blessingway, which are pretty much the same ceremony.

The Blessingway centers around a major image that helps the couple practice holiness. The husband avoids doing anything wrong by staying on the right path. This causes everything to come in smooth, nice, and gentle. The baby will be well formed and there will be no complication during delivery. The entire family will think this way so that the blessings can start

Awééts'ááł

Cradleboard Teachings

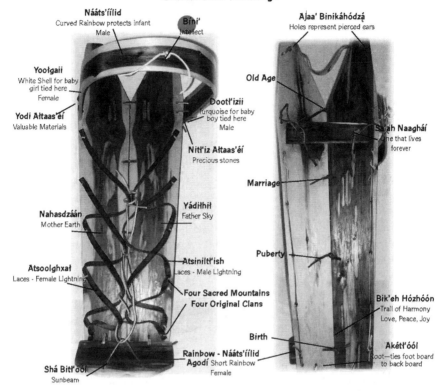

Nááts'íílid
Curved Rainbow protects infant
Male

Bíní'
Intellect

Ajaa' Binikáhódzá
Holes represent pierced ears

Yoołgaii
White Shell for baby
girl tied here
Female

Old Age

Yodi Altaas'éí
Valuable Materials

Dootł'izii
Turquoise for baby
boy tied here
Male

Sąʼáh Naagháí
The that lives
forever

Nitł'iz Altaas'éí
Precious stones

Marriage

Nahasdzáán
Mother Earth

Yádiłhił
Father Sky

Puberty

Atsoolghxał
Laces - Female Lightning

Atsiniltł'ish
Laces - Male Lightning

Four Sacred Mountains
Four Original Clans

Bik'eh Hózhóón
Trail of Harmony
Love, Peace, Joy

Birth

Shá Bitł'óół
Sunbeam

Rainbow - Nááts'íílid
Agodí Short Rainbow
Female

Akétł'óól
Foot—ties foot board
to back board

The juniper cradleboard is both a physical and spiritual protection for a newborn child. Calling upon the forces of earth and sky, identifying the various stages of life, wishing for prosperity and intellect, this object enwraps not only the baby in these positive things, but identifies important goals in the future for "long life, happiness." (Courtesy San Juan School District Media Center)

to happen. The mountains are sung to; the earth, the sun, air, and winds are also brought in to help. There are a number of songs that cause these good things to take place.

The four elements enter into other aspects of birth. The baby's spirit is represented by air. The spirit people are the wind and air, and so when a baby is born, the holy ones are present. Wind, water, and light come together and become one. They say the spirit goes into the baby, entering with the first breath. The infant inhales, crying starts, and that is when the spirit in the form of air becomes part of the body. The holy one is there, bringing new life. Sometimes the baby needs help with a spank on the bottom so that they can catch on to that spirit; this is when the air goes in, the child lights up, and life on earth begins. Water is also part of the process, giving the baby an initial opportunity to grow as well as supplying future nourishment, but the spiritual part comes with the light and the air—they are spirit people. The birth of the baby is set by these four elements.

Giving Birth to a Holy Being

The holy people step in to help with the birth just as they do in any ceremony. A person marks the day when the event is anticipated by speaking words of invitation for the holy ones to participate. The husband and wife are themselves holy ones who make it known that a birth is going to occur and that the spirit people approve. The holy beings say, "Alright. We're being called for that day to be there, and we will be present." Important holy people gather for the event. They will wait the first day, second day, or third day, whenever the baby comes, they will be there. As with a ceremony, the parents should not change the time or means of delivery (cesarean section) through modern medical practices because the holy people will be left sitting there offended. When events happen naturally, they will be present to assist and entice the baby to come out because they have been called upon to do that. They are an important part of the process and life itself.

Sometimes things do not go as planned, and there are miscarriages. During the first three months of pregnancy, people talk about the Water People controlling much of what happens in forming the baby. The infant is not yet put together, and so if it is lost during this time, it is let go through a water ceremony. A "cooling" ceremony is performed that "unravels" the problem. Amid songs and prayers, the grieving mother is marked in seven different locations (healing points) with lightning designs placed on her with ashes. These are eventually washed off with water, and then she is encouraged to live a normal life, putting this event in the past.

After the second trimester, the baby is considered a human being, and so a short ritual is held to bid the infant farewell. It is now part of the family and has entered into the world. People talk about the holy ones when this happens, and even though the baby is primarily formed, it has been brought out with nothing but blood. The fetus has a special plant, cliffrose (awééts'áál—baby cradle—*Purshia mexicana*), that is rubbed between the hands, shredded, then put with the remains before tightly rolling the cloth, wrapping the bundle with leaves, and placing it in a tree. A miscarriage is never buried in the ground the way a fully formed person is. The reason for this is that the child was never completed and so is not considered a human being but only one that was in the process of development. These remains belong to the Bird People because when the different creatures came into the second world during the time of emergence, there was an agreement made that these spirits, connected with water, would belong to the inhabitants of that world—the birds. The birds believe it is their right to have these remains, and so the Feather People take the spirit back.

When the baby becomes restless, it is getting ready to be born. The mother notifies a medicine woman or midwife who comes in to help with the birthing process. Usually this woman or women are important elders in the community or family members who are experienced, powerful, and respected leaders. The woman appointed to be in charge will check the mother's stomach and ensure there are no complications. After the mother's water breaks, the midwife will take a heavy wool sash belt and tie it to a horizontal beam in the hogan, then fasten two loops in it so that the mother, who is now squatting on the floor, can slip her hands into them. The laboring woman strains against the belt while the midwife and medicine man begin to sing. The lead woman may put a sash belt around the mother's waist then release it, repeating the procedure around her neck, arms, and legs as a blessing to accompany the songs while the medicine man sings. This is to unravel the pathway that the baby must follow and ease the passage out of the mother's body. The midwife might also take a weaving batten stick (bee ník'í'níltłish) and sit behind the mother so that she can place it under her breasts and press down a little bit here and there to push the baby downward. This is called Chasing the Baby Out (awéé' hanilchééh). I used to perform this a lot, and in the Shiprock area became known as the love doctor. When a woman had complications, I would get a call to come and help. I would bring my sash belt and put it on the different areas of the body to release and unravel the places that were holding the infant back. Sure enough, the baby would slide right through the birth canal within a half hour. This was another way of reconnecting with the child through song.

I received this special gift song from my mother's mother's sister, my great-grandmother. She knew a lot about being a midwife in her community and had the sacred songs and words. There are people like that in every family. I received it, as a medicine man, to help the mother in delivery by having the baby listen to it, reconnect with the mother, and follow the directions to come out. When this song is chanted, unraveling takes place, and the delivery goes very smoothly. The sacred song makes a sacred path and chases the baby from the womb. I have been doing this for years and years and never been disappointed.

The holy beings are present and sit in the song when it is performed in a sacred way. There is no single holy person associated with childbirth, but the song summons at least four to attend. As I understand it, the white body, yellow body, blue body, and black body holy beings from the four directions are there participating because they have been called from their homes in the mountains. They cannot be seen or heard, but they live in the songs and prayers and so are in attendance, representing other more powerful gods— the light, air, water, and ground. Shortly after the birth, they depart. The process is touched with supernatural power (álílee k'ehgo) as expressed through the song and events. The mother, for this brief moment, becomes White Shell Woman so that both she and the child are holy ones who come together through the song. Once the baby enters the world and assumes its role in the family, it is on its own.

Establishing a Course for Life

As the mother gets closer to the actual delivery, the women keep telling her to breathe deeply and push. Soon the infant starts to drop down, so the women sing songs praising the child for its efforts and encouraging it to continue. Once the baby is flushed out and the umbilical cord is cut, two important activities are set in motion. The woman directing the birth process is the one responsible for cutting the umbilical cord and caring for the placenta. This is her right. In the old days it was said that the cord should be cut with an arrowhead or stone knife to give protection to the infant from evil. A piece of it, about two inches long, is given to the mother for her to do whatever she likes with it as well as to make an offering. For a month or two she may carry it, thinking all the time where she would like to have it put so that when the child is full grown, his or her thoughts will return to where she had the cord placed. She ponders about her son being a rancher or an excellent weaver if a girl. Perhaps she will have it buried around the livestock corral or near a loom in a favorite weaving spot in or near the home. She might find a baby horse and tie it to its mane or tail; whenever it falls off, there is a blessing that goes with it. This is so the boy will be very good with horses, have a large herd, and become skilled in caring for them. The same can be done with sheep, goats, or other animals. The umbilical cord can be tied to a ram's horn so that there will be many animals that comprise the family flock. Whatever the mother wishes for her child, she entices to take place.

A woman may want her daughter to be a good housekeeper. Her umbilical cord may be brought to the home of a pack rat (łé'étsoh—big rat— *Neotoma cinerea*) and left outside of its dome house. This animal really

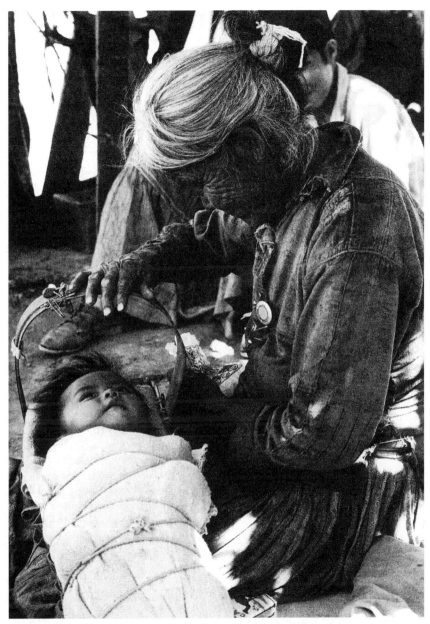

Older, experienced women take charge and supervise the birthing process. Except for the singing of a medicine man to urge the baby forth, birthing is a female activity. In a matrilineal society, these older women wield strong influence with adult and child alike, mixing wisdom and practical teachings that keep those younger on the pollen path.

cleans its home, spick-and-span, even near its entrance where he sweeps. He is a different type of rat that does not leave any dirt behind and is one of the cleanest individuals around. So the mother will take the baby's umbilical cord and tie it by the rat's doorway, so the child will be blessed to learn how to clean her home often and take pride in where she lives. These thoughts are given back to the mother, who thinks of what is going to be best for her baby.

There are some people who do not pay a lot of attention to where they put the baby's umbilical cord. Neither the father nor mother was careful in its placement. Around the age of two, the child will start digging around in different places and go through the stage called by some the "terrible twos," where they get into everything, make a mess, and disturb the peace. The mother may say, "What are you looking for?" But the grandmother knows. She will ask, "Where did you put his umbilical cord? That's what he is trying to find and why he is digging. If you just left it behind, he is looking for it and is going to unearth it. If you had given it to the horse or another animal, he wouldn't be doing this." The placenta is different. It is placed back in nature, wrapped in a cloth, and given a white corn offering before it is put underneath a rock or in a tree. The midwife or a relative is the one who takes care of this. The placenta is said to belong to the clan people, but there is no ceremony or prayer offered when it is set in its resting place and let go. So there are prayers with the umbilical cord but not the placenta.

Once the baby is delivered and cleaned, the midwife places the child with its head toward the fire so that the heat will come into the body from that direction. This is how the baby came into the world, head first. Next he is blessed by the sacred element of heat. An aunt or uncle will place their hand on the earth on the east side of the fireplace in the hogan and transfer that heat through their hand onto the baby's foot. Next, they warm their hand in the same way on the south side and put it on the baby's legs and body, then the west side on the shoulders, and the north goes on the head. Four times the baby is blessed by doing this, bringing the heat from the four directions provided by the sacred fire within the home. In the old days before stoves, the fire in the center of the hogan had wood that was sticking out in the cardinal points. The ends of these logs were pushed toward the center to burn, making the fire bigger and warmer. Everything had to be blessed in this way using the four directions, especially when performing a ceremony; this is how the practice came to be. Every time there was a ceremony, the same actions took place. In the morning, a relative would take the baby outside and put him in the sun for a while to be blessed by its beams. The infant would also have an arrowhead given to him for protection, water sprinkled on him for a blessing, and a prayer for the future before being given back to his mother. This is how childbearing and birth were done in the old days, but now, with hospitals and clinics, it is very different.

From Crying to Laughter

The first three or four months of a baby's life requires intense work by the mother as she meets the infant's needs. Crying, for some babies, seems constant. As the situation changes, Navajos recognize an important step of maturing through the First Laugh ceremony. This practice occurred initially a long time ago as a mother grew weary from the demands of her newborn. The people nearby wanted some type of response, some indication, that all of the fussing and tears would end. The baby seemed to be in constant pain and never stopped wailing, which scared some into believing that the situation was not only desperately wrong but permanent. Relations became strained, nerves on end. The people did not understand that it took time for the baby to move out of this stage and into a more settled lifestyle. Every cry just convinced them that something was wrong, the irritation would never end, and nothing could be done to remove the problem. Stress led to depression. Medicine men were called in, but they could not effect a change. Eventually the people's thinking changed from "Oh no, not again" to accepting the noise as normal and everlasting. They did not realize that a baby's disposition—as seen in the ability to laugh—took a certain amount of time to develop.

One day, the distracted mother noticed an unfamiliar movement by her infant. She thought she heard a chuckle. This couldn't be, but she waited and listened. "Did I hear that right?" She sat still and watched the child stare back just as intently. The mother looked away for a moment, turned back, and there it was—a smile and little chuckle coming from the baby in the cradleboard. The mother's whole body changed as she cried out in disbelief that the baby now made a different sound. She ran from home to home announcing, "The baby made a different sound. She isn't crying anymore, her face is no longer screwed up in pain, and she actually broke into a laugh!" Everybody stopped what they were doing and came to see what seemed impossible. They waited for the child to do something other than cry, but there was nothing. Everybody started making faces and actions that might get the infant to smile. The antics worked. Soon the baby was laughing, which made everyone—the whole community—happy. No doubt, this was cause for celebration, so the people went to Talking God to let him know and get his advice. They asked him what he thought and what he wanted for this newborn child. Someone offered, "We want her to grow old, live a good life" and Talking God agreed. He answered, "Okay. The main ones you need to talk to are the Salt People. They have white hair, are old, and represent long life to an old age. This is what we want for this child. The Salt People will bless you in that manner." The people asked, and the Salt People consented. The blessing came to this baby for the first time and the practice has continued ever since. Following a prayer, the people ate and celebrated. Everyone joined in trying to make the infant smile or laugh. This was also the time when the baby song was developed and medicine men started using it. They sing, "Hai ai haghai haghai haghai haghai haghai haei yą́ą́ haghaa éí éí éí haghai haghai haghai haghai"—which is really just mimicking the sounds a baby makes when crying. The name of the melody is The Smallest (or Newborn) Baby Song.

Eventually another child entered this world, and so people began asking, "When are we going to eat again and have another celebration?" The initial event became a custom and ritual now called the First Laugh ceremony (awéé' ch'ídildlohgó bána'a'niih). The first person who makes the baby laugh is responsible for putting on a large feast, during which the infant is protected and blessed with wealth by having salt rubbed on him. Each person attending also receives a small portion of salt, which represents becoming an elder. As a side note, a young man who has moved into puberty and had his voice change but has not been blessed through a First Laugh ceremony, can find some salt water and jump into it. This is a way he can bless himself. Salt has a way of giving protection and bringing wealth.

What Is in a Name?

Shortly after a child is born, they will receive a sacred name that is used only in ceremonies. By this title, the holy people recognize the individual. Family members will also know what it is, but outsiders, especially those who might use it against the person, should never be aware of it. When an individual is going to offer a prayer and talk to their creator, this name is used by way of introduction. It is an original, sacred name. For instance, if I were praying, I would say when I started, "You know me, I am Blue Boy. I am the one who is talking to you as Blue Boy in this sacred manner. This is who I am." Then I explain myself, why I am talking to the holy people, and what I need. If you just use your daily name as you pray, they will not know who you are and will not grant your request. But if they know you by your ceremonial name like Blue Boy, they will say, "Oh, okay. We heard that in the medicine over here, so we know who you are." If you really need to be understood and are serious, that is when you say your name. This first sacred name is given by the parents. It may be used up until a person gets married, but often it is dropped before that. It becomes worn out and loses its power.

One time when I was reaching puberty, my father and I were cutting willows for a bow and arrows. In the prayer that he offered, he used my sacred name, Blue Boy, which my mother had given me. As I cut the branches, my father prayed, "This is my son, Blue Boy." Nobody calls me by that old name anymore, not even my mother. About the time I was in the seventh grade, people stopped using it. Then for a while I only had the name Perry because I had lost focus with many of the traditional ways. I had outgrown it. Later, after I returned from the military, I received another medicine name that is used for ceremonial purposes, a second sacred name. The medicine man I was working with at the time said, "You are going to be Warrior Coming Back for the rest of your life." All of the elders sitting there agreed that that should be my name. We all thought that it was appropriate, and so they sang a song. From that day forward, I became Warrior Coming Back and cannot change it. When I perform a ceremony, this is the name that I use to introduce myself to the holy people. The patient will have their own sacred name, which they will tell me before the ritual starts so that I can introduce them also. A lot of times, people do not know anything about this.

Regular names, beyond kinship terms, are also chosen by the mother and father, who draw on relatives from either side. The mother may look at the child and say, "Your father is Metal Belt, and this baby is going to need a godfather or uncle or someone to assist him as he grows up. Who shall it be?" The family will talk about possibilities, and examine who he looks like and how he acts. After a while, the baby might start having an attitude, throw things around, or have some characteristic that set the child apart from others. The mother may say, "You know, his father has a brother over there who has the same attitude, and so we are going to name the baby after him." The first name given to a boy child came from the relatives on the father's side. For instance, my name came from my father's cousin's brother, whose name was Deswood Many Beads. The name was one of endearment given to him when he was a young boy. It had no particular translation or meaning, but was passed to me as a youngster. When he came to our house, my father said, "We gave my son your name, and so will you act like a godfather and help raise him? You will be this man. I will give you my blessing that you will be with my son this way." This practice has a name: The One That You Were Born For (báshínílchíní) and is done when the adult's name is given to the child. The person who accepts the honor and willingly shares his name has this responsibility until the day he dies. A godfather's duties are primarily that of a teacher. He will take his charge into the sweat lodge to instruct him, bring him to ceremonies to observe and help, and may be involved in discipline if necessary. In Navajo thought, "he stands there for you" and acts as a second father.

The same practice takes place for the baby girl, but the family will look to the mother's side of the family for an aunt who will serve as a guide and helper for the newborn. It is always your original clan that determines where the name comes from. All of my brothers were given names of relatives on my father's side of his clan family, and all of my sisters' names came from my mother's side. These were the first names given to all of us.

Another time that a name can be given is during the Enemyway if a person does not already have a sacred name. This ceremony is held only if there is a sickness. For instance, men returning from war, a person who has come in contact with the Anasazi, or those being bothered by the spirit of a dead person may need this ritual performed. During the ceremony, the spirit that is causing the sickness is destroyed, and the patient receives a powerful blessing that drives away all evil. At one point, the medicine man says, "This person has to have a name, and so I'm going to give it to him so that it will shoot against the enemy. Every time you call him by that name, it will be his protection, and the evil ones will know that this individual was named after the great ones. They will leave him alone." That is what happened to me following my return from the military when I had my Enemyway, and I have not been bothered since.

Both men's and women's names make mention of war, fighting, or qualities pertaining to warriors. Often men are called the "mean one" or something to do with anger or a fierce animal. For example a man might be known as the bear or the angry one, the hostile one, or mountain lion because they are fighters, quick to anger, and can be mean. The term used to describe this quality is hashkéhee, meaning "in an angry manner" and literally "it's going to bite you." Many years ago there was a woman kidnapped by the Utes and brought to their country. By the time the Navajos got her back, she had lost part of her mind. People asked what was wrong and why she had changed so much. They decided to hold an Enemyway ceremony for her, but they could not give her a name because she did not understand what it was for. Finally, the medicine man performing the rite said, "We have to have a sacred name for her in order for her to get better. Let's call her Hashk'é Binaat'áá, The Mean One or Mean Leader." Finally she got well. Later, all of the young women were named The Mean One's Sister, Aunt, or something else that connected them to this woman.

Many years later, the Navajo and Utes were at war again, and The Mean One accompanied some men into battle. The enemy was lined up on one side and the Navajos on the other, with both groups ready to join in combat. The Utes launched an arrow colored red with a snake painted on it high into the air. The missile traveled deep into the sky until the wind sent it spinning

A good mother directs her daughter's behavior to ensure success. By burying a child's umbilical cord in an important place, such as at the foot of a loom; by bestowing a name that identifies positive characteristics; and by teaching at an early age the skills and abilities necessary to succeed in life, a mother prepares that child for the future.

back toward the enemy line. The Navajos called out to their enemy, demanding that their leader appear. Then they brought out Mean Leader, who raised her bow toward the sky and launched an arrow colored blue, with its middle painted yellow and white, and the area around the feathers in red. On one side were the markings of the sun. This arrow traveled far beyond the Utes' line, indicating to them that their weapons would be powerless against those of the Navajos and that they would lose the battle. The woman, wearing a red dress, jumped on a horse and galloped toward the enemy. They saw her fast approaching and began yelling "Shoot her, shoot her down." Arrow after arrow tried to find its mark, but she remained untouched, riding through the enemy's line before wheeling her horse around and charging back again to the Navajos. She remained untouched. Now the two lines closed in hand-to-hand fighting, with the Navajos emerging victorious.

For her actions that day, her name changed to The Warrior Way of Going into Battle. Other women, then and now, take names dealing with fighting and being a warrior such as Going into War (Dahdiibaa'), Went to the Enemy Line and Returned (Ahéénibaa'), and The One Who Stood Up to the Enemy (Ch'iníbaa'). Whenever you see the word baa' in a name, it has something to do with war. She had gone into battle in the warrior's way, and so she earned her name change to reflect her role. These women's names are all about protection. From the beginning, including the nine months that they carry a baby, they are protecting family and the people around them. Throughout our lifetime, our mother and Mother Earth are our protectors and will always be there to help. This is where the women's names concerning war came from. Whether it is a quality surrounding war or being a "mean leader," either type of name can be given. Every woman who can bear children will be called this way and is expected to be a leader for and protector of children. This is why women have war names.

CHAPTER TWO

Changing Woman

The Pattern for Motherhood

As a youngster moves from childhood to adult status, physical and social changes are marked by a puberty ceremony that establishes positive growth and role development for the future. Steeped in traditional teachings that ensure good health practices for a long and productive life, these ceremonies combine spiritual and physical qualities that clearly define what an ideal man and woman will be like. They prepare youth for the many challenges and responsibilities of adulthood. This chapter discusses the training given to young women during the kinaaldá ceremony, which is particularly rich in instruction, as well as her introduction to the tools she will use for the rest of her life. Principles of good health, spiritual sensitivity, allegiance to posterity, and gender responsibility are all part of the directions given during this four-day ceremony that prepares the young initiate for motherhood. The young man's entrance into puberty is discussed in the next chapter.

There is an extensive literature concerning the kinaaldá ceremony. Among the best studies are *Kinaaldá* by Charlotte Frisbie, and *Molded in the Image of Changing Woman* and *Blood and Voice*, both by Maureen Trudelle Schwarz.[1] These works each have a particular emphasis—Frisbie on the songs and prayers, Schwarz in the symbolic meaning of the ceremony, aspects of female physical change, and traditional responsibilities. Perry's teachings below expand on what these authors have shared, but he also emphasizes different elements of the ritual. The reader is encouraged to investigate other works for additional information.

Following the arrival of White Shell/Changing Woman (abbreviated to Changing Woman for this discussion) in First Man and First Woman's home at Huerfano Mesa, the baby grew at a rapid rate. "A day was the same as a year. The second day the baby sat up and when two days had passed, she looked around. She was then dressed [in all manner of white shell]."[2] That same day she walked, the third day she danced, fourth ran, and on the tenth received the name White Shell Woman. On the thirteenth day (actually year) she began menstruating, telling First Woman, "Mother, something is passing from me." This set in motion the activities now associated with the four-day ceremony called Kinaaldá held for pubescent girls. Changing Woman established the pattern of the ceremony through which she became "the very essence and personification of regeneration, rejuvenation, renewal, and dynamic beauty [as] the Supreme Mother of the Navajos and the most blessed, the most revered, and the most benevolent of all the Holy People."[3]

Young women who follow in her footsteps become like her. As with Changing Woman, whose first period (kinaasda') came as a surprise, it may be the same for young girls who have not been instructed by their mothers, and like "the Holy People, though great, become embarrassed at this kind of blood."[4] Perhaps that is why Tall Woman, as her mother before her, postponed the inquiries of her prepubescent daughters, always changing the subject. Eventually, she did sit down and explain the physical changes, but one gets the impression she was not comfortable.[5] Once the young woman has her second period and a second ceremony called Kinaaldá Bik'í Dah Naaztání, she is able to bear children and is now under what medicine man John Holiday called "The Woman's Ruler"—menstruation (chooyin).[6]

A girl's initial menses launches preparation for the first kinaaldá ceremony. Each of the four days follow much the same pattern, with intensified activity on the last day. Combing hair, running, grinding corn, singing Blessingway songs, and food preparation teach skills and attitudes for her future role as a wife and mother. On the third day the men dig a large pit in which a fire is built to heat the soil for baking a cake (alkaan) made of ground cornmeal. The last day there is the washing of the kinaaldá's hair and jewelry, a final run, the cutting of the cake, the molding of her body, and the blessing of participants. All of these activities are embedded with teachings and symbolic action, and are done in the presence of the holy people. The women's tools (habeedí), which she is introduced to, form the basis for her future traditional life. A couple of examples (hairbrush and grinding stones) used during the ceremony and the loom with its tools, used later, illustrate how these and other implements hold symbolic depth.

Men and women have defined roles in Navajo culture that can be performed only with gender-specific equipment given to them by the holy people. Changing Woman, when formalizing the transfer of these materials to the earth surface people, emphasized the sacred nature and use of what she now gave them. "You may address your petitions to all things, none excepted. When you plead with this wind [soul] that stands within you, you will make pollen application to it. And you may petition your hogans, you will make pollen application to them. And you may petition your fire, your utensils of every description that serve you for meals. Petition your food woman, your food man . . . the same holds true for water."[7] All of these are sacred instruments and preserve life. They are also paired, just as First Man declared: "There will be the entrance [mat] woven toward each other, and the entrance uprights with the curtain. There will be the fire with the food, the pot with the stirring sticks, the earthen bowl and the gourd ladle, the metate with the whisk broom."[8] Each tool has its power and awaits to bless people.

Perry spends a lot of time teaching about hair care, hair ties, and the hairbrush—all of which play an important role in the ceremony and in daily grooming thereafter. One's blessings are tied up and sealed in the "knot" (hair bun—tsiiyééł), which is the means by which the holy people recognize an individual. The hair is bound to keep thoughts whole and unified with the coils of the scalp facing toward the heavens. The black stripes left by rain on the mesas and the water laden clouds that blow across the desert are compared to hair that has been allowed to hang down. The only time the hair was left loose in the old days was either during a ceremony or at the time of death and burial of an individual.[9] Elder Ben Whitehorse recalled the sacred nature of these connections between the land and sky, husband and wife, life and death, when he said:

> The man's wife shall care for his hair, likewise the man for her. They will sit one behind the other as they brush one another's hair. . . . The hair is strands of rain by which the holy people recognize us. It is sacred and through this symbolism, the rain gods—one male and one female and also the lightning knows of us as we live on this earth. They will bring no harm or threat to us. . . . Likewise, our earth is the female and the things made in the heavens are male. The male brings forth the water to replenish the earth with living vegetation and thus we humans and animals are continually reproducing. This is how they interact with each other.[10]

Florence Begay warned that "If you ever start cutting your hair, we will have little rain. I think this is true because we do not have much rain. Back then, men and women always wore their hair in a knot. It is considered male rain and so one should not cut it short."[11] The same brush that is used to care for hair is also used to clean the mano and metate after grinding and for straining materials from liquids. Once the brush is used in food preparation, it no longer serves as a hairbrush.

In the past, women spent a lot of time working on their grinding stones. These implements were fashioned from hard igneous rocks that were indented by chipping to obtain the desired shape. Often, they were left slightly pitted to make a good grinding surface. Some people might perform a short ceremony for a new metate during which white corn was ground, sprinkled on the four main posts of the hogan, then spread clockwise about the room.[12] The stones became important family items passed down from mother to daughter and were at times referred to as a mother. Tall Woman viewed them as able to kill the Hunger People. "Collectively the stones are seen as Lady Warrior; many say that the bottom stone is the woman's bow, and the top stone is her bowstring. The corn kernels or whatever else is being ground are the arrows. . . . It is said that with grinding stones, a woman can overcome hunger and poverty, just as a man traditionally did with his bow and arrows. Together, the woman and the man plan how to fight hunger and prepare to do so with complementary actions."[13]

Another important item in a woman's life is the weaving loom, an object that defeats poverty. The Navajo explain how this item originated as gifts from Spider Man and Spider Woman. There are a number of versions of how the process started, one telling how before the Navajo emerged into this world, Spider Man and his wife obtained the seeds of a fine fibrous plant they called cotton. The couple instructed the People to grow this plant to make clothes and get away from wearing animal skins. Once they obtained the fiber, the women made a spindle with a round disk to spin it into a strong thread for weaving. "Then the chief medicine woman said: 'You must spin towards your person, as you wish to have the beautiful goods come to you; do not spin away from you.' For it was in their minds to make cloth which they could trade for shell and turquoise beads and she knew their thoughts. She said: 'You must spin towards you, or the beautiful goods will depart from you.'"[14]

Spider Man assumed the task of making the loom, just as this is often the responsibility of men today. The upper cross pole was made from the sky, the lower one from earth. He fashioned the warp sticks from sunrays, the upper strings holding the warp to the pole from lightning, the lower strings from sun halo, and the heddle from rock crystal and sheet lightning, which he secured to the warp strands with rain ray cords. A comb of white shell; spindles of cannel coal, turquoise, abalone, and white bead; spindle sticks of various forms of lightning; black, blue, yellow, and white winds powered the spindles, allowing them to "travel all around the world."[15] Hence the title for weavers that Perry mentions, "Keeper of the Storm." Little wonder that with an object so powerful, women were cautioned to weave in moderation. Other customs arose: when a girl baby was born, her hands and arms were rubbed with a spider's web found over a hole in the ground so that she will not tire from weaving; a woman should not hit a person with her weaving tools or the one struck will become paralyzed; spanking a child with them will make him or her sick; and the loom should not stand too long—it will tire and hurt the weaver.[16] On a more positive note, the loom became a mainspring for industry, creativity, and economic viability—a powerful tool in the hands of Navajo women.

Alerting the People, Inviting the Holy Ones

When a girl receives her first menses, family members become aware of her situation, and a short blessing prayer is offered that notifies the holy people of her status. The first menses is the most important one, but the second one is also significant. There are two ways the ceremony takes place. The first time it happens, it is called Talking God Sings the Hogan Song (Haashch'éíyáłti'í hooghan biyiin neidi'á) because he is the one singing over the young woman. When the second period comes, it is called the Holy Mountain People Sing the Hogan Song (Naat'á hooghan bee bijíí łeh), since the Mountain People have the responsibility for overseeing the medicine practices. These are the two possible times for this ceremony, and if a person has both, then they are especially powerful. The young woman can make a cake, a central focus, at each of these ceremonies; the more elaborate the ritual and extensive the participation, the better. My daughter had both, bringing together the best of everything. My mother was there, insisting everything was done perfectly.

Nothing is more important than the health and strength necessary for the busy life of a Navajo wife, mother, and leader who will, in the future, guide and assist others. The term kinaaldá is applied to the girl at this point in her life as well as the ceremony that transforms her from a child to a woman capable of bearing children. The word means puberty, and in some instances may be applied to a boy going through the same growth stages, but with a far different ceremony. When the term is connected to a male, it is usually accompanied with qualifying statements, indicating it is much more appropriate when used to discuss female matters.

The young woman's kinaaldá ceremony came from the holy people, who felt it necessary to separate roles and responsibilities between girls and women, childhood and adulthood. Talking God and White Shell Woman could see the changes in the youth taking place—deeper voices, greater abilities, shifting sociality, courting, and sexuality—and decided the new circumstances needed to be recognized. The two agreed that there should be a ritual in which the female becomes Changing Woman, able to fulfill her role and bless the people. This is when White Shell Woman became

Changing Woman as she evolved, just as her children and grandchildren would undergo similar changes. She established the activities and teachings for this ritual. When a girl has her first monthly period, the family is supposed to drop everything that is going on, tie the young woman's hair in a bun, and prepare for the ceremony. Her elders sit down with her and explain that this change is normal and desirable but that now there will be different expectations for her, because today she becomes a holy one.

This change is something that has been passed down through the generations, just as the young woman, for a short time, will later become and hold the powers of Changing Woman. The day she has her first menses, she is told that she received a "visit by the grandmothers," meaning that her cycle had started and that she became very special that day. My mother, who is now 103 years old, shared a very, very sacred teaching with my daughter when I visited her and she told me of my child's situation. My mother said, "You will do your 'man' thing and go to work doing your part, but stay out of my way. This is mine. This is my way of doing things and if I need you, I will call you. But please stay away and do not interfere. It has nothing to do with you." She also told my wife that her daughter belongs to the Edgewater People, saying, "This is my thing, my grandchild. I'm going to do it." Grandmothers are like that. They assume total control and do not allow anything to get between them and their duty to their granddaughter. Whatever needs to be done will happen. Most grandmothers are very strict about these responsibilities.

Many of the attending grandmothers and mothers, in addition to the ones of the kinaaldá, bring their traditional cooking utensils and medicine; they are there to counsel with all the other women as a group, sharing teachings and female skills. You hardly see any young people around, but there are many grandmothers. They are often medicine people, and when they gather together, they sew a medicine pouch for the young woman and put together herbs for her. These women put in salt, red powder (chííh), and different types of medicine that they have obtained during their lifetime, then mix and grind it together before placing them in the pouch. The girl runs with it four times in the four directions. By the end of the ceremony after the stretching and other activities are completed, the young girl hands over the pouch, which is emptied into a bowl and divided between the medicine women to take home and the young woman who keeps a portion. This is like a sacred circle that goes back to the grandmothers, who use this medicine for the grandchildren to cure them of sore throats, colds, and other common ailments.

One reason that grandmothers are considered medicine people is because they are too old to have their monthly period. This is why, when it comes to this type of help, they are the ones, not the mothers, who get

Grandmothers and older women conduct the kinaaldá to teach the young woman about married life and womanhood. On the third night of the ceremony, all of the ground corn is turned into batter for the cake baked in the ground. Wooden stirring sticks and hands process the thick batter to achieve the right consistency.

involved. If someone is in surgery with complications like inflammation and is not getting well, the grandmother gets called in because she carries the medicine for that. She sings her songs, puts red powder in her mouth, and then blesses the sick person on their feet, arms, and other places before she walks away. When she gives the medicine to that person, the swelling goes down quickly. This is what these women are like. They handle much of the medicine for females, while grandfathers perform this type of healing for boys and young men. He can also help a girl with medicine as long as her sickness has nothing to do with her monthly. If it does, then it goes back to the women's side for healing. He can give the medicine to another woman, but he cannot administer it. Here, the issue is female blood, and he cannot cross that line; it is only for this matter that men cannot become involved.

Adults are warned to never disappoint their children by not holding a kinaaldá. Whenever their daughter or granddaughter has her first monthly, a celebration should be held for four days. The correct time to have it comes only once in a lifetime and so they should never cheat their daughter out of a ceremony. This is one thing that a mother gives her young lady; this parent has been forewarned to anticipate and plan for the need long before it arrives.

"If your daughter is twelve years old, start putting things together for her because you don't know when it's going to come. Be prepared for that day. You cannot hold off for a day or a week or until it comes again. Once that happens, you have ruined the whole thing. You have cheated your child if it passes; they will not get the blessings the way they are supposed to."

Learning Women's Ways: Hair Care

From the beginning, the young woman's hair is tied in a traditional bun (tsiiyééł); she is no longer allowed to wear it hanging freely, signaling to others that she is now part of the adult world. The fastened hair represents darkness, rain, and traditional order. Her role is now to take care of people and not to run around with her hair loose like a child. The only times the hair is taken down in public is for a ceremony and when there is a death in the family. If it is for a ceremony, it has to be wet. The medicine man conducting the ritual will make sure that the patient who has her hair down has washed it in yucca plant suds and that it is still wet. Later, it will be blessed with corn pollen, but following the prayer, the hair is tied back up.

One of the household female tools (habeedí) dealing with the human body is the hairbrush (bé'ézhóó). It is made from the ends of stiff desert grasses that are bound with a thong or string approximately eight to ten inches above the even-cut ends of the stalks of grass. The hairbrush is very important. It addresses the negative things in life and helps to remove them. For instance, when a person is sick, injured, or depressed, there is an influence or pattern that is established, and it rests upon the hair and head. In preparing for a ceremony, the patient washes their hair in yucca soap or shampoo. If it is under the direction of a medicine man, he will sing certain songs and say a prayer to encourage the cleansing that is taking place. If a person is using yucca soap just for everyday purposes, it is not necessary to have the songs. After the shampoo has been rinsed from the hair, the brush is used to straighten the hair and remove any kind of bad thing that might have accumulated over time. There is a song about straightening things out that is sung as the hair is brushed. This is like removing the grease and dirt that has built up over time, but by straightening the hair and having a fresh, clean start from the uneven and negative things that have taken place, the patient is helped toward recovery. The head is the place that many of these problems accumulate and have to be removed. The more the hair is combed, and the straighter it gets, the quicker and better the healing.

The brush has its own song and prayer. The grass that makes the brush used to be a living plant on the land before it was selected to be one of the holy people. The honor that goes with that is always about healing, for they have been chosen to remove evil by brushing it away. They have made the hair straight so that now it can be put back in a bun, where good thoughts and identity are kept safe and protected following the ceremony. The holy people are there, and they're participating in the combing. The brushing even gets to the point of becoming a massage with the healing part mixing in with it.

Another important aspect of taking care of hair is the teachings concerning the hair tie (tsiitł'óół) used to fasten the hair bun. The tie is made from spun wool, string, or unwounded buckskin that is between eighteen and twenty-four inches long. It is thought of as a sunray serving as a message from Sun Bearer to both men and women to remind them of his promise. Just as his hair is bound with a ray, so are the people's. He tells them, "I work every day from east to west and as it was agreed upon at the beginning, I shall be paid with one human life every day. If you should ever dream about the sunray tying your hair bun, then you will know that something bad could happen in the near future. You had better have a medicine man correct it." Dreams connect people who have left this world and who are trying to tell a living person a story or to warn them that something is going to happen soon and that the individual needs to act differently. The holy people are trying to give a warning. A lot of times when a man or a woman dreams about their teeth, eyes, hair, or even their reproductive organ, it is serious. This is especially true if the dream is about fingers, fingernails, and toenails. These are very important parts of the body and are not dreamed about without a reason. One of the most significant dreams that will come true is about an individual's hair tie. If a person ever dreams about it, then the Blessingway ceremony must be performed to correct the problem before there are consequences.

The hair string is considered to be one of the holy ones and with every ceremony performed for a patient, they should wash and brush their hair, and then put their tie on their neck or shoulder so that the holy people will know them and hear their prayers. The hair string is never left on the ground, but is handled with respect because it is an individual's identity. Even if a person has only a little hair and the hair string is short, it should still be placed on his or her shoulder. For someone who is having a Windway or Lightningway ceremony, an abalone (men) or turquoise (women) bead is tied to their hair string, adding to the sacredness. This is how people are recognized, as is a medicine man with his bandana. He also may wear a bead, or if the ceremony is for him, a hair tie.

Children learn at an early age to take care of their hair by using a brush made from stiff desert plants. Cleanliness is important to the Navajo people, and so by washing and brushing one's hair, not only is dust and sand removed but also evil and pent up emotions.

Run to Catch the Sun

One of the first events in the four-day kinaaldá celebration is the early morning run during which the young woman, with boys and girls of all ages, runs to the east on the first day to meet the sun. The exercise is vigorous and indicates how much power and stamina she will have later in life. Equally important is the air the runners breathe. Talking God, at the time of creation, explained: "The more you run in the morning and the earlier it is, you will capture that special air that is clean, chilled, and crisp—the good air that lives there." This is important because with it comes stamina, agility, balance, strong thoughts, and good feelings. During each of the next three days, she will run in a different direction, breathing in the twilight colors (white, blue, yellow, black) and cool air to fortify her body. Every time she runs, she brings in different breaths of air with their various qualities from the direction in which she travels. Her goal is to take in the very thin air that lives in the morning with the coolness that sits inside of it. This is what she is running for. Talking God spoke of this saying, "The more you run in the morning, the earlier you are, the more unique is the air that you capture. It sits in the air of the morning chill and has crisp, coldness in it. That is the one you need to gasp in and bring it into your body. It is the good air that lives there. When it warms up, it feels different, and as the day wears on, it seems tired and normal. Capture the one that is really early in the morning to the east and it will give you stamina, agility, balance, charisma, strong thoughts, and good feelings."

Medicine men talk about the silver lining of things. They take the young woman outside of where a ceremony is being held after the ritual in the evening or at night, and tell her to stand before the doorway and look. She is to stay in one place, turning her head to observe, then say, "There's a silver lining. Even when the sun goes down and darkness comes in, there is still light from the earth to the sky, a little line that sits between the two. Go look at it, capture it, and bless yourself with it." That silver lining lives in the east and is part of the crisp cold, cold air that sits there and is very good for a person. The line that she blesses herself with becomes her old age. This is where the old people's homes are located along with the old people's road. As she walks that path, she will have white hair, and every time she spends another year on it, she has been given that time for life until she becomes 102 years old. Eventually, she will be given a full reward of light. The whole goal of running in the morning is to capture part of that line and have it become part of her body. That is why the young lady starts running to the east. The following days she will go to the south, west, and north to bring in their benefits and teachings about planning, working, and thinking. She receives these old teachings as she moves in those directions. Everything becomes a teaching that was sitting there the four times that she ran, giving her many necessary perspectives that she will need as a woman.

The Grind of Daily Life

Every time she returns to the hogan, there will be a sheep skin or goat skin, turned wool side down, that holds dry corn and two grinding stones—the mano (tsé daashch'iní) and metate (tsé daashjéé'). The kinaaldá then begins to grind corn as the gods watch her. She might start grinding it in any old way, but her grandmother, as teacher and guide, cautions, "No, no, no. You have to face east. You have to face east and sit with your legs underneath you. Bend your toes and sit on them. Let your toes curl and sit on them. Let the flat end of your foot expand as it curls and stretches. That way your feet are going to get stretched more so that they will be thin and longer, making it easier to walk. This will make the arch in your foot bigger and stronger. You have to exercise your feet for that and so curl your toes." This is why she sits on her feet, curls her toes, and strengthens her arches. Next her teacher talks about developing her calves. "Your calf muscles have to be tightened. So when you are kneeling down, push more to the east with your knees, which will give your thighs a good workout. Sit back. Every time you pull the mano back, sit back to your heels, and then push the entire length of your arm until your stomach starts to hurt. When that happens, your waist will get exercise so that you will have muscles in your stomach as well as your underarms and arms." This is how the young woman is taught.

As she grinds the corn, her thoughts are on what she is doing and the purpose of her work. The different colored corn representing the four directions—white, blue, yellow, and multicolored (north)—need to come together with good ideas, good thinking, good planning, and good living. These are the hopes for the future that will come to play in a woman's lifetime. This is why she is preparing the food, which is one of the most special meals that has ever been made, because the medicine people will be there participating. Some of the holy people are already observing during the day—the gods from the east, south, west, and north—in the form of Holy Winds and air people. They are invited by the kinaaldá running in the different directions, so they return with her. While they are there, they are blessing the food during its preparation, especially the cake ('alkaan) that is made from all of the ground corn. Even the children participate by chewing on some kernels of wheat then spitting it back into the growing amount of batter. This causes the starch to break down into sugar, sweetening the cake.

The individual nature of the children has a lot to do with how sweet the cake turns out.

Although everyone has a part to play in preparing this four-day celebration, the grandmother is the central figure. Toward the end of the third day, when the cooking pit has been heated for a long time to receive the batter that will bake into the cake, the grandmother directing the activities will see that the hole is lined with corn husks and then take four stalks of sacred corn and lay them out in the four directions with a fifth one coiled in a clockwise circle as a bottom centerpiece. Taking white corn pollen, she sprinkles it in the form of a cross to the directions, blessing it for the people before pouring all of the batter into the pit. Once the mixture is in the lined hole, a second blessing—going from east to west and south to north—is given before covering the batter with cornhusks followed by a layer of dirt with a fire built on top. Everybody helps to put things back together as the holy cake begins to bake.

On the final morning, the medicine people come from different directions and start singing a blessing over the cake. All of their songs are chanted, completing the part of the ritual. The young woman runs a final time, and when she returns, she meets the rising sun and has become Changing Woman. It is said that the sun looks at her and says, "My, my, my, you are so beautiful." As this happens, a relative stands between the sun and the Changing Woman. The sun's eyes are capturing the young woman and the people know that the last time this happened, the Twins, Monster Slayer and Born for Water, were conceived. This time a relative has stepped in to prevent that from happening again. He tells the sun to back off, assuring the people, "Now, we get the blessing." White Shell/Changing Woman smiles, looks at the sun, and warns, "You're not going to play that game again. You played it before with me, but not her. She is a holy one here among the earth people." This is kind of a funny story that goes with the ceremony, but it holds teachings about attitudes and behaviors that will help in life. Here it is about jealousy and how a woman will talk to her husband and tell him to stop looking at another young woman, when he is caught staring at her beauty. The man gets stopped right there and told to remain faithful.

Acting as a Holy Being

After this "interfering," the people get ready to continue with the blessing. An older woman, such as a grandmother or a medicine man respected for their skills and wisdom, are selected to bless, "stretch," and mold the kinaaldá into the form of White Shell Woman: "Who's the handsome lady

The batter is poured into a hole that has been heated, cleaned, then lined with corn husks. Depending upon the number of visitors present, the cake should be adequate so that everyone can have a piece, a gift from Changing Woman.

here? Who's tall, straight, and strong?" The people bring a number of skillfully woven blankets or deer skins upon which the girl now lies face down. The grandmother, elderly woman, or medicine man uses a weaving batten (bee ník'í'níltłish—straight lightning) to "stretch" or "mold" her to grow straight and tall, starting with her feet then moving to her legs, back, shoulders, neck, and head. The grandmother takes the wooden stick and pushes upward against the girl's legs, arms, and muscles to bless her with strength, agility, and a new life. Next, medicine (white clay—dleesh) is placed on her cheeks and forehead. This again blesses her, showing that she has already been spoken for as one of the earth's beings and that the sun should not interfere with this.

Now, she has obtained down-to-earth beauty that will remain with her, and for this short period of time, has become a holy person, ready to enrich the lives of others. After the stretching, the kinaaldá stands up and blesses with an upward movement, elders, children, everybody, while she is at this point still Changing Woman. The gesture signifies continued growth in knowledge, wisdom, stability, and the important things of life. Navajos always think about growth, as with a tree with its roots on the bottom. The blessing starts low and progresses up toward the heavens where the holy people live; this is why it is done. People look at the ground and see dead trees and stumps that are not growing, but those plants that are upright and growing into the air, are green, filled with life, and adding to their stature. Upward means growth. Dead branches are on the ground, but living things are in the air where birds are singing, the sun shines, winds blow, and rain falls. Everything in the air is lively, so this is why the kinaaldá makes this upward movement.

At the end of the ceremony, the women uncover the cake, and the kinaaldá distributes portions of it to those attending. The center piece is given to the medicine men and grandmother who conducted the ceremony and guided the girl. This is considered the heart of the cake and so is given with appreciation and respect. The remainder is divided out first to all those who helped and then to everyone present. People are to walk away with good feelings, knowing that they have been blessed by both the young woman and the holy people. Now all are free to eat, talk, and counsel. "This is a new day, a good day, and one we shall celebrate again." Everyone should feel renewed, just like the kinaaldá, by the fresh cake. Some might even take a piece of it to a relative that lives far away and did not attend. "This is the medicine that was part of a ceremony, so we share a piece of it with you."

Importance of the Kinaaldá Ceremony

A lot of people like the idea of being rejuvenated or renewed. Some may feel old and frustrated, unable to live life the way they used to; others look forward to new things that are coming. People like this are always attending puberty ceremonies, thinking "I want to go there to renew myself." They become energized when participating and feel good about themselves. At night, when attending the ceremony, they might sit there and cry about their youth. When somebody sings a good song, they may start crying about their health, life as it is or was, how they used to look, and go back to a time when things were better. The ceremony helps them work through issues and provides comfort for the future. It is also special for young people because of the good teachings on how to prepare for life and the support given by the clan people. Rituals were developed to do just this type of thing.

Today, things are changing and parents do not always make holding this ceremony a priority. Young couples and children who should be doing this say that they do not have the money or the time. They may argue that they will not get paid for a couple of weeks and so postpone it until it is too late. It is not about them; it is not about the money; it is not about time; it is about the girl and marking the event. It is on that one day, and it should not be taken from her. If you do not perform the ceremony at the correct time, she will fall short of the beauty she is supposed to have, of the good things to learn, of the agility, health, and happiness she could receive. You are taking that all away and depriving her of those rights. Nowadays there are a lot of missed opportunities. Perhaps it is because children have problems in school, do not finish or learn well, or are embarrassed. Maybe their parents are separated or are taken away from them. Maybe they marry too young, and create a situation of children having children. There are also too many domestic issues. Whatever the reason, it is a shame. No one is there to see that these good things happen for the child. This should never, ever take place.

The people in the Black Mountain area are very strict about this. I can't speak for the rest of the Navajo Nation, but those from around where I was raised know of this ceremony's importance. Mothers, grandmothers, and family feel good about their young woman once they have this ritual. They are told that everything comes in pairs, and this is true of good and evil, just as we have two brains, two eyes, two nostrils, upper and lower teeth, two arms, hands, legs—everything is in sets of twos. It is alright to make mistakes on one thing, but it needs to be corrected the second time. The Creator gave people a female and male side, one from the mother, the other from the father. They are giving you a part of their lives both physically (left and right side) and mentally (personality). Everything is in pairs. When you make a mistake with one side of your brain, the other side will be there to correct it. One balances and checks the other. The correction is made with the other side, which is your second chance to fix the problem. If the male side makes a mistake, the female side and thinking will correct it, or vice versa regardless of whether I am a man or woman. This is how young men and women are told to go through life and make decisions. Still, everyone should think twice about things before doing it. If the ceremony is missed on the first menses, it must be corrected and held on the second.

The molding of the young kinaaldá is the height of the ceremony, after which, for a short time, the girl-now-woman becomes Changing Woman. At this point, she is capable of having children and nurturing those who come to her. The elder selected to perform this molding must be highly respected.

Women's Tools (Habeedí)

One important aspect of the kinaaldá ceremony is to ensure that the young woman is proficient in the tasks expected of a woman preparing for marriage. There are a lot of traditional teachings surrounding the use of women's tools that the holy people have provided to fulfill her role as mother, wife, and housekeeper. They are designated for female use and hold responsibilities by which the woman of the home is judged by her peers, while the male, with different responsibilities, has his own tools that are strictly for his use. The woman's equipment of the home includes fire, water, and grinding stones, and the hairbrush already discussed, and cooking pots to be looked at in a later chapter. Here we will learn about stirring sticks, fire poker, bedding, and the loom with weaving equipment. While most of these objects are simple in design, they all hold significant teachings that outline the role, nature, and responsibilities of womanhood.

Take the stirring sticks (ádístiin) used to mix batter and other foods, for an example. These sticks are made from peeled greasewood stalks that are about two feet long with varying thickness. If there are nine of them, the traditional number, then they would be thinner than if there were fewer. The reason for nine is that this is the number of months that it takes for a baby to be created and born. Each of the nine sticks represents one of the months of pregnancy, just as there are nine different corners around the inside of a hogan. One travels around to them in a clockwise manner that represents the time the child is in the womb, ending with the doorway and birth. This completes the circle and opens the door to a new life. The same thinking is seen when a pregnant mother folds her hands, with interconnected fingers, over her stomach where the baby is living. Nine of the fingers are on top and joined together while one of the thumbs is tucked underneath a hand, representing the umbilical cord. When the child is born and the cord is cut, the last finger—the thumb—returns, making it ten fingers again. This is how the elders taught about childbearing and why there has to be nine stirring sticks.

The main image associated with this implement is that of defeating or killing hunger through cooking. A story gives reason for this. There was a Navajo woman whose husband had gone on a long hunting trip. He and a number of other men ran into an enemy war party that eventually killed him. The survivors brought his body and possessions back to the village and explained to his wife all of the events that had taken place. She mourned her loss, buried his body, but insisted on keeping his bow as a remembrance for her son. The men removed the string and gave her the bow to put in storage until the boy matured enough to carry it as his own weapon. She resumed life with her children until word came once again that the Navajo were at war. Soon the enemy neared the village, sending people yelling and warning that an attack was imminent. "Grab your bows! Get ready! Soon they will be in camp and if you are not prepared, you will die." She was startled when she heard this but quickly leaped into action. Grabbing her husband's bow, she searched for something she could use as a bowstring. Suddenly she thought of her hair ties, took three of them, and twisted the yarn into a cord with a loop at each end that gave the bow its tautness. Now she needed arrows, but there were none. Looking about she saw her stirring sticks, nine sitting near the fire so grabbed them. There was also a ceremonial bullroarer (tsindi'ni') made of a piece of sharpened lightning-struck wood. She planted it right in front of her, grasped the bow and stirring sticks, and waited. It did not take long for the first enemy warrior to appear in the doorway. Drawing back the bow, she let fly the first of the sticks, killing the foe. Eight more appeared, each one meeting a similar fate. They all went down. The tenth one, a chief, entered to be met by the woman striking him with the bullroarer deep in his chest a number of times before he died. She had killed the last enemy.

Once the fighting ended, the Navajo warriors went through the village to see who had survived. They did not expect the widow to be there, thinking that she had been killed or captured, but they were wrong. Upon entering her house they found her with ten slain enemies lying about. The men backed out of the home, called for the people to come and see, and danced in delight over what she had done. They announced, "We have a new warrior today," adding that this woman was really good at what she did. Everyone heaped praise upon her, declaring that women will carry their stirring sticks as a weapon of defense against physical and invisible (hunger) enemies. In honor of what she had done, they changed her name to War (Baa'), meaning that she was a warrior. Women now began to take on personal names that had something to do with conflict. This woman became the first female warrior, and so they sang her song and made her famous because of this incident.

There are two types of fire pokers (honeeshgish), ceremonial (often made from lightning-struck wood) and those for daily use, both of which can be made out of juniper or piñon. This same piece of wood is also used as a planting stick that tickles mother earth when placing corn or other seeds in the ground. Selecting a dried branch from a tree to make one is considered an honor. The old tree is viewed as a grandfather, and so Navajos address the male and female fire poker as a grandmother (used for cooking and tending the coals and so is longer) or grandfather (used to straighten wood and stoke the fire and so is shorter). They leave offerings at the grandfather tree, thanking it for its assistance. The stick is involved not just with food preparation by keeping the fire going, but also with protection, and therefore is kept by the doorway to prevent evil from entering.

Many stories and prayers revolve around the fire poker, while twenty-one songs tell about its power. It is one of the holiest objects that can be used when praying. A fire poker touches the red hot coals without really burning, yet directs them to do their job while cooking. It is always represented as one of the most sacred of all the material objects kept in the home. This device is thought of as the main person who opens the door to new things such as the puberty ceremony. It starts the process of healing and feeling better. Just as in a wedding, when a grandmother sits on one side with her relatives and the other grandmother sits on the opposite side with her relatives, they counsel the couple together. The elderly women are referred to as fire pokers and have the task of preparing the bride and groom for the hardships of life that lie ahead. They serve as doorways that open up to the realities of life, and like fire pokers, remain steady and do not burn up or perish in hard times. This is what they teach. Just as the planting stick brings forth things to harvest in the field and the fire helps feed and warm those in the home, there are many things for this new couple to harvest and feel—in a positive way—during their lives together. Many good things lie ahead if they practice the rules of proper behavior.

Another example of the power and teachings of the fire poker is when a person is praying over their sheep or horses or cows. The animals are contained in a corral, and some small fires are lit with sacred herbs that produce a little smoke. The medicine man offering the prayers starts with the fire poker, holding it as he speaks to the holy people. This is done to remove sickness, protect the animals, encourage growth, and calm them. Just like humans, the animals receive a sense of well-being.

Bedding, in the old days, was made of sheep and goat skins. They play a particular role in the home and speak strongly to the relationships and responsibilities of those living in it. When a husband sleeps next to his wife, she will be on the south side and he on her north, or as it is said in the teachings, the left and right side of the bed. If you are unmarried, then there is no concern, because both sides—male or female—of a person's body are then open. If an individual is married, then there are certain areas that they are supposed to be in. If together, the couple sleeps toward the middle or western area of the hogan, but still the woman is on the south side and the husband on the north where his bow and arrows, saddle, and other equipment are located. If an enemy enters through the doorway in the east, the husband will jump up, seize his weapons, face the threat, and place his wife and children behind him so that he can act as a shield. That is why he sleeps on that side.

In the old days, Navajos used to pay a lot of attention to this idea of the left and right side being divided between male and female responsibilities. The south side is where women, children, food preparation, and other female activities take place. When a woman walks beside her husband, she will be on the right, just as the right hand is used when praying with pollen for good things. A man, as the leader and warrior of the household, works on the north side of the home, wears his bow guard and holds his bow with his left arm and hand, and keeps the woman on his right side when walking so that she will not interfere with his male task of defending her. On his right side he prays with corn pollen and performs peaceful activities. This is why the Blessingway   emphasizes   the   right   or   south   side   and   the

Enemyway/Protectionway the left or north side. If the woman sleeps, walks, or in other ways crosses over to her husband's side, she will dominate and assume the role that should belong to him. He has lost his authority, been turned into a woman, does women's chores around the house, and takes care of the children. She will now become the one who kills the enemy, as her war name implies. The husband has traded places with his wife.

If this happens, the couple will have many disagreements. It is important to stay on the correct side of things, otherwise, the marriage does not work well. Today there are a lot of blended families. The mother may have been single for years after her divorce, dictating to her children what she wants done and how life should be. Even when a man enters the picture, his new wife may continue to act as the head of the household. She feels that she has to direct everything about the family in a proper way because her first man walked out. Often she does not give respect to her second husband and compares him to the first. If the second husband acts similar to her first husband, she will treat him the same and not respect him. This is also difficult for the children. These problems can come about because a man allowed a woman on the wrong side. This is also why a man does not let a woman or child carry or touch his bow. You tell them, "Stay away from there. Yíiyá (scary). Don't touch it. You're going to get hurt."

The loom is a very important part of a woman's habeedí, which includes a number of associated tools that allow her to support the family. The ability to weave becomes a serious undertaking after a young woman has her kinaaldá ceremony and the grandmothers have visited and explained about how this is one of her responsibilities. Prior to this she should have learned the fundamental techniques by watching her female relatives ply their craft in the home and perhaps even having tried to weave a small rug or blanket. With more maturity, however, she is told that she is now "the keeper of the storm," learning about the tools of the trade. Even during her puberty ceremony, she might be working on a rug, as the elders sing and talk about it. To get her to think about the colors and how weaving is part of life, they ask, "What is one of the things that you see in the first part of dawn and that is also part of life?" and she would respond, "the color black." They would ask, "Why black?" and she might reply, "Because I like my black hair." One of the first things that she might weave onto her loom at the bottom was black yarn, representing the predawn light, her hair and eyes, and things made beautiful by this color. White yarn might be the next color, representative of White Shell Woman. Wind, rain, and kindness are positive things that come with this color and are set in the white to the east, a direction tied to fresh beginnings, new horizons, songs, stories, and entering a different phase in life. Even the warp (vertical) strings on the loom are white, representing all of these new things through which life is woven. The young woman might say, "This is how we see things. And this is how I want to put it together."

Another part of her training is to understand the power of the tools used in weaving. The juniper weaving batten was taken from the center part of a tree and is used to separate the vertical strings on the loom. The comb used to tamp down and tighten the horizontal wool woven into a design was carved from a different tree. These were made of hard wood that could withstand a lot of use, just as the weaver should withstand the trials of life. The tree is also associated with lightning (but not struck by it), which visits it in a compatible way. This entire storm that is part of an underlying metaphor about weaving has a lot to do with how the earth is sustained on a daily basis. When one looks at a typical day, there is also going to be blue skies, mountains, trees, animals, and other things that will be put together through the colors that are used to create the rug or blanket. The elders speaking of these things say, "This is all going to happen, but before your weaving ends, you will be visited by many storms. You will also become like a holy one and be the keeper of the storm." This is reflected in the actual weaving when the woman takes her batten and inserts it between the strings, which vibrate when they are slammed down and tightened by the comb, making a brrrrr sound. This is like a storm with its thunder that is coming in. She controls it. And when she inserts more yarn between the warp, this is the lightning flashing through the sky. This is how she put her loom together and used her comb, all of which is done in order.

People say that whichever arm and hand is used, whether weaving with the right or left, designates the woman's killing side. She is told, "If you want to have a man, if you want to have a life, don't ever hit your children with the hand that you weave with. If you do hit your child on the head with part of that hand, even just a light tap, their sensibility will go away and not come back. You have destroyed those qualities. If you hit your man with that hand, especially if you use the weaving batten to hit him on the back, that man for sure will die from a disease that can never be cured. Do not ever do it just because you have a killing point." The woman's hand, because she becomes a keeper of storms and its elements through weaving, is very holy. She cannot hit with it, or else what she strikes will start to bleed or sicken. The elders counsel the woman that she has strong powers and not to abuse them—her hands could be lethal if used in the wrong way. At the same time, these hands, through their holiness, can also hold a baby, provide cures for sickness, and cook food for the welfare of family and friends.

CHAPTER THREE

Monster Slayer and Becoming a Man

A young woman's kinaaldá ceremony is a highly publicized and widely attended event that heralds in the change to womanhood. Not so for the young man going through a similar shift in maturity. Indeed, many Navajo people today do not know much, if anything, about a male's ritual transformation to manhood, and very little has been written about it in the literature.[1] One reason for this is that the male puberty ceremony (yilzííh) is kept a private event, and is conducted by the older men (grandfather, father, uncles, etc.) on the male side of the family, while women get involved only at the conclusion, serving as support staff with cooking and some advice. A second reason is that the majority of the activity centers around a sweat lodge with limited capacity and is designated for male gender use only; third, much of the ceremony is tailored to the individual and his circumstance, lasting anywhere from one to four days, some proceedings being more elaborate than others. Perry presents here a full account of what this ceremony entails. He does not, however, provide much of the story behind the teachings, which will be the emphasis of this introduction. For background information concerning the Twins—Monster Slayer and Born for Water—as well as Changing Woman at this time, see volume 1, chapter 9 of this trilogy.

As monsters roamed the earth devouring Navajo people, Changing Woman gave birth to her two sons, each with a special mission. The gods foreordained these newborns to "take care of the ruination on the earth and to kill all of the monsters after which peace would be restored."[2] These boys, like their mother, grew rapidly so that in eight days they were eight years old and ready for instruction. Talking God (Haashch'ééyáłti'í) and Water Sprinkler God (Tó Neinilii) invited them to a long race, but by the time it was half over, the holy people were running behind the boys, scourging them with mountain mahogany branches, urging them to move faster. Talking God won the race, promising to return in four days to give the boys another opportunity to compete.

The lads were sore, tired, and discouraged, wondering how they could ever triumph against the powers of Talking God and Water Sprinkler. The Holy Wind (Nítch'ih), which had been placed on their ear folds, learned of their concern and told them that if they practiced, they could beat the older men, because youth was on their side.[3] For four days the boys trained hard, maturing into strong competitors. When the race started, the confident runners began passing the two deities so that by the time the run around a mountain was half completed, roles had reversed and they were behind the gods, scourging their backs and encouraging them onward. The oldest of the Twins, Monster Slayer, won. The gods were highly pleased at the progress the two boys had made, laughing and clapping their hands in praise of their success. As for Monster Slayer and Born for Water, their fitness opened doors that prepared them for future events.

Soon the Twins set out on their journey to visit their father, Sun Bearer, to obtain the weapons needed to defeat the monsters. After an arduous journey fraught with death-dealing danger, they arrived at their father's home only to be confronted with a new set of challenges of proving they were truly his sons. He threw them against sharpened arrowheads, ground them with a mortar and pestle, had them smoke poisonous tobacco, and sit in a superheated sweat lodge, but with the help of different holy people, they remained unharmed. Finally, Sun Bearer realized that these two young men were truly his offspring. He bathed and fed them royally; highlighted their facial features to make them handsome; molded their bodies into strong physiques; dressed them in flint shoes, socks, pants, and shirts; gave them bows and arrows for killing the monsters; sprinkled them with "shake-offs" from four of his protective animals; and provided each a life feather.[4] With these experiences and equipment, they were ready to return to the earth and cleanse it of the evil beings threatening their people. A close reading of Perry's description of the male puberty rite makes apparent the origin of its practices.

From a historical standpoint, until the beginning of the twentieth century, Navajo men were constantly on alert for enemies—whether Native American, Spanish, Mexican, or Anglo American—who could show up at the hogan door on a slave raid, killing spree, or scorched earth mission. Response to the threat had to be immediate, and so training for it began early in life. In W. W. Hill's classic study "Navajo Warfare," published in 1936, the author captures what this preparation was like.

All of the able-bodied population were potential warriors. The training of children for war and for the general hardships of life began at the age of seven or eight. Boys were awakened early in the morning by their fathers or maternal uncles who said, "Wake up, be lively! If you are not up early, the enemy will come and kill you while you sleep." They were forced to take long runs, roll in the snow, and dive into icy water. As they grew older, they took runs at noon when the sun was hot. At a still later age, they were given purgatives and emetics, followed by sweat baths. Boys were told that if they did not do this, the first thing that came along would kill them because their systems were filled with ugly things that they should have gotten rid of: they would be quick-tempered, have weak minds, be unable to stand life's hardships, and therefore disgrace their families. . . . The old men said to the boys, "If you train right, you will be killed by an arrow in the chest and die like a man. It is not a disgrace to die defending yourself. Otherwise some weak enemy will kill you with an arrow in the back and you will disgrace your people."[5]

The imagery and metaphorical thought that Perry uses in his description of the ceremony is an intense mixing of the elements portrayed in the story of Monster Slayer and Born for Water and the preparations, weapons, and techniques necessary to prepare a young man for the warfare of life.

On a more positive note, instruction in the ceremony points out that there are important practices that lead to harmony and long life. As with the kinaaldá, a man should marry and be faithful, physically fit, devoted to family, good at providing and protecting, actively opposed to evil, energetic, responsible, and spiritual. The sweat lodge and protection songs used during the rite are to be learned and followed as a pattern for life. Approximately a month after this initiation, a Blessingway serves as the capstone event. This future husband, father, and grandfather is now ready to assume a mantle of responsibility and respect based upon his now informed actions.

Perry touches on a second topic of the hermaphrodite/transvestite/gay/lesbian collectively known as "nádleeh," a word translated as "being transformed," "changed," or "one who changes repeatedly."[6] At times, they are referred to as "woman who never gave birth."[7] In traditional Navajo culture, the people with this orientation are treated with high regard and often viewed as gifted problem-solvers, someone who has a wide range of skills, and is knowledgeable in spiritual, sensitive topics. The mythological reason for this view is offered in the next chapter; here there is a brief discussion on how these individuals function in society. The Navajo, in traditional culture, distinguished between the hermaphrodite and the transvestite. Anthropologist W. W. Hill determined that hermaphrodites were called "the real nádleeh," Navajo informants suggesting, "'You can tell them when they are born.' The transvestites were called 'those who pretend to be nádleeh.' 'A boy may act like a girl until he is eighteen or twenty-five; then he may turn into a man or he may not. Girls do the same thing.' Male and female transvestites were about equal in number."[8] One thing that was consistent throughout is that they were all treated with respect and honored. Adults cautioned children to always be kind and accepting. Please note, in the dominant culture, the terms "hermaphrodite" and "transvestite" have been updated to "intersex" and "cross-dresser." But because the older terms are used in traditional Navajo culture and in quoted literature on the subject, we are using them here for consistency and clarity.

Nádleeh were viewed as having knowledge that led to wealth and solutions to problems. Their innovative thinking could at times cross boundaries that a regular man or woman would not ordinarily approach, but through keen observation, contemplative attitude, and gentle spirit, these gifted people worked with the holy beings to solve problems. Perry's story about the origin of the pipe and pottery is a good example. No doubt the best-known Navajo nádleeh who exemplifies this venturing beyond bounds is Hosteen Klah (1867–1937). While he was not the typical individual one finds in this social position, he illustrates the various roles and skills that were possible to achieve. Franc Johnson Newcomb, friend and worker with this powerful medicine man, gives a detailed account of his activities in her book *Hosteen Klah*.[9] As with many nádleeh, he was involved in using both herbs and ceremonies to heal the sick. Constant study increased his knowledge to the point that he mastered over a half dozen complex ceremonies with their additional variations, many of which required numerous sandpaintings. He also became a highly proficient weaver, a skill that many nádleeh practiced. By combining his knowledge as a medicine man and weaver, he went far beyond the traditional practices of his day by creating not only large weavings with Yé'ii in the design, but also entire sandpainting images. Community members were shocked at this breech of protocol of making in permanent form pictures of holy beings and sacred rites. Yet as a nádleeh, he felt free to explore this unknown territory and its effects. Newcomb explained it this way: "The Navahos believed him to be honored by the gods and to possess unusual mental capacity combining both male and female attributes. He was expected to master all the knowledge, skill, and leadership of a man and also all of the skills, ability, and intuition of a woman. Klah during his lifetime lived up to these expectations in every way."[10]

More typical nádleeh, in addition to weaving and medicine, were well known for working hard at daily tasks normally assigned to women and accomplishing more because of their male strength. They were often placed in charge of planting agricultural fields, and at ceremonies, supervising the preparation and cooking of food for crowds of people. Other skills such as knitting, tanning hides, making moccasins, raising sheep, creating pottery, and fashioning baskets brought further wealth and prestige. Hill reported one Navajo stating, "They know everything. They can do both the work of a man and a woman. I think when all of the nádleeh are gone, that it will be the end of the Navajo."[11] Another person said, "If there were no nádleeh, the country would change. They are responsible for all the wealth in the country. If there were no more left, the horses, sheep, and Navajo would all go." And a third, "You must respect a nádleeh. They are somehow sacred and holy."

Their status in daily life is that of a woman. When an infant, the nádleeh receives excellent care and is viewed by the parents as a special child with a promising future. As an adult, transvestites had the potential, due to their physical makeup and social status, to outperform regular women. This could lead to friction and jealousy.[12] Nádleeh often dressed as females; served as midwives; danced and joked femininely; acted as a mediator during disputes between men and women; followed clan incest taboos; used female kinship terms; and did not participate in war, hunting, or politics. Sexually, a transvestite could play either role, depending upon the clothes and identity assumed at the time. John Holiday, like Perry, was aware of a ceremony that publicly recognized the change of status from man to woman, by giving a man the gift of female skills. John was, however, unclear on the procedure. "Rug-weaving equipment, such as the weaving board, weaving comb, loom, yarn, and special loom ties, were bestowed upon the person during this ceremony, enabling the man to become like, and work like, a woman. He has his own songs and prayers for that special sing, but I am not familiar with them. . . . He is still a man and a husband who has children, but since weaving is truly a female art, it is out of the ordinary. The special sing 'made' him that way."[13]

This chapter is about changing the status of males—a boy becoming a man and a male shifting into the role of a female. In both instances, there were new expectations. Perry provides seldom-discussed information about both, and when joined to that which is in the next chapter, gives a much clearer understanding of foundational beliefs concerning the Twins and the two nádleeh at the time of creation. Just as Changing Woman provided the ultimate pattern for females, so too, do these men for males. All have their place in the Navajo universe.

Indications and Preparations for Manhood

As a boy matures, he begins to feel different as his voice assumes the qualities of a young rooster, he grows taller and stronger, and might sprout a little peach fuzz on his face. The youth may start talking about more adult things, his circle of friends shifts, and he may push the familiar surroundings of family away because he wants to be different. This is when his father sees the changes and needs to guide the boy into manhood. Around the age of twelve or thirteen as a boy reaches puberty and his voice changes, his father will take steps for him to make the transition from boy to man. To start his initiation, the father or an uncle will bring him to the beginning of a five-night ceremony where a fire needs to be built. There, the young man is given an opportunity to prove and accept his approaching manhood. A fireboard (bee'elk'ą́ą́h) made of a piece of cottonwood six to twelve inches long with indentations carved in the side with a slit in the side of each notch is given to the boy with a fire drill (woolk'ą́ą́h) made of cottonwood or sagebrush around seven inches long. The drill is inserted into the indentation and twirled until the heated wood starts to fall through the carved slit in the side, creating a coal that ignites the tinder at the bottom of the hole. The smoldering ember is placed in a nest of tinder and kindling made of crushed juniper or sagebrush bark and is blown upon until the smoke turns into fire. A young man, in order to prove his ability, had to at least obtain smoke. At some ceremonies, there might be a line of youth waiting to pass this initiation test, and if they fail, they are to go home and practice until they can attend another ceremony and publicly perform the feat. By achieving this goal, they are now eligible to court. Like the kinaaldá ceremony for a girl, this is a required practice for a boy. This is part of the teachings of the Enemyway.

The symbolism of the fireboard and fire drill has sexual connotations. The board with its indentation represents a woman and her physical makeup that allows her to have a child, the fire drill stands for the male penis, and the ember that smokes is a baby. Once the embryo is created, it is like the fire, it needs to be fed and cared for, have its demands met, and also controlled. It is a fire that will never go out. This teaching accompanies the practice of not letting one's belly button (ats'éé') be seen by a female. There is an attraction between the man's and the woman's navel so that if they come together, a baby will soon be arriving. This is to be avoided.

As the boy assumes more and more manly characteristics, there are a number of steps he needs to take. The first time these changes were ever noticed, Talking God raised the question of how they should be managed and exactly what qualities this young man should have. A boy's situation

In the past, one of the first steps of a boy moving into manhood is to have the ability to effectively use the hand drill to start a fire. Friction between two pieces of wood produces an ember, which when placed in fine tinder, is nurtured into a blaze. Used now only for ritual purposes, the fire drill belongs to the grandfather or elder in the home, regardless of who made it, although it can be used by both men and women.

was far different from what women experience—so what should he become
to be a successful male in Navajo society? Talking God often relied upon
the wisdom of the Mountain People to answer questions, and so he talked to
them and the Water People to hear their thoughts. The mountains suggested,
"We have a representative with us who is straight and true. Every time we
see him, this man is always standing on top of a hill." They were actually
talking about a tree, saying that it was a good example of how a man should
be. The tree has limbs, puts on tall straight growth, and is handsome. They
were describing a warrior. The Mountain People and the plants talked among
themselves, trying to decide which of the trees had the most desirable
qualities. One type stood out—the pine tree because it was much more
flexible than most trees whose limbs broke easily. "I have different moisture
on me, my body bends backwards more so I won't break." Since all pine
trees are considered male, its moisture or sap burns hotter and quicker than
that of a female tree like juniper; the tips of its needles represent a penis,
helping the holy ones to choose it as a representative for the young man.

Talking God recognized that male youth eventually became hunters,
ones who cared for their families and protected them. As the holy people
examined the young man, they noticed his two black eyebrows. They
represent black bows that every male is born with for protection and hunting.
Through these he would see his enemies, but this was not enough, and so
they went to Cougar to see what he could offer. As one of the main Mountain
People, a courageous fighter, and as a holy one, Cougar knew what would
help, since he already had a group of boys that he was teaching to be hunters.
The mountain lion said, "I share a lot of things with my boys and so they are
becoming good hunters. When they make their first kill, I pass on to them
my black mustache. Let's do the same for young men after they prove
themselves. A mustache will be something that I will give to them as a gift
so that they can become better hunters." The black whiskers around the cat's
mouth and beneath its chin became the present to men following their first
kill. A man's mustache is often referred to as his black bow.

This comes from the Enemyway ceremony, during which the enemy
spirit that is bothering an individual is killed through words and sent to the
north or the land of the dead. A medicine man's mustache is the black bow,
while his arrows tipped with black flint are the words launched by his
tongue. Once that spirit is destroyed, it will not return to the people because
the words curse the thing that is evil. The medicine person knows how to
kill those spirits with words, just as an evil person can destroy an individual
through witchcraft. There was a man named Curly Beard/Mustache
(Dágháshch'ilí), who had a long, curly mustache. As a highly respected
medicine man, he had every right to kill with it, but he only used this against
the enemy. He chose not to curse his own people. If this way of killing is

used too much, then the person should get rid of his mustache. This power cannot be overused or abused.

The black beard on the chin has to do with the Mountainway and the cougar, while the mustache is tied in more with the Enemyway ceremony. If the beard starts up by the ears and goes down to the chin, then it is associated more with the north, rain, and the Black Body holy people. When a person wears a beard, it must be taken care of and not be allowed to grow too long. If someone wants to have it long, they must learn more medicine and prayers. If it grows an inch or two, then they have to obtain more prayers to sit with it. This is tied in with the bell or goatee of the buffalo, which is a powerful medicine animal as already discussed in the Lifeway. His beard carries songs, prayers, and medicine with it, and so if a person takes or copies that thing from a buffalo's chin, it becomes very sacred medicine. This is how it was always talked about.

A lot of people do not want that kind of responsibility, and so they just chop it off and keep clean shaven. But if you see an elder, an old man, who wears it long, that is what it stands for. He has additional medicine powers. You can just tell by looking at him that he carries more medicine than normal.

Curly Beard was the one who told stories about this. People asked him why he had such long whiskers that blended into his mustache and hung down low. He taught, "This is not just for show. This is for the thunderstorm that comes in, the snow that comes in, and all of the other types of weather. I speak with the mountain this way. It is all about the roots to all plants that grow in the ground like this. That is how I make connection with them." He meant that this was how he prayed for rain and the thunderstorm in the holy way; as a medicine man he carried these prayers in the length of his beard from his chin down to his chest. Just as he sat there and talked, then prayed for rain or snow, the moisture would come down, just like his mustache and beard, following the same pattern. Through this water he made connection with the plants. When he talked to them, they understood him because it is through this moisture that they grow. The plant puts its roots into the ground, and that is where the medicine is that brings about healing. He and his beard grow just like the rain falls. When a male is old enough to grow these things, then we will know that he has become a young man who can hunt for his family and protect them.

Remember that a very delicate point is the indentation under a nose covered by a mustache. If that little spot is not developed, then something is wrong. This is where the senses of a man—his skill and wisdom—are located to determine if he will be a good hunter or not. If a person does not have that channel beneath his nose, he will struggle as a human being. This is because one's language would be different and he could not talk straight.

This is another thing the mountain lion talked about. Next the lion directed that even before the facial hair grows, a man needs to cut an oak tree (chéch'il) for the boy. He will do this after making an offering of sacred stones to the other trees of this kind. When an oak is cut, corn pollen is put on the stump and a prayer is offered, then the piece of wood is removed and a bow carved from it. As the wood is being worked, it is soaked and placed in the ground to cure, then sinew from a horse's neck is softened and wrapped around the bow to give it extra strength. This is called a black bow and is very special. Lion helped carve and form it and once finished, he told the people that it was time to start a formal ceremony, now that the bow was complete.

Teachings of the Sweat Lodge and Altar

The next step is to put a sweat lodge together and place some sacred stones inside. Outside the people build an altar to bring in the powers from the four directions. The builders create a round structure with a hollow middle and four indentations, one in each of the four directions. There are seven to ten stones placed on the east side of the altar with an opening in that direction; the same pattern is repeated on the remaining three sides to the south, west, and north. This altar represents the Four Sacred Mountains, while the openings are the four sacred rivers, just as is found in the Navajo game of tsidił. This is where a man will hunt and never get trapped or lost. The opening in the center of the altar is where the young man places his bow vertically, while in the game of tsidił, the rock represents all of the wealth of the Great Gambler, who was defeated by playing that game. The altar is also organized the same as a human body with its two arms and two legs, but here it represents how the water runs and the mountains sit. This is where a man will pull a bow and let an arrow fly to its target. A hunter will find game in one of the four directions. When he kills an animal, he associates that creature with the direction in which he found it. For instance, my grandfather would tell us, "We are eating meat from the north," meaning that the holy ones in that direction provided it for his use. His arrow had killed in that direction.

During the ceremony, the altar plays another important role. Depending upon where the men sit in the sweat lodge, they will place their medicine in the niche of that direction—if sitting to the south, they will put their medicine in that opening. Any worldly possessions are placed in the center by the vertical bow and the boiled medicine that the young man will drink. All of this adds to the power of the blessing that he receives during the

Intense heat, intense teaching, and intense commitments are part of the sweat lodge ceremony for a boy entering manhood. Just as rolling naked in the snow in winter, running long distances, and sleeping little are part of preparing the individual to meet life's challenges, so is this "graduation ceremony" with its emphasis on becoming a warrior. (Drawing by Kelly Pugh)

ceremony. The medicine man conducting the ritual also gives each of the participants an eagle feather and an arrowhead to provide protection and to carry the prayers to the heavens. All of this was talked about.

The medicine man places the finished bow in the center of the circular altar and the ceremony begins. The young man comes to the sweat lodge that day with nine rocks that are to be heated and placed inside. The reason for nine rocks on this first sweat was that they represent the nine months that are required to form and give birth to a baby. The second time these same rocks are heated, only seven are used—each one standing for one of the seven healing points of the body addressed during a ceremony. The healing points are discussed in chapter 6. The third reheating of the rocks used in the sweat lodge goes back to nine while the last or fourth time uses seven. The numbers seven and nine represent two things. First there are two constellations—Pleiades and the Dippers respectively—that are formed by that number of stars. In Navajo medicine thought, odd numbers are used instead of even ones because the odd number allows a holy being to be present to make up the final pair. The gods use odd numbers that sit between the things that humans do in pairs. People have two of everything—arms, legs, sets of teeth, and so forth, so even numbers are not special. For example, when decorating a staff for the Enemyway ceremony, things put on it are in odd amounts such as one, three, or five, but never two, four, or six. One does not count like that. Another example is that a hunter will carry two arrows and have the third one fitted into the bowstring. Having only two arrows readily available is risky if the first shot misses, but three provide a better chance. On the arrow itself, there are three feathers, two to keep its flight stable and the third in the center to guide it.

Another physical preparation for the ceremony is making a drink from boiled medicine plants that cause vomiting for purification. As the young man sweats and then goes out four times, he drinks some of this mixture, which cleanses him internally while the sweat on the outside washes him externally. As the mixture of medicine boils, the water starts making noise, singing and talking to the people performing the ceremony. The singing says, "Nei éí hada'eizghánee ai nei éí hada'eizghánee ai nei," meaning the water and earth sing together. This is in the language of the birds. These songs came from the second world where the bird people lived. As the people emerged into this world, they realized that the bird's language was special and holy and so they learned the songs and prayers that the feathered people taught and saved them for ceremonies. There were other songs gathered along the way—those from the heavens; a third set came from the mountains, and the fourth from a lake that sits still—all of which are represented in this ceremony. All of their sacredness comes together as it goes back to the time of emergence of the people. The first sacred sweat lodge sat in the south, and that is where the teachings say that the Navajo came into the fourth or White World. Now all of these teachings were put in place with songs.

When everything is ready, the young man takes his sacred bow and runs to the east for a good distance and then bends toward the south, the west, and finally the north before returning in this circular pattern to the sweat lodge. All of this time the medicine man and elders are chanting on his behalf. Quickly placing his bow vertically in the center of the altar, still huffing and puffing from his run, he enters the sweat lodge for instruction. At this point, he can hardly breathe from the exertion and the heat, but he remains quiet, listens, and absorbs the teachings of the elders and the lessons of the Water People (sweat). The men talk to him, saying, "My son, one day this is going to be the way things are. Right now, your heart is beating fast because you just ran. Suddenly when you entered, the hot rocks confronted you and made it even harder to breathe. Life is going to be hard like this, but you are the one who is going to have to overcome difficult times and still hunt for your family. You will have to be the one who will have to be out there chasing deer and making things happen so that others can survive. This is why you are changing and are not a child anymore. You are becoming a young man, an adult. Today your heart is going to be a lot stronger and you will be able to do many difficult things." They also spoke of stamina that was sitting in there and was becoming a part of him, teaching how he should act among the people.

He is now blessed by the prayers and songs of Monster Slayer who spiritually outfits the young man from foot to head in black jet armor. Inside the lodge, he sings with the medicine man the words: "I am Monster Slayer. I am Monster Slayer from the east with my dark metal shoes. I say with the dark metal tip of my toes, lightning comes out" (Áá naayééneezghání nishłį naayééneezghání nishłį ha'a'aah biyaadéé' béésh diłhił shikee'go ádishní béésh diłhił shikee'go bilátahdóó shitsájígishgo). The songs dress him in protection for his entire body and head. He continues praying about the holy ones, saying, "I am the Monster Slayer. I represent the darkness, black shell, and the black flint of everything." He does this until all twelve sacred medicine prayers and songs are completed after which he leaves the sweat lodge.

Now it is time for him to depart on his second round, running in the same direction, following the same pattern, entering the sweat lodge upon his return, receiving more songs and prayers, emerging from the lodge, and drinking more emetic. While in the lodge this time, however, he is blessed by the powers of Born for Water and is dressed in turquoise (blue) armor, receives (figuratively) a turquoise bow and arrows, as well as new prayers and powers. On the third circuit, after carrying his oak bow, he enters the lodge to receive the prayers and teachings of One Who Was Raised in the Ground (Łeeyi'neeyání) and is dressed in yellow armor made of abalone shell with a yellow bow and arrows. This story tells of how he survived a fight with his sister Changing Bear Maiden by hiding underground before coming out and killing her. He later brought his brothers back to life. After completing his fourth and final circuit, he is dressed in white armor made of white shell and receives the teachings as the Child of Born for Water, also known as his Great Grandchild. Things that grow in the ground are represented in these prayers, and abalone shell with an abalone bow is how they are addressed. He prays to the Last Grandchild (Tsóí Nádleehé) who stands for future generations of grandsons that will eventually become grandfathers. They are spirits who will be made mortal in the future, but the chain of existence goes two ways, with the one who is now a grandfather at

The Twins, in traditional Navajo teachings, are the ideal expression of manhood and the "superheroes" that every young man should strive to become. In this artist's depiction, each has a bow and arrow for protection, a bowguard and bracelet on their wrists, a medicine pouch hung on the right side, and a life feather received from Spider Woman. (Courtesy San Juan School District Media Center)

one time having been a grandson. All is connected. These are spoken of as the rough edges of all arrowheads (bééshdzoolghas). This refers to two different types of arrowheads, one smooth and sharp and the other jagged and rough like lightning. They represent two different types of protection. Each time the young man prays, there is another sacred bow and arrow added with its four sacred colors, as well as the four sacred birds that sit on the tips of the arrows coming from the four directions.

During the fourth cycle of running, he carries his bow as he did in the first run. Following this next sweat and prayers, the young man is ready to be "stretched." He lies down on the ground with his arms spread-eagle while the medicine man or elder puts his feet underneath his arms by his shoulders and pulls upward to stretch him. Repeating this on the other arm and then the two legs, the young man is now ready to be molded. The elder takes the bow, and starting with the legs he pushes the muscles of the young man in an upward motion, just as the weaving batten was used to stretch and push the muscles of the young woman during her kinaaldá ceremony. The bow molds both legs, the body, and arms, all the way to the top of the head. The young man next stands up as other participants form a circle around him. The medicine man takes the bow and moves it from left to right and then places his lips on it, inhales its essence, and then walks away. The young man does the same, then blesses all the warriors according to the powers he now holds that come from Monster Slayer.

This is also when he receives his sacred medicine name. All of this is done with the help and in the name of Monster Slayer, who is the main holy person overseeing this rite. When I had this performed for me, I received the name of Haské náyoo'áál (The Boastful One Who Brings Things Back In). I was given this name by another warrior, my uncle, who passed his name along to me. The name is referring to the idea that as a warrior, you bring things back from the enemy like livestock, women, and other forms of wealth. Every young man receives a name, one that he will live with for the rest of his life.

At this point, the initiate is given his bow with instructions from the elder or medicine man who tells him, "The herbs that we brought in and put in the fire, and the ones that you drank and vomited were to cleanse you and to give new ideas and new ways to see things. The bitterness of that medicine is bad, just as life is sometimes. The heat that we endured in the sweat lodge is how life can become. Nothing is always going to be easy for you as a man, but you will go through it with your bow and arrows. The bow will sit by your doorway so that when you are ready to move into the world outside each morning, you will look at your bow and know that there is protection. When you return in the evening, you will be reminded again. Be honest with your bow and arrows today because if not, you will not be able to kill with them. The arrow will not fly straight unless you are truthful with them. Your back and arms have to be strong in order to give your shot power and accuracy. Your physical ability has to be up to the tasks you will face, otherwise you will not have a straight shot at life." All of this was given to the young man about how his teaching is supposed to sit. From that day on, he became one of the men and stood among the warriors. So that is his story about how he sees things.

There were also teachings for a left-handed person who has to hold his bow with his right hand. The young man who is like this is told that even though he may shoot differently and release the arrow with his left hand instead of his right, that his left hand is still considered the killing hand associated with death. The bow guard is supposed to be on the left arm to protect the flesh from being struck by the bowstring. Regardless, the kill is always associated with the left hand and arm. The bow is doing the killing, but you will be the one holding it. The right hand will be free and will not get hurt as much. It has a choice—either to release the arrow or to hold on to it. The left hand has no choice—it is the killer. No one will ever say, "Put your woman on your left-hand side," but only the right side because this hand has a choice—you eat with it, hold your corn pollen and pray with it, and keep your wife and children on that side. As mentioned in the last chapter, they stay on the right and behind so that the left hand is free to handle the bow. The bow guard is only worn on the left arm, never on the right, regardless of which hand holds the bow, indicating "No Woman Here." Even if a man is left-handed, he should not wear a bow guard on the right arm. This is the only story given to men as to how to manage their life; otherwise there will be problems between the couple all of the time.

Just as in the female kinaaldá, there are many teachings that tell how a young man should act. Many of these use the metaphor of the bow to explain important concepts of life. For instance, there is a Navajo saying: "This is how we carry our bow." What that means has nothing to do with actually carrying one, but instead refers to how a male person acts or presents himself. Just as when a young man grows into adulthood and cuts his first bow, the father and the uncle go with him and perform prayers and make an offering to it. These men have the knowledge and experience to shape the wood and are constantly inspecting it from every angle. After it is finished, the young man is given it at the sweat lodge ceremony and told, "This is the direction that is coming from the bow, here it is, this represents you. Now we have done our part in instructing you, so from now on, you have to carry the bow on your own.

Remember the teaching about the two black bows that sit above the eyes—the eyebrows—the gift from the Creator so that one can see better. Through them a person can learn what their enemy is about and how to avoid

Photographer Edward S. Curtis named these three holy people the "Yeibichai War Gods." The designs on their forearms, legs, and chest denote that the lead god is Monster Slayer with the bow as his symbol, followed by Born for Water wearing the design of two triangles with points touching. The last Yé'ii is unidentified. (Courtesy Library of Congress—Photo 39005)

harm. It is important to be mindful and watchful. When I was about nine years old and my grandfather Short Man was about 101, he gathered all of his grandchildren. He did not know how much longer he would live (he died two years later) but wanted to share an experience. He began by saying, "Every day I swallow my saliva and cough with it until I can hardly breathe. Maybe I'm not going to make it another time. I need to talk to you. I had a dream last night about all of you children and I want to share it. When I say 'you,' know that I am talking to each one of you. In the dream there was a war in which there was a big battle. People were dead and scattered with smoke and blood all over the place, but now it was quiet. I awoke as a god and there were other gods with me; the elders were there, standing to one side saying, 'I wonder whose grandson this one is?' I looked and identified your moccasins. You were lying face down, but I recognized you by your moccasin, turned you over, and sure enough, it was you. I pulled you over because the arrow was in your back, then looked at you. The arrow was made crooked, and the feathers on it belonged to a common bird. It appeared as if you were running away from a fight when you were shot. Somebody had killed you this way. I felt badly and thought to myself that I must not have taught enough. My words had not been used, so I walked away feeling sad that my grandson was killed this way.

"Then I had another dream that occurred in the same place, the same spot. The gods were there again and this time I was one of them. I wondered whose grandson was lying before me. This time I could see the moccasins pointed upward and they were yours. I made my way over to the body, and sure enough, it was you. This time the arrows came in to the front and there were a lot of them—at least twelve. These were straight and fletched with the feathers of the bald eagle. As soon as I saw the feathers of this bird, my heart soared and I started dancing. 'Haho (meaning victory), my grandson has fought well. He must have been taken by a chief. This is the arrow of a war chief. My grandson was not running away, but faced his enemy. He must have killed many foe before he went down. Not one, but at least twelve arrows it took to kill him. He must have fought well and been a good warrior. Haho!' I danced, then walked away."

After he told his dream, he said nothing else and left the room. I sat there pondering, "What's the moral to the story? What is this all about?" It took me four or five years to really understand what these dreams were saying. The first one spoke of crooked arrows made by children and feathered by common people, something anybody could do, and I was killed when trying to escape. I did not survive, had given up too easily, and died from unimportant things. I should not have died from the arrow of a child. In the second dream, I faced the enemy, looked him in the eye, and died at the hands of a high chief, while fighting well and receiving many wounds.

That is why he danced and praised me for what I had done. Grandfather later said, "So it is in life. If you should die with black hair that means that you did not do too well. If you die with the bald eagle, with white hair, you lived a good life on this earth. That is where I am going, and you will walk with me there." This is how he talked about some of these things. I could never forget that story. Today, I cherish it.

These teachings of the bow are important, especially when it is time to court and marry a woman and have a family. My father and grandfather said, "Okay, now you will be on your own. We have set roots for you, and now it is time to practice what you have been taught every day you live. You will be leaving the nest soon, independent and on your own, and will start to build a nest that is yours. Remember, if you fall with one leg, there are two, and so pick yourself up with the other one and keep going. There are two sides of your brain, so think about things twice before doing something. See things two times, hear of two different ways before deciding. Everything comes in pairs—two ears, two eyes, two nostrils, two sets of teeth, two arms, and two legs—one of which represents the negative and the other the positive. Because of this, there is always a way out, and you will never be cornered." A lot of this is summarized in the phrase "It is up to you" (t'áá hó ájít'éego), meaning we all decide what we become. Live up to what you say, and do what you intend to do.

This teaching also goes back to the time when Monster Slayer allowed the four monsters to live. They still exist and are there to confront and challenge a person each day. They are here to teach one how to be a better person. Too much sleep is not good; if you sleep too much, you will not fulfill the responsibilities that you have. It is important to be up in the morning and work until sunset and fend for the family. Even when old age comes, it doesn't matter, one has to continue to work. When a bad situation arises, it must be met with a positive approach and attitude. Whether a person is a son, daughter, in-law, parent—regardless of one's position in life, he needs to improve himself in that role. People cannot quit just because things do not work out as wanted. It is up to every individual to find a solution that fits the situation. Today a lot of young people suffer from depression, and so they go to a hospital to receive medication to solve their problems. Twenty or thirty years ago, there was no such thing. If a person got depressed, the elders would tell them to go chop firewood, haul water, herd sheep, or do something else, but not just sit there and think about it. Keep busy. Back in the old days, there was no such thing as a young person with depression. There was always plenty to do besides lying around worrying and crying about life's problems. Go to work, then go from there.

Where a Man Belongs

In the last chapter, there was a discussion about the woman's place in the hogan and how the east and south side are generally her domain and the north and west side is that of her husband, with the west side being the place of honor. The Blessingway ceremony is about kindness, peace, and the good things of life that bless us. It is based on an east-to-west direction that includes the south, where food and children are kept. This ceremony belongs to the gentle female side of healing and helping. The area from the north side of the door in the east around to the west side of the hogan belongs to the men. This is where evil, sickness, and things that are harmful are handled through ceremonies like the Evilway and Enemyway. This division of space is emphasized during a wedding ceremony. When the bride enters the hogan, she will carry a wedding basket filled with blue cornmeal mush. Moving from the east, she will circle about the hogan to the south and west where she will sit. The groom enters from the east but goes to the north and then the west to sit by his bride. By doing this, each marks their own part of the home. The man's belongings—arrows, bow, saddle, everything that he needs—sit on the north side. If one day he leaves, he will make his way back out in the same way that he first entered. He has no business on the women's side; on his side, everything has to do with the enemy or harmful elements found in life.

When ceremonies are taking place, this is the only time people will switch sides so that the women can sit on the north and the men on the south. This change is made so that the medicine powers can visit on the children's side during the ritual ensuring that growth, change, and protection will also be there. Once the ritual is completed, the normal division of space is resumed. This way the entire area in the hogan has had a ceremony performed in it. People are just living there, then it is the opposite, and that's because of the darkness and the daylight of what the people encounter in this world. Medicine is generally set on the north side and kept away from children.

Men Thinking Like Women

There is one place where the world of the female and male are fused together, and that is in the roles and teachings of the nádleeh, when a man assumes the position of a woman. Their story goes back to the world beneath this one during what is called the separation of the sexes. Part of their story will be told in the next chapter on sexuality and marriage, where the men and women, because of a dispute, were separated for four years by a large river called the River of Death. During that time, both groups suffered because the women took their knowledge and practices with them while the men held on to theirs; both had large gaps in understanding how to do things. As the men thought about their situation, they realized that there were two males that were different from most others. These two had at times been shunned because they enjoyed doing the tasks of women like caring for children, cooking, and staying around the home. They were in no hurry to go someplace or do something, and were accused of thinking like women, carrying themselves like women, and so had actually become women when they were really men. Nobody wanted to be with them, and so the two were pushed aside.

Still, they were highly intelligent, solving problems, understanding how things worked, observing, and never hurrying off on some adventure. They listened to the wind, fire, and water, making songs out of the things they heard. At the same time, they gathered herbs and healed little wounds. As their knowledge grew, these two nádleeh learned the power of many plants that reduced swelling, cured sickness, and relieved pain. They made offerings and gathered ceremonial knowledge. By the end of the four-year separation between the men and women, they had become very respected spiritual medicine people, helping and teaching the men many things. All of this was accomplished because they had been initially pushed aside and had not participated in the normal activities of male life. Now they were highly valued and held a place of importance with all of the people.

White Shell Woman recognized their ability when she held a meeting to instruct the holy beings before her departure. The people were gathered in a large hogan, sharing with her various stories, songs, and prayers that held helpful teachings for the future. When all had been said, White Shell Woman focused everyone's attention back to the center of the hogan when she appointed the two nádleeh as her leaders. The men protested, saying that those two did not hunt, did not act like men, were always serious, and never joked. How could they be spiritual leaders? She did not agree. The nádleeh knew a lot and had helped the men during their time of need, including with basket-making, pottery-making, and using clay, as well as with creating many medicines for healing. They were the ones who knew how to prepare and cook food and make the men's homes comfortable. Now White Shell Woman had a question and she needed their help. She asked, "How do we do this? There's tobacco here, and we need to use it as a medicine that can cure sickness. Can you tell me how we can get this tobacco to the patient?" The two nádleeh sat down and talked it over before saying, "We will give you something, but first we must go down to the river to get what we need."

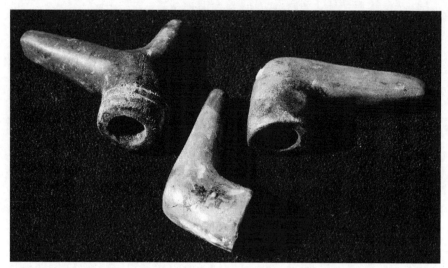

Gifts to the Navajo from the nádleeh. Pipes are used with different types of tobacco, depending on the ceremony. For instance, the white clay pipe has corn, clouds, and rain (small insert of turquoise) markings and is employed in the Blessingway. The two darker pipes are used for people with mental issues in Protectionway ceremonies. One has an extension beneath the bowl to hold if it gets too hot. Each contains the four elements—earth, fire, air, and water. (Photo by Kay Shumway)

The akéshgaan rattle is a symbol of power. Made from the hooves, skin, tail, and tendons of the left and right foot of a buffalo, and with a braided handle, the rattle represents the spiritual and medicinal power this animal holds. When the rattle is shaken, the ground begins to rumble. Only medicine men who practice Lifeway ceremonies are able to carry one; when petitioners desire a ceremony, they bring turquoise, which is inhaled by both parties before starting to plan. (Photo by Kay Shumway)

After a while the two returned carrying a fired clay pot and tobacco pipe. The fire had colored both the pot and pipe with its black and red markings. This is one of the stories that teaches about the very sacred nature of fire. It creates something that can be used with medicine or as a tool when formed and baked correctly. The object will help in a good way, just as a pipe makes the healing smoke of mountain tobacco available to help a person.

There is a ceremony that is performed for an individual who transforms from being a male with manly types of responsibilities to a nádleeh who now weaves, cooks, and functions like a woman. I do not think a lot of ceremonial people now know how to do a ceremony for them. Today only old, senior medicine men who may carry an akéshgaan rattle are aware of these things because they have the knowledge and background from long ago. They would know what to sing and how to pray, and they would tailor it to the individual. A medicine person needs to know what he or she is doing to bring about this type of change. It is all in the songs and prayers, and if they are done incorrectly, the holy people will not recognize what the medicine person is trying to perform. You have to know what you are doing.

To carry this rattle (akéshgaan) signifies that the individual is not only extremely accomplished, but that he has received it from another medicine man who has been equally endowed. For instance, Little John Benally was such a man who grew old in the service of healing people. With age he was losing his sight and some of his memory of songs and prayers for healing, and his thinking was less focused, so he knew it was time to pass some of his medicine along. He was not related to me and lived in another part of the reservation, but he had seen me perform ceremonies and liked the way that I did them. I traveled to his home, and with his family members sitting around us in a circle, he explained to them that he was transferring his akéshgaan rattle to me. He then blessed me from feet to head and instructed me in its history and use. A number of years later after his passing, his family members wanted to have this powerful object given back to the Edgewater Clan people and so demanded I return it. We went to the Navajo Tribal Court where the judge determined that the transfer of this property had been done correctly according to tradition, and so I was able to keep the rattle.

A normal person in a ceremony receives a basket to drink out of or to wash in, but nádleeh use a clay pot. That is a change that takes place. Also, at the beginning of the songs used for them, the main lyrics are a little bit different, as they recognize that the nádleeh was the one who developed many of these songs and the ceremonies. They are acknowledged in this way and are considered two-spirit people closely related to the holy ones, and they have healing skills as well. They do things perfectly and control powers, placing sacredness in everyday objects. They do not worry about daily, mundane things but focus on the sacred, learning slowly and with patience in order to achieve excellence. They are seldom in a hurry. At one point, the holy people became concerned as the nádleeh moved toward god-like perfection in the things they were making and learning and so were told to slow down before they became too good for themselves and got in trouble.

Their medicine and songs, when compared to those used for regular people, are different. As they talked to the wind, water, and so forth, they learned their teachings for healing; these elements' songs were first used by them. We are reminded of the importance of these people, who hold a lot of spiritual power and even placed sacred designs of the wind and other elements on their pottery or in baskets. This can be a dangerous thing for others to do. These very patient individuals had designed the basket in cooperation with the elements as the nádleeh sat, watched, and listened during the time when they were left behind by the people and told they were only good for taking care of children and watering the crops. While they sat there, they invented the basket and later the clay pot. That is why in a ceremony being held for a nádleeh, they are able to use both the basket and clay pot, as part of a right that others do not hold. For a regular person having the same ceremony, they would just use a basket unless they were involved in an Enemyway ceremony. At that time, they would use a gourd for drinking and a clay pot only for a drum. A nádleeh can use both because they were the first ones to develop them.

CHAPTER FOUR

Marriage and Sexuality

Teachings from the Holy People

A defining characteristic of Navajo culture is clearly understood gender roles—male and female—and in no part of the creation story is this more clearly explained than during "the separation of sexes" that occurred in the Yellow World. This story, while well known, has a number of versions as to how sufficient conflict developed to cause a split between men and women so that each went their own way. Some accounts blame the women for neglecting their duties and disrespecting their husbands, others claim it was the men who fractured the relationship spending too much time in self-aggrandizement, while others tell of an unfaithful, argumentative wife who convinced the women to join her in separating. Some accounts say it was the men who left, others the women. Whatever the case beyond the details, this narrative identifies the origin of major traditional practices and issues in Navajo society. The introduction of gender roles, jealousy, infidelity, family responsibilities, division of space, sexually transmitted diseases, nádleeh, and certain social, political, and economic procedures are still part of Navajo teachings today.

Eventually the two warring factions realized that life was much better together than apart. Both sides understood that they depended upon each other and had unique skills. Neither the helpful roles the nádleeh played when assisting the men nor the skills of the women could replace the companionship and effectiveness of being unified. Both agreed to fulfill their responsibilities without interfering with those of the other sex, while at the same time living a life of self-control bound by the laws of the holy people. Although the problems of the past were now forgiven, there remained a residue of issues unleashed by this four-year argument. The creation of the monsters, each with their own characteristics based upon what the women had used for self-gratification, would soon plague the earth surface beings. Still other monsters arose from other practices given to assist people. What had been good had now become perverted and harmful. Some of these problems were quickly overcome such as the monsters killed by the Twins. Other, less tangible issues lingered to tear at the fabric of Navajo families and individual lives. Marriage and sex were two powerful forces that both united and divided people then and now. Perhaps this is why Perry chose to spend an entire chapter on these subjects.

These are sensitive topics—ones that go back to the time of creation, as First Man and First Woman planned for male-female attraction. The men were to have as their responsibilities hunting, gathering wood, and planting fields, while the women were to prepare food, work about the home, and tend children. Still, First Woman believed there had to be more than just drudgery. She wanted to have something that would attract and bond husband with wife. That is when Coyote appeared, declaring that he was married and that others should be like him. First Woman decided to give males and females medicine that would draw them to each other.

She made a penis of turquoise and rubbed loose cuticle from the man's breast. This she mixed with yucca fruit. She made a clitoris of red shell and put it inside the vagina. She rubbed loose cuticle from a woman's breast and mixed it with yucca fruit. She put that inside the turquoise penis. She combined herbs with waters of various kinds, which should be for producing pregnancy. She placed the vagina on the ground beside the penis. Then she blew medicine from her mouth on them. That is why when people marry nowadays the woman sits on the right side of her husband.

"Now you think," she said to the penis. It did so and its mind extended across Mesa Verde. When the woman's organ thought, its mind went nearly halfway across and returned to her hips. That is why her longing does not extend to a great distance. "Let them shout," she said. The penis shouted very loud, but the vagina had a weak voice. The penis had lost its voice. "Let them have intercourse and try shouting again," she said. When they tried again, penis could not shout loud, but vagina had a good voice. The penis had lost its voice. As the organs were being put in place between the legs, Coyote came. He pulled some of his beard out, blew on it, and placed it between the legs of both the man and woman. "It looks nice that way," he said.[1]

As with Adam and Eve leaving the Garden of Eden, humankind was ready for procreation, the ability for which could be both a blessing and a curse.

In traditional society, Navajo people were reserved. They dressed with extreme modesty—face, head, and hands were the only places where skin showed. Nudity, except in ceremonial functions, was shameful and to be avoided. While language used to either joke or be serious could be ribald, the culture defined according to gender, social standing, and relationship when such language was appropriate. Otherwise it should not be spoken. Many large families living in a hogan scheduled times for people to wash and change clothes in order to avoid embarrassingly inappropriate situations. Even sexual relations between husband and wife were low key and at night as others slept.[2] Still, there was individual choice and character that came into play. While the ideal is taught, reality may be quite different. A good example is found in Walter Dyk's *Son of Old Man Hat* and its sequel *Left Handed: A Navajo Autobiography*, both considered anthropology classics.[3] The man, Left Handed (Tł'ah), sharing his life story, told of having many sexual escapades with little remorse, leading Dyk to conclude, "Clearly the Navajo are not romantic or sentimental about sex. They do not believe indulgence sinful or shameful. Dangerous it may be, but with care, its dangers can usually be avoided. Sex is a pleasure to be enjoyed like eating and drinking. . . . It is evident the Navajo can be extraordinarily reserved as well as extraordinarily frank."[4]

As mentioned in a previous chapter, some families were reticent to talk about sex, postponing a "birds and bees" discussions when possible. Two formal times—the kinaaldá and the wedding ceremony—provided possibilities, as did more adult versions of the Coyote tales told during the winter, but there was no guarantee.[5] Other families were straightforward and wished to avoid potential missteps. Medicine man John Holiday had the benefit of having such a relative. His grandmother, Woman Who Owns the House (Asdzáá Bikinii), was an herbalist and much-sought-after medicine woman who specialized in female cures. She took her young grandson on a number of extensive ministering efforts, teaching as they traveled. John recalled as they rode near Tsegi Wash in Arizona, "Grandmother showed me a formation of rocks, pointing with her finger and outlining what she said was a woman's placenta and uterus. It was hollow, she said. Right next to the uterus was the birth canal, a narrow ridge of rock, which is where the baby originates. Beside that rested the male's buttocks [pelvis], she said as she pointed to the landscape. She never mentioned anything about this until we were actually on-site."[6] The two then proceeded to pick medicine plants used to cure sexually derived ailments.

Woman Who Owns the House was well known for using plants and herbs to heal women struggling with the effects of venereal disease. John vividly describes one procedure he witnessed, although he was not supposed to be present.

When we arrived, we saw a very sick, thin lady lying in the hogan. She had received a serious infection through sexual activity with her husband shortly after the birth of their baby. She was now in danger of dying. Grandmother treated her with herbs, having her drink the medicine for the next four to five days. At one point, some of the women grabbed blankets and carried her out to the ash pile to the north of the hogan. Out of curiosity, I went to watch from afar. I saw them holding the sick woman upside down, as they poured some herbal medicine between her legs. They then put her upright as it washed her out. They kept doing this for some time. She continued this treatment at intervals for seven days. After four days, she showed great improvement.

Eventually, her husband returned home on a big black mule and entered the hogan. My grandmother told the healing woman, "Go to your husband, my daughter, and see what happens this time. He will not harm you; he is not as great as he thinks he is. I will continue to treat you with these herbs until you are healed. Why don't you go and get some more of 'his medicine' [sperm] and see if it will work." This was considered medicine, too.[7]

Grandmother taught that there were four main types of venereal disease. They are syphilis labeled as "the Man"; "the sore"—gonorrhea—as "the Woman"; "internal bugs" is the "Young Man"; and "the itch" is the "Young Female." The origin of these diseases goes back to the time of Monster Slayer, when he was hunting. He mistakenly hung a deer on a tree while butchering it and noticed something moving in the deer's groin—venereal disease. Something told him to use four different plants—white ground corn, chokecherries, spruce, and sumac—which caused the sickness to leave him alone. He was told that someday the human race would experience venereal disease, and these plants would serve as a cure.[8]

One of the greatest defenses against problems like these diseases, jealousy, selfishness, and divorce is a strong marriage, as outlined in the Navajo wedding ceremony (iigeh—"Two Come Together"; iiná—marriage). To supplement Perry's detailed description of the ritual below, some contextual information is added here. The first wedding established a number of procedures that are now practiced. Briefly, White Shell Woman one day was out harvesting seeds when Sun Bearer appeared on his white steed and gave her directions. She was to go home, have First Man build a brush shelter away from the family hogan, remain there alone for four evenings, prepare the seeds she had gathered in a specific way, then place them as mush in a woven basket. She went home and told her foster parents about the necessary preparations, ground the seeds into a fine meal with water, put it in a white bead basket, then sprinkled the mixture with pollen. Following instructions, she drew a line from east to west, turned her hand

and drew one from south to north, then drew a line around the outer edge of the container. When all was ready, she brought it to the recently fashioned hut and remained all night. Although she claimed no visitation, there was a single track pressed into the dirt, and some of the mush on the east side of the basket was gone. The next night, a second track appeared, and mush from the south was eaten, but she saw no one. The same thing happened on the third night with mush from the west, and on the fourth night with mush to the north and a fourth track added. Four days (months) after this, she felt a baby moving within. This is why women today, after four months of pregnancy, can feel the stirrings of their infant and why in the old days, following the marriage ceremony, the bride and groom separated for four days to their previous homes, before coming together as husband and wife.[9]

Details of marriage arrangements, the gift exchange, ceremony, and traditional teachings can be found in a number of excellent sources that all point to symbolic meaning and the value of establishing such a relationship.[10] A few examples follow. Take for instance, the "bride price" or presents given to the young woman's family. In the past, one of the main items was livestock, horses in particular, the number of which could range from three to twenty. The woman, who could be as young as twelve or thirteen, certainly appreciated the groom's family extending itself through a plentiful gift. Hence the informal name for a wedding—"driving the horses in" (łįį' neelkaad). The mush that the couple ate was made from white (male) and yellow (female) ground corn, blessed with pollen, not only signifying the union of the two, but also planting the seed for future children in a basket that represented a new life together. When the young man arrived at the wedding hogan, he brought his saddle in and set it beside the doorway, indicating that he was there to stay. If the marriage failed, the wife could place it with his other possessions outside the door, making divorce official. But for many Navajo couples this was unnecessary. Life, just like an arranged marriage, was what husband and wife made of it, staying together their entire time, "until death did they part."

Separation of the Sexes

The people were tired and ready to rest, following their emergence into the Yellow World. The men and women each had their own ways of relaxing and enjoying the companionship of the same sex. Indeed, as they spent the days performing their various tasks, there was plenty of time to strengthen their bonds of friendship with other women or for the males, with other men. Both groups lived a bounteous life. The women grew corn while the men had real success in hunting—the deer were fat, their cooked meat dripped with grease, and the hunters took pride in their accomplishments. That was part of the problem. The men were caught up in their achievements, so to see everyone happy just fueled their pride to become even more successful. The family became less important and the men more boastful saying, "I'm going to thank myself because I am so good," as they greased their hands and ankles after feasting. To do this was a way of showing appreciation for food and a sign of thanksgiving. Still, a man would brag of his exploits reminding others, "I hit this one deer as it was running away from me and I got him good." They praised each other, kept telling themselves how accomplished they were, and how they were the best hunters. Now when hunting, it is wrong to boast about killing a deer and not have respect for it giving its life.

The women first looked at how the men were acting and then at each other. They did not like what their husbands were doing, complaining that they talked too much. The wives scolded, "You think you might be good, but the only reason you're good is because I'm here for you. Because of me you sleep well, eat well, and are dressed well. Sexually, I am there for you, and that is the reason you behave." Some of the men laughed, claiming that they could live without their wives, there were other women that they could find, and that their lives would be just as good as ever—with or without a wife. The argument boiled over. The women countered, "Well a woman is a woman, and you need one. You're not all there by yourself. You need a woman for you to be good. That is what all your pride stands on. One thing you have to realize is that you can never live without a woman." All the women agreed that this was true and that the men only behaved because they had a wife. Only after they have had sex does a man return to being normal. The men became increasingly angry. They felt that they could live just fine without the women and disliked their control over sex. They could find happiness in just being with other men.

The arguments grew, each side becoming more convinced that they did not need the other. Sex was not the only issue as the men told the women that they would not hunt or share meat with them; the women countered that they would not cook or care for the children. "Maybe if you don't need my sex, then you don't need to eat with me. Maybe I shouldn't cook for you. Take the kids, too. You can be a mother." The men escalated by insisting, "We can wash our own clothing. We'll take care of the kids. We're fine. We'll do okay. We can cook for ourselves with our own two hands." Now the women were mad, shoving the children toward the men and saying they were ready to leave. The men were smug, pointing out that they had two

Frequent travel by men in traditional society was necessary for ceremonial, economic, and extended family responsibilities, which took them away from their wife and children. Just as with the separation of the sexes in the Yellow World, this could lead to marital problems, fragile relationships, and divorce. While the culture encouraged togetherness, daily life raised its own issues.

nádleeh who already knew how to do many of the things that women did. Separating the two groups was just fine with them.

Angered by the deteriorating situation, the men boarded a boat and paddled across the River of Death to the north side, vowing that they would not go back to the women on the south side for four years. The gods watched what transpired and felt that this would be a good opportunity for all to learn. The holy people decreed that everything had been going well until these attitudes developed. "Now we are going to put our own rules down. Anyone who gets into the river or tries to cross it will die. This one time you can do it, but we will not allow you to come back over. The river will swallow you if you do not have our permission. This is the lesson you need to learn, for these rules you are trifling with are holy ways. All of this is happening because of pride."

For four years, the men and women remained separated. Their ability to work and care for themselves steadily diminished. The first year the women planted full crops of corn and had abundant harvests. The next year, they did not work as hard and planted less while in the third year there was only half as much; the last year they did not even bother. Now they were eating corn that was old and moldy, left over from the two previous years. They grew tired of having the same thing, the corn's flavor was poor, and the women became consistently weaker. They sought wild plants, especially berries, but collecting them was too much work; soon starvation set in. They hungered for meat but did not know how to obtain it. Some of the women started eating rabbits, but those certainly did not taste like deer or buffalo. On the other side, the men wanted something else besides meat. That was all they had, no corn; they hungered for kneel-down bread or anything made out of corn, anything that would bring variety to their diet.

Even more troubling was the issue of sex, one of the main issues that had caused the separation in the first place. This is when sexually transmitted diseases began in both groups. The River of Death kept the men and women apart; those who tried to cross perished. Not until four years had passed could the two sides get together to live. Neither group controlled their sexual urges, but for the men it was worse. Men and women started masturbating, using different objects to increase their pleasure. The men killed deer, cut out their livers, and used them for sexual gratification, simulating a vagina. They also used a deer's buttocks and the female deer's reproductive system to fulfill their urges. There are a number of reasons why deer were chosen over other animals. First, they are common, abundant, and well known to the Navajo. Although they are considered somewhat promiscuous and often associated with doing things in excess, they are a very clean animal. It is one of the four-legged creatures that remains high off the ground and presents itself as gentle and female. They are very quiet and submissive and do not have an attitude. If it were a lion or bear or badger, a person would have a struggle on their hands. Deer do not fight back. They do things in their own way. That is the reason why the parts of a deer were used.

Very few people talk about these things nowadays. Some of these teachings come from the Coyoteway, the Deerway, and the Excessway (Ajiłee), all of which are interrelated and have a lot of similarities. They are also connected to the Mountainway if someone is involved with incest or something happens in the family that requires a more intense ceremony to correct an aspect of sexuality by using a sweat lodge. This is the only time that this story is brought out to teach the person who needs help. Sexually transmitted diseases like gonorrhea, which Navajos call The Pain on the Bottom (aa'dinih), need to be healed but also used to teach how to prevent it from reoccurring. To correct it, there are the Deerway ceremony teachings that can go back to when the men had sex with deer livers.

Little did the men know that all of the sexually transmitted diseases that we have in the world today were in this animal. Navajos are very opposed to having sex with an animal; it is viewed as having sex with your own food and is totally against the way we are taught. But these men did it, and so they started finding blood in their urine, suffering from rashes and itching, their scrotum swelling, and pus dripping from their penis. Urinating was a big problem because of the intense burning sensation. They just did not know what to do.

As mentioned in the previous chapter, there were two nádleeh, who had become accomplished medicine people as well as masters of tasks performed by the women. The two set to work, helping the men through herbs to correct their problems. They did not perfect it right away, but experimented with different types of plants to see what combination worked most effectively. Some herbs they boiled and used in the sweat lodge. Rocks in boiling water with herbs provided a lot of intense therapy while the people drank the liquid medicine and then washed with it. Eventually, they discovered the right combination of plants to defeat these diseases and cure the patient, but it took strong treatment to do so. Today medicine men use these same herbs as medication to heal illness from sexually transmitted diseases.

The women did not suffer as much or in the same way as the men. Their misbehavior came about by masturbating with rocks and roots and other things found on the ground. The women did not get involved in this type of wrongdoing until the later part of the experience during the fourth year. The first three years were dry, but during the fourth year, big rains soaked the ground and left everything soft. Even the rocks absorbed the moisture while plant roots absorbed it and became soft and fleshy. As the women used these rocks and roots for gratification, they did not understand that the moisture in these objects was actually causing them to conceive. Like the men, the women fell prey to sexual diseases, but it did not bother them as much as their counterparts. For men, the urges for sexual activity were stronger, diseases bothered them more, they became sick quicker, while the women carried the diseases much better without the rashes, bleeding, and itching. Even today, men have a lower tolerance than women once infected. Disease was now a fact of life and something to be avoided.

The four years passed slowly, but once the men and women reached the end, they were ready to cross the river and return to each other. The holy people allowed them to reunite, both sides agreeing to forgive each other and behave themselves. The gods taught that there were now rules that needed to be followed by showing respect and listening to other's thoughts. No more pride or arguing or thinking one is superior. Respect for the opposite sex must be learned, or else this same type of thing will happen again. Because of this experience, there is also life that ends before it should, when a couple is untrue to their mate. There may be a husband who dies before his time is through, leaving a widow. From this time forward, if a man or woman becomes involved in extramarital sex, it will cause not only dishonor but possibly death. It may be the man or the woman or both, but this places a curse (íínísdziih) on the couple as well as the person or baby born outside of the marriage.

Navajo women, noted for their beauty, also bring strong leadership to their marriage. Traditional clothing and jewelry accentuate many of the values recognized by the holy people such as obtaining wealth through hard work and maintaining modesty.

Living with Monsters

Another side to this was that when the two sexes came back together, the women did not know that they were pregnant from the rocks, roots, and other objects they had used for sexual gratification. Now they would have to face those consequences. The people began traveling together to Blue Water near Grants, New Mexico, searching for a new start, and as they did, strange looking babies were born. The first one had a triangle head with big eyes in the center. Another had a box face with eyes in the center. The people did not like them because they were ugly and so wanted to leave them behind. They placed these newborns in a hole covered by a big rock, put a lot of stones on top of them so they would die, and walked away. They had no regrets because these beings were not human children.

The people, however, had not counted on the rains that fell that year. There was a lot of water and some of it flowed under the big rock, dribbling into the babies' mouths as they faced upward. That dripping water saved their lives and gave them enough strength to live, grow stronger, and eventually push the rocks off of themselves and escape their grave. They asked the stones that had been covering them, "Can you tell me who put me there?" The rocks answered, "Look at the footprints. They belong to the ones who did this. Just follow the tracks of those people and you'll find the ones who are guilty." The two started walking, tracking, looking for those who had left them behind. When the two found the guilty people, they killed and ate them. The names of these two monsters were Big God (Yé'iitsoh) and Gray God (Ye'iitsoh Łibáhí). Since these Yé'ii were young, they started by eating children because they were jealous of them. "Why wasn't I loved? Why did you leave me behind? Any brother or sister of mine, I am going to kill and eat."

So Big God and Gray God walked among the people seeking children for their supper. They would wait to see if they could detect a child's presence or if one were about to be born. The people learned how these monsters thought and so began keeping their children inside, erasing any trace of footprints they made when they ventured out of their home, and never letting them out during the day so that the sunlight would make them visible. As these evil beings ate the children, life seemed to stop. This is why the Twins, Monster Slayer and Born for Water, were born, to defeat these creatures so that children could survive and life could go on.

At the same time, there were yet other monsters that came from improper sexual relations who were spread throughout the land and could not be defeated. For instance, there were the Slashing Reeds (Lók'aa adigishii), the Rock That Crushes (Tsé ałjizhii dóó'ak'áhí), and the Monster-That-Kills-With-His-Eyes (Bináá'yee Agháni) to name a few. Many of these were spread across the land and had been set in place to defend the Holy Trail that leads to Sun Bearer's home. Remember that even though all of these creatures were doing bad things, they were still holy people born through supernatural means.

Love with a Rainbow

Another story that teaches of birth comes from the Windway ceremony and talks about two winds. One of these was a human female spirit living on the earth, and the other was a male spirit-being that came from the east. This young woman sat on the edge of a rock ledge, admiring the beauty of the land and the far distant scenery. The canyons that stretched before her seemed a welcoming sight as the wind blew gently on her face. Soon this same wind started caressing her and singing, almost as if it were a person. She closed her eyes and started saying that she liked the way the wind touched her. She spoke louder, "I don't know if you're the wind or if you're a human, but don't stop. Talk to me." Soon the wind began blowing in a different way and began to speak. She continued, "I like that. I like that," and started playing with it. The male wind said, "I think I'm being accepted by a human being."

The relationship started to develop. The wind offered, "I'll come as a spirit to you and you can listen to me." The two came together and formed a bond; each time she talked to the little wind she closed her eyes and meditated. She really liked the way they were talking. As for the Wind Boy, he was actually beginning to understand this human woman because they could talk together with their minds and speech. Wind Boy spoke of a very nice place where there was clean air, how small droplets of water were caught by the wind, that there was a rainbow that sat beyond the flowing water, and how he wanted to go with her to this place called Rainbow Land. He offered, "Let me take you over there. It's a really beautiful place." She closed her eyes and they both started meditating and picturing themselves walking to this secluded spot. The wind brought her down into the canyon then told her to open her eyes. Sure enough, they saw the rainbow and a beautiful waterfall cascading over a rock ledge. The mist spraying into the air made her very happy. The young woman smiled, laughed, and showed pleasure at being at what is known today as Havasupai Falls. The couple stood in the rainbow until Wind Boy passed through it and turned into a young man whose name became Turquoise Boy (Dootł'izhii Ashkii). After this they climbed back to the top of the canyon and returned to the ledge where they had first met.

Now, however, there was a difference. When she looked around her it was through rainbow eyes that cast different colors on everything she saw. She watched the varying shades of color play across the land, creating scenes of intense beauty as the kaleidoscope of hues washed the countryside. The young couple sat at the top of the Grand Canyon on a ledge in the early morning, watching the entire gorge turn blue. As the sun rose higher, the color shifted to purple, and as the day progressed green, and in the late afternoon yellow. At sunset it turned to orange and finally purple. This was made possible because the rainbow was upon the two lovers who were viewing the colors and atmosphere change upon the land. If a person now sits on the edge of the ledge all day, he will see seven different colors before the night arrives.

With this new perspective, she and Turquoise Boy wished to return to the bottom of the falls, a place of unspeakable charm. This time they actually walked together holding hands. As they now physically descended to the canyon floor, the couple picked their way to the small pool at the base of the falls. There they made love in that pool and on top of the large rock nearby. All night they lay together, starting to create children. These offspring received names that spoke of their parents' experience: Baby Little Water, Baby Little Wind, The Wind That Has an Attitude, and The Wind That Has Little Behaviors.

Many of these youngsters became known as the rainbow children, some of whom still live in that area. Their descendants are known as the Havasupai people. The songs and prayers that go with this story are really beautiful. They tell of rainbows, mists, and fog with a little bit of rain that comes off of them. My father talked to me about them and said they live down in the canyon bottom, and if a medicine man wishes to perform a Waterway or Windway ceremony, he should go and visit these people. They are the holy ones who live down there, and so even though they are human just like you and me, they have a holiness that is part of their being. This is not to say that for every Windway or Waterway ceremony one has to go there, but if special powers are needed for a certain situation, a pilgrimage there to obtain water from the pool is especially helpful. Telling the story that goes with it is also important, and if you share it with the Havasupai people living there, they often give a gift, although they are not involved in the ceremony itself. Other times the practitioner might bring a gift to them or make a trade with food, especially for the bread they bake. The same is true as Navajos exchanged bread with the Hopi and other pueblo people. This is the symbol of friendship and general relationship (k'é) that ties into marriage and sexuality because it is made from corn and was cooked in the ground. As one of the first foods made out of corn, it also represents fire, the earth, plants, and almost everything that goes into the water and that falls with it. Bread is said to be one of the most complete foods because it was cooked in the earth by the holy ones. This is how a medicine man is hired by cooking bread in the ground (łeehyilzhoozh).

Teaching about Sexuality

Today, Navajo teachings about sexuality start at an early age, but the lessons are indirect and often veiled in the activities of daily life as opposed to specific dos and don'ts by the mother and father. There are times when the topic is approached directly, usually by the grandmother or grandfather, but for the most part, sex is not a normal topic. In traditional culture, animals and people are born all of the time, so the process is visually out in the open. Starting around the age of nine or ten, a child becomes aware of what is happening around them. Diapers are changed, physical differences between males and females are noted, and everyone sleeps in the same hogan and is aware of what goes on. If there are brothers and sisters, maturing becomes more visible as each grows older; this is not a bad thing to become aware of the differences.

More formal teaching often falls to a grandmother and grandfather, who do a lot of joking as they talk to their grandchildren about the future. Sometimes it is just a spur-of-the-moment lecture, but other times they joke about it by using the phrase, "Let me eat my grandchildren" (Shinálíyishdeeł— I eat my grandchildren [on father's side]). The youth has to figure out what this means as they go along with what is said. It is kind of funny when you speak about it, but today in the western way of talking, it would be almost like a sexual reference that would cross the line of appropriateness. What is really being communicated is that sometime in the future, that person is going to have a child, and that elder will be its godfather or godmother. This is spoken in a nice way with a sense of humor that has a lot of love to it. But if one were looking at it from a contemporary western view, it could be interpreted as child molestation. It could mean that the elder is suggesting he or she was ready to touch the youth. By saying, "Here, here, let me eat my grandchildren" (Hah hah éí shináłíyishdeeł), a person would want to run from that. The elder might get up and chase the youngster around as if they were going to do something, but they are really just playing. This was a way for grandparents to express their love by suggesting, "This is my granddaughter. This is my grandson. In the future you will have children and they will have children that will be my grandchildren. So I am telling you that you are my grandchildren and from you will come others. In a spiritual way, I want those grandchildren, too." In the old days, there were

Symbolized in this prayerstick are important teachings for men and women. The figures are carved from cottonwood, with a piece of turquoise (hidden beneath) for the male and white shell (lady) for the female; the yarn covering their torso is a medicine bundle, while the yarn at the base is red for healing; the other colors represent the beauty of a "short cut" rainbow. The bluebird feathers (m) and yellow feathers (f) are in front of a white bald eagle (messenger) feather, with a turkey feather (emergence) behind. The buckskin bundle, which "sits in front of the prayerstick," has inside a colored mirage stone, plant materials, and herbs, while on the outside is a black arrowhead for protection. These objects used in Blessingway and Protectionway have a multiplicity of meanings concerning social behavior. (Photo by Kay Shumway)

not the same kind of boundaries when talking like we have today. The rules have changed so that now we cannot talk like that. It is very hard to understand this type of Navajo joking if you have not been raised in the culture. But this was one of the ways that young people were introduced to the idea of different generations, how they were connected, and that they were important.

The mother and father did not really sit down and actually talk to their children about sex, leaving it to the youth to figure it out by themselves. Nothing was said about where a baby comes from and how a birth takes place. There might be some broad hints in preparation for the arrival of a newborn. How I learned about birth is probably a similar experience that others had. I was only six years old when I saw and participated in my first one. My mom did not have a babysitter, but she was one of the mothers or midwives that had to be there to assist. This was in the winter and cold. When we entered the hogan, I saw a rope hanging from one of the logs in the ceiling, and beneath it was the woman who was going to give birth. She had her hands wrapped around both ends of the rope so that the women could hoist her up a little bit off the ground. At the same time they did that, she was pushing to help the baby come out. She was well dressed and fully clothed. One woman who supervised the process, sat in front of her at the west end of the hogan, away from everybody else. Another one of the mothers sat on the west side facing her, while two others sat—one on the south and one to the north—each holding the ends of a belt that went around her. Now part of her skirt was raised while a large bunch of juniper leaves that had been boiled were spread beneath her on the ground with steam flowing upward. The entire hogan smelled of juniper as she tried to give birth with one of the mothers guiding the baby and standing ready with blankets.

Suddenly the baby arrived and soon began crying. One woman quickly cut the umbilical cord and made sure that everything went in its proper place. The new mother moved to one side of the hogan and laid down to rest. This was all a family event, a good thing that was not hidden from me, but they also never spoke about what had taken place. If I had asked my mother or father to explain what I saw, they would have said, "Don't talk about it. You'll get to know what it is. You'll figure it out." So I was never taught about how a baby was born. In the medicine way, the story goes back to Gobernador Knob, where White Shell Woman was born, wrapped in a cradleboard, and found by First Man. The baby lay crying, covered in four different clouds and secured by sunrays. This is how they talk about it in the medicine way; this story always goes back to the female hogan where we are still in the mother's womb. This is a holy hogan, and the next day when the sun comes up, each of us will exit that door (birth) and are reborn.

This happens every day as we go forth to meet our father, the sun. He will shine his light on us, and we will take the sun's rays and once again put them on us. This way life is given again every day, and so Navajos say that one is born again each time. At night one goes into the holy hogan to sleep, but in the morning a person goes through the doorway and is reborn after resting in preparation for a new day. A new day is a new life. This is how a lot of medicine people used to teach. If a person had a bad dream or thoughts during the night, then they would make an offering to correct it because the next day that individual had been born again, so there is no need for them to have a bad time.

I believe that young women were taught differently than men. We have already discussed the intense training that the grandmothers give during the puberty ceremony. I listened to my grandmother teach her granddaughter at her kinaaldá about proper behavior and being careful around men. She taught her granddaughter how to sit with her calves beneath her body with both knees straight in front of her, with her toes curled and the soles of her feet pointed upward. The granddaughter complained that it hurt, but grandmother said, "Yes, it is going to hurt now, but your calf muscles and thighs will be exercised, as will your hips. The same is true of your waist, which really has to be muscled because one day you are going to give birth to a baby who will require all of your strength to push it out. As your child grows older, you will need to first carry and later walk with him. You may have to go miles to do things with them, and that will take a lot of muscle to do that."

Animals, when giving birth, provided another opportunity for a young woman to learn about birth. Usually a mother and daughter are together at the corral during lambing time, bringing lambs into this world, cutting their umbilical cords, making sure that they can stand up, and wiping out all of the placenta. A mother and daughter share these experiences and talk about it. Men, on the other hand, are not involved and had to figure things out for themselves. Clan people also talk about it in their own way because they have medicine that they deal with, but this information is not given to the men, just to the young girls who are instructed by the older women. Men are not allowed to be part of this and are told, "You stay out of this area." We only get involved in the birthing process when songs and prayers are needed.

A lot of this kind of knowledge is being lost on the reservation. In the Black Mountain area around Piñon, people still talk and teach in the older Navajo way. The medicine follows a traditional pattern, the old people's way. But when a person moves down toward Kayenta, the teachings stray from the traditional ways, and there are more modern rules that need to be followed. For instance, when Navajos go to Black Mountain, they are often surprised and sometimes shocked by the way things are done—everything from cooking to the conduct of ceremonies. Lines are being drawn in different communities about what is and is not acceptable. In the old days, there was not really any confidentiality. How people carried themselves was more strained than it is today, because if they had a ceremony performed in the Black Mountain area, they might be sitting there with no clothes on and just shorts or a G-string with people coming in and out. The door is open to the ceremony so that anybody could enter at any time. It is just an open session where people would talk about the patient's problem in front of community members. The person being treated had probably done something wrong and so that was discussed, too. Everyone was there to help with the songs and prayers, and so the entire issue was opened up as part of the ceremony. Now, in a lot of places, things are kept much more private.

Marriage: A Family Affair

Preparing for marriage in traditional culture was serious business and could be accompanied with harsh teachings. Once a young woman had her kinaaldá ceremony, everyone was aware that she could bear children and was eligible for marriage. In some cases, she may be promised to a man but did not marry him until she was older. Both families are involved in this decision as to the suitability of the boy for the girl and vice versa. There was also the problem of having sexual activity before marriage, which was something relatives wanted to avoid. For the young woman unfortunate enough to have a baby out of wedlock, her value as to how she was viewed decreased. The young man's family that she would be marrying into may be skeptical as to how faithful she may remain with their son. Also the exchange of gifts given to her family was lower. It was all about making and keeping promises then and in the future. Along those same lines, if a wife was divorced and then remarried, the question was asked about why her previous husband left her and if there would be similar issues with her new spouse. How will she care for him and why did they separate?

In good homes, family members were very cautious in guiding the unmarried young woman. There may have been arguments about where she was going, how long she might be some place, and whom she was going to be with. These same questions were also raised for a married woman involved in questionable activity. Virginity was important because the family said, "I want my first child to come out of that one. I'm going to claim the first one. Besides, I will be taking someone else's children." That is why there was a lot of emphasis placed on self-discipline being taught before there ever was a baby. I watched my sisters growing up and how my mother trained them. Sometimes she would borrow some children from other families just to have one of my sisters take care of them and learn what to do. One time I heard the baby crying about three o'clock in the morning. My mother had to wake my sister up and say, "Go help her. Change the diaper; quiet her down and make some milk." All through this process Mother would tell her: "I know you want to sleep now, but I'm teaching you something that you're going to have to take care of when you have a baby. If you have a child, you're going to have to do it this way." These hands-on experiences were not fun, and my sisters did not like them. They backed my sisters off from having a child early and caused them to think, "Maybe I can't handle this."

Another teaching time was when a ceremony was taking place. If a neighbor was having a squaw dance, Mom and a daughter would go there to help and cook. By the end of the day, my sister was tired, but Mother would counter with, "This is family business. This is how you are going to have to live, and this is how you learn. You are going to have to be here, even though the sun is up and it is hot out there. You are going to be making fry bread in the sun by the fire. That is what having families is about and what life is like. If you can't deal with it, then don't look at the boys." Mother would always push, push, push. Sometimes the girls started crying about these hard things, and that was when she would say, "If you want to have a family, this is the way things are. I'm just showing you. Life will not stop because you do not want to be a virgin all through your life. You are going to have to practice self-control."

This is how she pushed my sisters. They did not like it, but she persisted. Even at the time of birth, when my mother was assisting, I heard her talk to her daughter about what was happening. My sister was crying and screaming, so my mother, in a loud voice, reminded her about the consequences of life. "This is all your doing. You thought having sex was just fun, but this is part of it, so stop screaming. Shut up and let's get the baby. Give a push. Push more. Stop crying. Nobody asked you to have sex. You thought sex was all pleasure but the other side is on this end of the deal. This is how much pain goes into having a child. You are probably going to be in bed with your man again and trying to make another baby, but think about it here, how hard it is." She would stand there and tell her, "Men don't go through these things, but they sure will get on top of you and have their time with it. You may enjoy it, but you're the one who is going to be doing all of this. You're the one who is going to be cooking, making milk, up at three o'clock in the morning, taking care of the baby while your man is sleeping." Mother put everything in order and did not mince words. This is how older Navajo women taught. They did not hold back on anything, and although it was harsh, the lessons sank in.

When a young man was ready to get married, the father or mother or one of the grandparents approached the prospective girl's family. This came after a long, hard look at her extended family and their reputation. Whoever received the request for the girl's hand in marriage would say, "Alright, we want this amount of sheep, cows, horses, silver, and so forth for this wedding to take place." The boy's family member would go home and announce, "This is what they are asking." If the amount seemed too high, then one of the ladies from that family would visit the girl's household and say, "Okay, if you're asking this much, it is a lot. I want to know if she can make bread and clean the house and take care of a child. Can she do all of this and that?" Once an agreement was reached, she went home and obtained approval from the family. Now it was set.

Goats and sheep are trailed to the home of the family who is about to give their daughter in marriage. Relatives often survey the area for a potential husband or wife who is worthy of joining their family. For those women who have taken care of themselves and learned how to do things, the payment by the man's family could be substantial.

On the day of the wedding, the bride and groom sat down with Changing Woman and Talking God respectively. Both sides have agreed that the two families involved in the match were well suited for each other, and so the grandfather or medicine man performing the ceremony started by saying, "You both come from good families. You are representing them today in this wedding hogan." The mother of the bride entered in from the east and moved clockwise to the south then sat down on the southwest side of the home. Next the daughter entered, following the same pattern and bringing with her a wedding basket filled with cornmeal mush. She sat down next to her mother. The girl's mother's father (grandfather) next made his way behind the mother and daughter, sitting next to his wife in the rear. On the opposite side, the young man came in from the east, moved to the north, and then the west where he sat down. Next his mother and grandfather entered along with his grandmother, who sat in the same pattern as the bride's family.

The bride's grandfather primarily conducts the ceremony, blesses the mush, and gives the opening advice. He uses corn pollen to outline a full circle around the edge of the basket, then outlines an east-west, south-north cross. This made the blessing complete before anyone takes the food. The teaching of the cross is based on directions, signifying that just as the sun travels from east to west, so will this marriage that is about to take place. It is for the rest of the couple's life and is a journey that they will share with all of its happiness and problems. Once the journey starts, it is uninterrupted. Next, the girl's father or male representative from the wife's family places before the couple a gourd dipper (t'áá ádee) and a woven water jug (k'įį' bee élya) that has been sealed with hot pitch. The groom then pours water on the girl's hands so that she can wash them, and she, in turn, pours water on his, signifying that they are both clean and following good habits as part of everyday life. The holy people are observing.

The bride's father directs the groom to take some mush and pollen from the east side of the basket and place it in his future wife's mouth; she does the same for him. They follow the same procedure dipping from the south, to the west, and north in a sunwise fashion. The last part scooped out is in the center, which represents the home and place that they will live and return to each day. Others now eat some of the mush. The girl's grandfather addresses the couple, saying, "You will both be teachers and will be represented by two fire pokers. One is going to be sitting on the east and south side, the other on the north and west side of the doorway. These are two separate paths that you are going to take. The one that is going to sit by the south doorway is called The Teacher Who Sits on the South Side near the Doorway (Nahat'á yił náhoojijí). This fire poker will play the role of a grandmother and give guidance from the female side. The other stick represents the teachings from a young man's mother and is called The One Who Teaches in the Enemyway (Nahat'á yił náádiidááh ch'ikę́ęh naat'áanii). This is to confront opposition coming from the north side of the doorway. One side is the Blessingway and the other side is Protectionway." These two ladies or fire pokers were given the task to be the doorway to an unborn child that will soon be arriving and will become its teacher. The one that sits on the south side is called "Natsóí" (grandchild on the biological mother's side) and is told, "This is going to be your grandson"; the one on the other side was called "Nánálí," meaning the biological grandmother on the father's side. They are both teachers, but neither one will take sides in making final decisions, and both will remain open to different views. This unborn child will come into the world with these two teachers waiting, and it is formed by the corn mush taken in as a seed, which will go into the mother to form the child. This is what is being planted during the wedding, and this is why the couple eats the cornmeal mush. The four sacred sprinklings of corn pollen helped form either a man or a woman who will be called Tádídíín Ashkii, representing White Corn Pollen Boy (Naadą'iłgai ła'í Neiyoo'áłí Ashkii) or the Grower Child. These relationships exist before birth.

Then the father from the boy's family asks if the groom plans to respect his bride's family. This relationship is sealed with tobacco and corn. He will give his mother-in-law some yellow corn and she, in exchange, gives him some white corn. By doing this, the mother-in-law no longer needs to cover up and avoid eye contact with her son-in-law. Next, tobacco is provided by the groom's side, then smoked. The new husband lights and smokes it first, and then gives it to his mother-in-law, who smokes and passes it along until everyone in both families, except the bride, has smoked it. Now their relationships will be straight and honorable. Both families are represented because they all have responsibilities—the grandmothers, fathers, mothers, bride and groom, and the unborn child. Everyone is in agreement and plays a role in certifying that the marriage is good.

Once the agreement is approved, the groom's mother is given the wedding basket and water jug, after which the girl's grandfather announces that the gift exchange will now take place. "Now you can give the belt or the bracelets or whatever you're coming with to the family." The girl's mother receives the previously agreed-upon objects and livestock. All shake hands, sealing the agreement. Next, starting with the girl's mother, father, grandfather, and grandmother on the bride's side, they take an opportunity to give counsel, followed by the groom's mother. The wedding feast is now brought in, and as people eat, the groom's family gets to speak. Then everyone has a chance to offer advice and congratulations. This wedding always takes place at the bride's mother's home, the food is provided by her family, and the main role and responsibility are on her side.

CHAPTER FIVE

"To Be Navajo Is to Have Family"

Clan and Family Relationships

W hile marriage and sexuality in Navajo culture are fundamental when considering a stable nuclear family, there are also important roles played by extended kin and considerations concerning clan (dóone'é) relations. Unlike the newly wed couple in Anglo society, there are responsibilities and practices that reach far beyond the husband and wife. Perry provides an excellent insider's view of what this means and how it looks. For those who live outside of Navajo culture and do not understand what a clan is, how it functions, where it came from, and how it links seemingly unrelated groups together, it can be confusing. The same is true when considering the different roles and responsibilities of extended family members when compared to the simplified nuclear family structure embraced by today's dominant society. A clearer understanding of both clan and family is the goal of this chapter.

A formal explanation, with interspersed clarification, is a good place to start. Anthropologist William A. Haviland defined a clan as "A noncorporate [does not work as a unified body] descent group [tracing ancestry] whose members claim descent from a common ancestor without actually knowing the genealogical links [physical connections and personalities] to that ancestor."[1] Returning to the beginning roles of Changing Woman, she formed four foundational clans from elements of her body. There is disagreement as to who some of these original groups were, but not about the process. The Franciscan Fathers, who did extensive research with Navajo elders about this event during the creation, related:

With the skin which she removed from her breast, she formed [a man and woman for] the Kin yaa'áanii (Towering House) Clan; from the skin of her back, [a couple for] the Honághâanii (One-Walks-Around) Clan; removing a particle of skin from below her right arm, she made [a woman and man for] the Tódich'íi'nii (Bitter Water) Clan; and from below her left arm [came the pair for] the Tótsohnii (Big Water) Clan. To each of these particles of skin, she added some of the skin taken from her hands, making of each the image of a man and woman, quickening them by chanting. And when they spoke, they spoke the language of Changing Woman.[2]

There are two other clans that are top contenders for being among the first four—the Hashtł'ishnii (Mud) Clan and the Bit'ahnii (Under His Cover) Clan.

The four men and women representing different clans first traveled with White Shell/Changing Woman, then drifted away on their own, each having a unique experience. As these groups journeyed about, they encountered Navajo and non-Navajo people who were incorporated or formed ties with those they met. Often there were supernatural events, important spiritual powers, and unique qualifications that caused groups to join forces. Perry provides a number of examples as illustration. Each clan has its own origin story and shared group traits that are often discussed as part of a member's personality. Some clans are considered older, others more recent; some are related, others are not—something to pay attention to when proposing marriage; and some are large with extensive shared ancestry, while others are small or have even disappeared. Gladys Reichard, in studying this conjoining of people through clan names, determined that there were those who obtained their title from physical places in which they lived; pueblos and pueblo clans were the next largest body, with a smattering of other alien groups (Mexican, Ute, Sioux, and Apache) at the end.[3] Anthropologists sharing in this interest want to know how many clans there were and how their derivation speaks to the Navajo historic experience. Washington Matthews recorded a total of fifty-one, the Franciscan Fathers at Saint Michaels fifty-eight, and Reichard sixty-four, although she combined and dropped some because of repetition.[4] In 2003 Ronald H. Towner summarized current scholarship by pointing out that 40 percent of the Navajo clans claim pueblo origin while Klara Kelley, another archaeologist, identified as many as "12 and possibly 16 of the 26 clans living in the Transwestern Pipeline project area [vicinity of Grand Canyon] may be of puebloan origin."[5] The same year, Robert M. Begay performed a small-scale research project through sampling to determine Puebloan linkage to the Navajo. He interviewed participants who ranged from elders who were medicine men to knowledgeable young adults. His findings indicated that nine of the twelve responding to his survey considered Ancestral Puebloans as having ties to the Navajo.[6]

In a cultural sense, the primary function of the clan is to regulate marriage and relationships spreading from that union. Due to this connection, the husband will often live in the area in which his wife and her family reside, hence her clan members are dominant. The women living there maintain much of the family property, the home, and staunch links in the line of descent. Strong female ties are again highlighted when a Navajo introduces him or herself to a stranger. The greeting follows a traditional format that underscores the female connection. First mention is of that individual's mother's clan ("born of") then the father's clan ("born for"), followed by the maternal grandparents' clan, and concluded with the paternal grandparents' clan. This introduction is as much a spiritual declaration as a biological, historical, and mythological statement. For anyone belonging to this individual's clans, there may be social, religious, or economic responsibilities once this tie is established. Strangers who meet by chance but share clan ties, at least theoretically are bonded to each other and should extend assistance if needed. That is why, as Perry emphasizes, "No Navajo is alone if there are other Navajo people around." Somewhere, through all of those networks of connections, a kinship tie will emerge.

At the same time, members of the same or related clans should not marry. Heavy sanctions are reserved for dating a person from one's mother's clan or father's clan. This is true also with linked clans that tie into an individual's primary clans. Each one is affiliated with perhaps five or six other clans, but these relationships may be unclear, especially for the younger generation.[7] Marriage into a primary clan is tantamount to incest, while the more distantly linked clans are not viewed as seriously but should still be avoided. Mental illness, disorientation, and blindness can result.

These consequences are similar to the mother-in-law taboo, whose origin began at the time of creation. Franc Newcomb explains,

> It seems that when the stars were placed in the sky, there was one group that was called the Mother-in-law constellation. Everyone was watching the placing of the stars when suddenly the eyes of all the young married men became stiff and refused to move in their sockets. "Why is this?" asked one, and the Coyote replied, "It is because you are looking at your mother-in-law!" When they understood this taboo, their eyes moved again and they could look in every direction, but from that time no married man has looked at his mother-in-law for fear of blindness.[8]

Warnings are provided as one or the other approach to prevent an embarrassing or harmful situation. There is, however, a short ceremony that can be performed to remove the taboo between the two.

While the emphasis is placed on the mother's line, making this culture "matrilineal" (not "matriarchal"), the Navajo do not discount the role of the father's side.[9] In Navajo thought, each person has four distinct types of blood coursing through their veins, inherited from both sides of that individual's line. Medicine man Avery Denny noted:

> There are four bloods and then you have the four clans. So everything is four in your body. . . . It all works together as one. . . . Your mother would be your nursing, you are fed on your mother's milk, so that is your digestive system. And then your father is the one that gives you support to stand up, that would be your skeletal system. . . . Your respiratory system would be your paternal grandfather, meaning he is the one that is going to teach you how to pray and all that stuff. And your maternal grandfather would be your nervous system.[10]

Few, other than medicine people, are involved in this type of knowledge, but it is something to consider when studying the emphasis placed upon marriage along certain lines while avoiding others.

In terms of understanding the roles that the nuclear and extended family play in the daily life of an individual, there are some excellent sources to turn to. For those who would like a scholarly, anthropological discussion of how traditional families on the reservation function, see Mary Shepardson and Blodwen Hammond, *The Navajo Mountain Community* and Louise Lamphere's *To Run After Them*.[11] For a less technical and more experiential view from an anthropologist who lived in a Navajo community on a part-time basis for years, visit Gladys A. Reichard's *Spider Woman*.[12] An insider's perspective is obtained from Charlotte Frisbie's *Navajo Blessingway Singer* and *Tall Woman*, two books derived from a husband's and wife's experiences with contrasting outlooks; Kay Bennett's *Kaibah* illustrates how many of the different family members played various roles as she grew up on the reservation.[13] Each of these books expands upon the strengths and issues of life in an extended family.

As one encounters the information in these works, it quickly becomes apparent that there are different interpretations—both in a broad cultural sense and also on a single-family level—as to how things should and do function. Personality, acculturation, economy, social surroundings, and many other factors enter in so that not everyone will agree with how one person identifies roles and responsibilities. For instance, some writers emphasize the part played by the mother's brother in providing discipline, while someone else will see it as negligible. Others view the mother's sister (also referred to as "mother") as being vitally important but in other settings not nearly as involved. This entire kinship system—known as the Iroquois system, which is one of six types found throughout the world—can be confusing to outsiders who see a number of "mothers" and "fathers" for the same child, while cousins—seemingly unrelated by Anglo standards—are referred to as "brothers" and "sisters." This widespread kinship system is totally logical but emphasizes relationships and responsibilities in its own unique way. Perry shares his thoughts as to how he sees the process from his traditional background.

Relationships are spelled out and "prepackaged" through Navajo kinship terms that provide rights and responsibilities to whomever they apply. They are often exact, specifying if a relative is on the mother's or father's side of the family, the general age, and the sex of the individual. This is true not only for close family members but also cross-cousins, in-laws, and those not even related, such as an elder being called grandfather or grandmother. These terms carry respect, recognize certain obligations and responsibilities, and define what should or should not be done when interacting. Indeed, these terms are the norm and are used so much that a person's "street" name may become irrelevant. When I was helping Navajo Oshley to write his autobiography, he talked a lot about things that he and his wife had done. I felt it was important to include her name, but he had trouble remembering it because he was so used to using the kinship term that the other name was unfamiliar. To an Anglo, this seems hard to understand, but between the use of kinship terms and the belief that an individual is not supposed to hear his or her own name a lot, Oshley's lapse is understandable.

Kinship terms also hold power. For example, Perry's discussion of how a son-in-law should act is instructive. The term can be used to keep a destructive wind away to protect people. By saying "naadaaní" (son-in-law), this word has power to push the wind aside. When a whirlwind approaches, knowledgeable people repeat this term, sending the wind on a different course that bypasses the group. On a more humorous side, a mother-in-law may be referred to as an owl. One woman noted, "In-laws are owls [associated with bad news] looking to catch a glimpse of anything. Owls have round staring eyes that never blink. They turn their head and bob up and down so as not to miss a movement and are perfect for hunting. In-laws look for negative things so that your family becomes their prey. That is why we jokingly say that one should 'shield the eyes from the stare of an owl.'"[14] Metaphorical thought has a way of creating mental images that capture the essence of relationships.

Land Based Relationships

If there is a single word that summarizes the complexity of Navajo thought concerning the world we live in, it has to be the term "k'é" meaning "relationship." The creation story is filled with animate beings who interacted with each other as they established patterns to guide the Navajo in proper behavior. Rocks, rivers, trees, animals, and land features have powers within that can be prayed to for assistance while offering various resources to those living in the area. Communities developed in certain regions where people gathered to use these resources and share daily life, and so even today, many traditional Navajos lump geographical territory on the reservation with its people according to where they live. For instance, I am recognized as one of the Black Mountain or Black Mesa people. This is the most traditional area on the reservation because of the Holy Hogan, which is considered the center of the reservation and the place where many of the meetings were held by the holy people when they were organizing this world. Much of the medicine teachings were put in place there as well as the original songs, language, way of dressing—just about everything came from Black Mountain. Right in the middle of the Black Mountain area sits Little Black Spot Mountain, which is the home of the Black Body Person. They say that is his doorway, and that is the reason for it being more sacred in that area than anywhere else on the reservation.

Navajo Mountain and its people are next in terms of traditional teachings. That area is isolated, and those living there are seen as holding on to their roots. They are strong in knowing their culture, while their language is just as good as that of the Black Mountain People. The way they dress, "carry their bow" (act), and practice ceremonies are much the same as my people. Grandfather used to call them The Ones Who Had Long Hair Buns, while others knew them as Wild People because they lived out in the mountains kind of like hillbillies in a good way. Then there are the Valley People who live below Black Mountain where Rough Rock comes out, Many Farms sits in the bottom, and Rock Point and Round Rock lie to the north and east, respectively. The people circumscribed in this area are called the Valley People. Next are the "Whities" who live around the Lukachukai (Lók'a'jígai—White Streak of Reeds Extends Horizontally Out) Mountains. They received their name because of white reeds that grow in the area and are called the White/Mountain People. This includes the Chuska Mountain area in that grouping. Those living around Farmington, Shiprock, and a lot of the northern region next to the San Juan River are called Along the River or Water People. Navajos residing on the desert land that extends south from the river to Gallup and Albuquerque then to Window Rock are known as Middle Line or Railroad People because of the railroad passing through their land.

Establishing the Clans

As the holy people placed the main elements of fire, water, earth, and air together, they saw that all four were related and depended on each other; they felt the same would be good for the earth surface beings. Once the people began wandering and separating over the land, different groups assumed names because of their qualities, experiences, homelands, or origins. The clan system began to develop, resulting in today's approximately sixty clans, an important part of the tribe's growing population. There is no reason for any Navajo to feel alone and depressed since the people and their world are filled with many different types of friendly relationships, the clan being one of the primary ones.

Understandings between these different groups evolved into rules that would decrease tension and increase compatibility. No one could marry into his or her own clan or another clan that was closely related. An individual's mother's and father's clans, reaching back on both sides of each, should be avoided in marriage. This guaranteed that prospective partners needed to seek a mate outside of their own group, creating a wide pool of related people with whom to share friendship, assistance, responsibilities, and new bonds in an ever-widening circle of friends and family. The relationship through k'é helps one feel like "I do belong to someone." Whenever a person encounters new people, they introduce themselves by announcing their clans and saying "I am coming from here," so that soon they will find someone from their home area or that belongs to their clan; this helps people to feel good about themselves. To be a Navajo is always to have family. The holy ones said that this was a good way for individuals to come together and provide a sense of belonging. This is why the clan system was developed; it is a way that will never die out—it has always been there.

Going back to the beginning, the holy people watched how Father Sun worked with the water, a female, and how male air connected to Mother Earth. Each one depended on the other to survive and prosper; remove any one of them and the others will fail and cease to exist. So the holy people said, "If we can live with all the things that surround us, why can't we have a relation with each other?" With this understanding, they told the people that they were once one family, but that they needed to be divided and go

Each generation of the three represented here have defined roles of responsibility designed to provide strength and unity. From the grandparents that provide sacred teachings to the mother who handles day-to-day training, to the child who can also draw upon extended kin, there is benefit for all.

different ways in order to spread across the land. From this came the clan system. As the people separated and walked in various directions, they eventually started to meet again the children from different groups involved in a variety of activities, living in special places, and having certain characteristics that made them unique from others. From this came the clan names, each having their own story as to how their name was obtained. For instance, if one group had Many Goats or drank some Bitter Water or lived on the edge of the trees so they became known as the Black Streak People, the group received that as their clan name. Their relationship would form and take on its own distinct qualities and characteristics. People would marry into one of these other groups, forming bonds between grandfathers and grandmothers, fathers and mothers, even down to the children. This is why through the Navajo clan system, there is no such thing as a person who has no relatives. All are connected in some way. That is why Talking God commanded, "We cannot leave anyone behind; everyone is included; there will always be a relationship with others so that no one is lonely."

As White Shell Woman departed to the west and wandered with her followers, the Navajo began this splitting and dividing process. For those people returning to the Southwest, the clans began to form. Many of their names recognized how they found water. One group dug a trench and discovered water but it was bitter, so their name became Bitter Water (Tódich'íi'nii). Another became known as The Water That Is Near (Tó'ahaní). One day, a group of people climbed San Francisco Peak, traversed the area, and decided to stay overnight. That evening they saw a fire that looked like a spark faraway to the east, down on the San Juan River. The gods told White Shell Woman that those who had built the fire were traveling in their direction and would soon join her group and add to her clan people. The next day her band started walking and went to a place called The Sun House (Shábighaní) near present-day Flagstaff. The Hopi had built it there to use as a seasonal calendar. It is made from rocks that have legs sticking out in a circular shape that casts shadows and allows people to measure the length to determine the time of year and appropriate seasonal activity as the sun shifts from north to south. When White Shell Woman's group arrived, the Hopi and Havasupai were using the site and determining that they were entering the hunting season. The two groups discussed the fire that they saw in the distance and tried to guess who those people might be.

Eventually those strangers encountered White Shell Woman's group, who learned they belonged to Near the Edge of the Water Clan (Tábąąhí) led by a chief named Big Knee (Agod Tso). He reported that they had found other people who were sick and wandering about before he took his group to the west and met White Shell Woman. Big Knee had four bows, each a different color—black, blue, yellow, and white—that hung in his bag. There were also arrows of different colors. He boasted, "Look at me. I wear the basket on my heart," as he pointed to the basket secured with buckskins wrapped around his chest as armor. After White Shell Woman had asked his name, she learned that he belonged to the Edgewater Clan. He offered more information. "I come from a place called Blue Water; I am a hunter heading west looking for big game." White Shell Woman looked at him and saw ten to fifteen women standing behind him wearing beautiful deerskin clothing. She commented, "You are really dressed well. You must be a good hunter," to which he replied, "Not only that, I have skills to teach people about counseling, how to talk, to manage things, and to care for animals and people. All of these are my followers and they are very healthy; the women who stand behind me are my wives." By any measure, he was a great leader. The people made a shelter (iłnáshjin) out of trees with the leaves still attached. This is the same kind of structure made for the fire dance. In the center, they built a fire with four sticks, each one representing one of the four directions. The holy ones began to visit as the people discussed how they could fix problems and the role each would play.

At this time, the first four clans had already been established, so Big Knee's group would now become the fifth or "thumb" to the five-fingered people, the one who would hold the four "fingers" steady. White Shell Woman agreed, "You will be the fifth clan, so we will adopt you, and you will be part of the people here." Unlike the four fingers who did everything "straight" and in four repetitions, the fifth was to strengthen the grasp. Compared to the act of holding a bow, the Edgewater Clan gave a more secure grip on accomplishing tasks. Big Knee explained, "I'm a better hunter because I can grasp my bow with five fingers, fit my arrows to the string, hold additional arrows in my bow hand, and release them when ready. My thumb is a killer and makes me a good shot. If we become part of you, there will be five fingers. We will be the big stubby one (thumb) that will make an important difference. When preparing the staff for the Enemyway ceremony, there will be a picture of a bow. All five fingers will be represented there, and as the bow is held horizontally, the thumb will be level with all the other fingers. When you unfold your palm we will all be level, and I will be the one that keeps everything steady. This is how the markings will be." That is how he talked about that. So Big Knee accepted the responsibility. Later, they all went back into the circle, back into the center of the Four Sacred Mountains.

Some of these stories say a lot about the Enemyway, but other medicine men will have different teachings. This one explains the markings on the staff and belongs to the teachings of my grandfather, but there are other people who tell Enemyway stories differently. The same is true with the migration teachings of other clans. Edgewater People say they are the thumb of the five-fingered people. We became the one that pulled everybody together, and so as we practice medicine, as we teach people through stories, as we share knowledge and go hunting, we will lead. We are on a higher level than most clans. To me, this is a lot of boasting, but I am proud to belong to this clan. Every other one has its own stories about how they formed and promote their clan people to a high level. It is all about carrying around these stories to show why their group is important and how it came to be.

Clan Members' Interaction

There are, of course, some people who may not be directly related to a person through a clan. When this happens, there are titles or names that can be shared to create a bond. Everybody who is not related to you can be referred to as either being "My Grandfather" (shicheii) or "My Paternal or Maternal Grandmother" (shinálí shimásání asdzą́ą́). For example, when a person travels from the Western Navajo to the Eastern Navajo Agency and is asked his name and clan, a relationship can develop from this first meeting. Let's say he answers, "I'm from the Edgewater People living in the west side over here." The other person might respond, "Oh, I'm related to the Edgewater People, so you must be my nephew," which opens doors to establishing an identity and ties. Clan people in the new area now become your clan relations and will provide help and friendship.

I saw how well this worked one time with a young man suffering from severe depression. He was crying and reaching out to a medicine man for help, saying that he had no family, that he did not know who his father was, how his mother had very early in his life put him up for adoption, and now nobody seemed to care. He had been pushed away from his community, had lived with some white folks who eventually let him go, and now had no place to call home. The medicine man sat there and did not bat an eye until the young man finished and then asked, "What is your clan?" The young man replied, "I'm from the Many House People." Another person sitting there said, "I am of the Many House People, so you must be my son." Now the depressed individual began to feel like he belonged to someone. His newfound relative replied, "As of today, you become my son. If you do not have a mother, you know where your mother is now. Come look for answers my way."

This is why every time a person goes someplace new, they introduce themselves—their clan and where they are from. Someone will probably be from that area or will be a clan relative. There will be a connection through k'é. I find that every time I do a ceremony someplace, a person will say, "Oh, you're my uncle or grandfather and I am related to you." This makes me feel good and that I belong. To be Navajo is to have family. That is why the holy ones developed the clan system. They said this is a good way of coming together, and you will belong to everybody and everybody will belong to you. K'é has always been there.

About seven years ago, I went to a conference in Billings, Montana, where a large group of Native American medicine men from seventy-two tribes gathered to talk about traditional practices. People wanted to know how their teachings and ceremonies were received and what kind of herbs they were using. I represented the Navajo people along with five other medicine men, each a specialist in a particular ceremony. The conference organizers gave us five tables to set up a lot of our medicines and herbs—all of which were named and had accompanying pictures, showing how and why they were used. I was responsible, in general, to answer questions. Most

Nuclear and extended family bonds are often close, and embedded within them is the responsibility to work and share together. Whether preparing food for storage as seen here; cooking at, paying for, or assisting with a ceremony; or caring for a family member—there is a strong sense of group involvement.

of the tribes did not have many practitioners and did not bring much in traditional medicine. The Mohawks did not have any medicine, and the Sioux had only a small amount, but the Navajos had 118 different kinds.

One of the things that really impressed the other groups was the Navajo clan system. We were the only ones really structured that way. Some people thought that scholars must have put this system together, but they were told that it was the holy people and that its roots went deep into our history and culture. When we talked about k'é, everybody liked it. Even the people from Washington, D.C., really appreciated it and admired that Navajos know who and where their clan people are. The problem with intermarriage that some tribes face is avoided through our clan system that specifies who can or cannot marry. Our system was highly respected and heavily discussed.

Grandparents: Counseling in Holiness

Daily life for a Navajo at home is often embedded in the extended family, where grandparents, mother and father, aunts and uncles, and in-laws contribute in preparing the next generation according to traditional values. Starting with the role of the grandmothers and grandfathers, each person ideally establishes a particular type of relationship in teaching, while avoiding tasks that are others' responsibilities. Grandparents are important in teaching about spiritual things. They avoid a lot of the instructing about mundane responsibilities where conflict or resentment might arise, and instead foster an atmosphere of peace conducive to discussing religious teachings. They remain on the outside of issues so that they can look over the whole family. They are like the gods who are concerned with spirituality and developing character as opposed to the concerns of the physical world. This is why family members turn to them for answers and ask them questions first before going to others. Even if they know the answer, people will seek out their grandparents first to ask about what kind of ceremony is needed, what has caused a problem, and how should they have acted. This shows respect for the elders and provides a second opinion. The grandparents' approval is important in the decision-making process because they look at things from a different perspective, outside of a short-term solution.

People in the family and community recognize the importance of these elders, whose names are often the family's identity. The grandparents' name is the first one said before that of the father or mother, son or daughter, or a grandchild is mentioned. For instance, a person might use a grandparent named Many Beads to identify a baby, son, daughter, or maternal and paternal grandchildren (Biyo'łání be'awéé', Biyo'łání biye', Biyo'łání bitsi', Biyo'łání bitsói, Biyo'łání binálí). These people were recognized through the grandmothers and grandfathers in the old days, not by their own individual name. If a young man is going to perform a ceremony as a medicine man, people would not use his name, but rather that of his grandfather, saying Many Beads' Grandson, just as a girl having her kinaaldá would be referred to as Many Beads' Granddaughter. Using this name shows that these elders are highly respected as "the big people on top." Even when introducing yourself, you always use them as part of your identity by saying, "My grandfather is Many Beads." Once the grandfather's name is mentioned, most people will recognize you and say, "Oh, you're the grandchild to that man," because usually the grandmother or grandfather have accomplished something for which they are well known. By following this practice, the people show respect to the family.

This same type of attitude is shown when a person picks a plant, addresses a river, speaks to a rock, prays to the stars, talks to a mountain, or sings to the air. The speaker identifies him or herself as being their granddaughter or grandson instead of daughter or son. This has always been done because those natural objects are much older than we are. Consider the tree that stood for all the plants. This is called The One That Stands on This

Earth That Has Roots in the Ground and Grows Straight before Me into the Sky (Ni' Yiyah Niizíní Yá Yiyah Niizíní). It will meet the clouds somewhere, so this is the one that we stand with as a plant. It was once a small sapling, but is now a mighty tree that has been there for years and years, watching and helping our grandfathers, generation after generation. Anything that grows on the earth is their brother and sister. Because they are so much older than we are, we always call them "grandmother" or "grandfather." When we pray to them, we identify ourselves as a young child, saying, "I am your grandchild. I come before you today and give an offering, because I'm asking for your help. I am requesting assistance so I will sing a song for you and say a prayer so that you will let me take some of this plant back to heal another individual." This is how you show respect and form that good relationship.

Grandparents are always the peacemakers, are not really into discipline, but may share some strong teachings to emphasize the right and wrong way to do things. They can often provide compromise when a son or daughter is at odds with their parents. For instance, let's say a daughter is really disciplining the grandchildren harshly. The grandmother might talk to her and tell her to take it easy on them, and then share advice as to how to handle the situation differently. To the grandchildren, the grandmother is a mediator, and to the daughter she is a helper. If things do not work between the children and parents, grandmother might say, "Let me take over. The children can live with me for a while so that I can teach softly, correctly, and more openly about things." Grandmothers and grandfathers are like that, never harsh, but always respected. Grandchildren should never talk back or fight with them.

Mother and Father: Trainers for Life

The relationship of the children with the mother and father is based in training for the practical needs of daily life. While the mother and father work together to raise the children, generally, the mother disciplines and directs the young daughters, and the father does the same for the young boys. If there are major decisions such as marrying young or other life altering events, both parents get involved in counseling. In an ideal situation, the parents sit down with the young person and talk through their plans and the consequences of their decisions. Discipline may or may not be applied by the father, but if there is no father in the home, then one of the uncles will step in. These men can be very firm: "I'm going to put my foot down. This is the way things are going to be" and the mother usually goes along with what is said.

Usually the mother plays the greater role in running the household and working with the children. One reason for this is the importance of her clan in providing identity. It is how one represents oneself. If it is an important situation that would reflect on the clan, then the mother would get involved. For instance, if there were going to be a squaw dance and some of the medicine people want to use one of the children to play a role in the ceremony, the mother has responsibility for deciding that. She may involve her sisters by coming together to decide then say, "Tell the father to stay out because he is on the outside of our clan and this is a clan decision that has to be made. We alone are the ones who stand here; we will make the decision as to how this will work, and this is how we are going to prepare." The mother's side can go much deeper in some areas.

If the problem is that someone is skipping school, smoking dope, or drinking alcohol, then the father is the one who enforces family law. This happened in my family when my sister ran away with some girls and my mother had to go and bring her home. She spanked her with the weaving batten used for making rugs, but it was not enough, and she ran away again. That is when my father got involved; he did not say much other than "I've got a little whip here that I'm going to have to spank you with." He grabbed that rawhide whip used for horses and really punished her. My sister was crying, wailing, and resisting; I felt very badly for her, but in the evening, after dinner when we were ready to go to bed, father sat us down. He talked kindly to my sister but made it plain that he wanted all of us to hear his thoughts and understand why he had done what was necessary. Father said, "The only reason I did that to you today is because you did things that were wrong. That made it necessary for me to spank you. I love you more than a lot of things, so I do not want you to get hurt. You cannot do anything you want; this is the reason I spanked you. If you do it again, it will happen again. Don't underestimate my power or determination. The whip is standing right there and it is not just to be looked at." Good enough. After that, she never did it again. Today, my sister is about seventy years old, and she still talks about that incident. She says, "If my dad had whipped me more, I would have been a different person. Because I learned from that, I'm glad that he did it because at the time, I thought I had the world in the palm of my hand. I was seventeen and ran away, but he brought me back and straightened my life out." She is really grateful that he cared enough to take that action.

Aunts and Uncles: The Ones to "Walk With"

Another group of extended family members who are important are an individual's aunts and uncles on both the mother's and father's side. While all of these relations are honored, there is a word in Navajo meaning "my uncle" (shidá'á) that shows the highest respect for a particular individual. One does not use that term unless they really know, understand, and honor that person. He is very dear to you, and you will never go against him. His teachings are highly valued, and so you stand with them throughout your life. That is how strongly you respect him and what he represents. Once you use the word shidá'á, you cannot take it back. It is a way of binding that relationship, and when that term is used, it has to be upheld. The word actually communicates more than just "my uncle" or "my mother's brother," carrying the feeling of "The Great One." If it happens to be my mother's sister, the word is shik'a'í, also meaning she is very special. She is the one I will really listen to and will represent her life by my actions. I will be like her and pray for her, and she will be my role model. These two words used for an uncle and aunt can be applied to only one male and one female person in an individual's life. I had a great aunt like that, who grew up with my mother and they were best friends. They were raised together, played with each other, shared toys, and slept beside each other in the hogan. Everything they learned was learned together and their work performed together, so they formed very strong bonds of sisterly love. That connection was also passed on to my mother's children. Even years after they both had their own families, this aunt would say when I got out of high school, "When is my son coming home?" She thought of me as her biological son and talked to me and my brothers and sisters that way. She loved us like that and at times cried for us when she was concerned, then would hold us saying, "My sister's child."

My uncle was the same way. I had a very deep relationship with him, even to the point that when I went away to work and then came back, I always had a gift for him. He expected it and would ask, "When is my nephew going to be home?" While he anticipated the present, he also loved us far beyond what was normally expected of an uncle. Once I returned, he would set up the sweat lodge, just for me, and we would sit in there and talk and pray and sing together. This is how a special aunt and uncle act when they really love you. This is an important relationship since there may be five uncles or aunts, but this is the one that stands out among all the rest and for an individual, either boy or girl, there is only one. They are the ones you walk with.

There is a difference between the roles that a grandmother and grandfather play as opposed to those of the special aunt and uncle. These last two act very much like a father and mother, getting involved in daily activities and teaching life skills, while the grandmother and grandfather share a lot of religious and philosophical teachings but do not usually handle discipline and day-to-day matters. Respect is shown to all, but I have seen aunts who take on more of the responsibility of raising the children than some biological mothers, even to the point of adopting their nephew or niece and raising them as their own. They do not get too involved with the grandparents, who spend more time on traditional teachings. The aunts and uncles help the father and mother in making decisions that guide their children. For instance, if a mother is having problems with her son, she might tell him, "Go talk to your uncle." The uncle then plays the role more as a mother or brother figure than that of a father, providing counsel on proper behavior and being compatible with other people. The father's teachings are always about the other side, the male or Enemyway teachings. His responsibility is what people call today "tough love" and the difficulties of life.

Not so for the uncle who is open and will not get after a person, or if he does, it will be discipline in a nice way. This is often couched in love,

These temporary structures, where cooking and socializing take place during an Enemyway ceremony, illustrate Perry's emphasis on keeping different clans separate even though everyone is working toward the same goal. At times, clan rivalry becomes tangible.

respect, and the teachings of the clan people, saying, "Okay, if you respect yourself, then this is the Edgewater way, my way and my sister's way. We teach this in the Edgewater Clan. Our clan has to be proud of its people and so I am stepping in to tell you that we're going to carry our bow and arrows this way. We're going to be straight people." The aunts and uncles all stay within the mother's line. Once in a while they may step up to be on the father's side, but they really do not want to do that unless his teachings have to go in another direction of his clan people. Usually he or she stays focused with their immediate family, pointing out that what he is teaching comes from blood or clan connections. Since we are the same people, we use those teachings.

In-Laws to Out-Laws

This brings us to the role of in-laws and how they are treated. Because of the Navajo marriage system, a wedding joins two different clans and teachings together into one family. Now, it becomes important as to how the young man presents himself to the family circle of another great clan. This can be very hard to do because there is often criticism and different expectations. For example, when I got married, I found that my mother-in-law's family and their lifestyle were opposite of mine and the way I had been taught. I had to really look at what was going on and say, "How do I make it easier for them to accept me for who I am?" This was not accomplished overnight, and there was a lot to learn and practice before I finally knew what was wanted. I felt like I was always being pushed off to the side as her family members waited for me to prove myself. How hard you try to get into the circle is what people are really looking at. They feel like you do not belong to their clan, which you do not, period. You have a different life, teachings, and family, so you come to them as a big stranger. The in-laws are saying, "Show me. Show me what you got. I'm not going to accept your words. Show me through action and prove yourself. That is what I want to know. Can you build a house for my daughter? Oh good. That is what I want to see. Now I'm beginning to see that you are worthy." If you buy a vehicle for them, you are on the right road, but you have not arrived yet. This process may take at least two to three years before people really begin to see that you're a good person.

This is so different from the Anglo world, when a son or daughter marries and is immediately accepted as a member of their spouse's family. They are called "son" or "daughter," given nice things, and treated as an equal by all of the new relatives. This is not the Navajo way. The first year of marriage is very difficult and the couple is on their own. Of course, both the husband or wife can go to their own family and receive help, but they will get little from the other side. Your mate's clan people view you as an outsider who does not have correct teachings. The love and understanding found in the western world for the newcomer are totally absent. Instead, the other side is just waiting for the new husband or wife to make mistakes or say something wrong and then be criticized. They are always looking at the negative side of what you are going to do. Once in a while, they might see something that they appreciate and thank you for it, but that is a rare occasion and should be happily recognized. The more the in-law works his or her way into family expectations, the better and sooner will be their acceptance.

When I first became involved with my in-laws, I was employed in Salt Lake City as a construction worker. No matter what I did for my wife's family, it was never enough. As my daughters and son came into this world, I showed her family that I could provide for my children and wife by buying vehicles, a house, food, and clothing, but it was never good enough. Finally, I was so bothered by their attitude that I went to my mother and asked her what I should do and to find out why I was being rejected. She asked, "Did you take some firewood over there?" I said, "No." She responded, "That's what you need to do. Take some coal, firewood, water and all of the essential things that she and her husband live by. They are not concerned about everything you are providing for your family; that is not their issue. Instead, do something for them. That is what an in-law does."

I went to Black Mesa and filled my truck with coal and dropped it off at their hogan. I did the same with firewood, chopping and delivering it. Next came the water, which I hauled in to provide for the animals before going to the store to buy a lot of hay, which I stacked near their corral. That broke the ice. My mother-in-law said, "Wow. I'm beginning to see a good in-law here." I learned that no matter what you do or how hard you work, you will still be an outsider, but you can move a lot closer to being accepted by helping your in-laws with the essential things of life including earth, water, and fire. People used to say, "My in-law is coming and he'll fix it. He'll take care of it" or "My daughter-in-law is going to cook. She'll take care of it." That is how it was put together and how people talked about them. Regardless, it still takes a long, long time before an in-law feels a part of the group.

Just how long was shown by an old man I talked to at a ceremony he was having performed for his family. All of his children entered the tepee including his daughter and his soon-to-be son-in-law as they prepared to be married during this Native American Church wedding. Everyone was involved and happy for future prospects, but at the end, the old man said nothing but just sat there. He had been this way all night long, and his wife had noticed his attitude. Now she was angry and ready to find out why he was behaving this way. After the last song and prayer in the morning, as the people were drinking water and things were quiet, she spoke up. "How come you're sitting there quiet? Say something nice or say something good to the bride and groom. At least say 'Thank you.'" The old man replied, "What should I be thankful for? I'm not going to say any 'thank you' to this man until one day I see my grandchildren, and one day see a house, and one day he gets good things for my daughter, and then we shall see. That is many years from now. It is too early to say 'thank you,' and so I am not going to say it. I'm still looking at him, to see how he's going to do. Just because we have a ceremony does not mean I have to do it." Everyone just looked at him and said, "Okay. Okay." Some people are like that with in-laws and are not ready to give in. Just because they are medicine people, that does not mean they will not be hard and demand things be shown to them. It usually takes at least five and sometimes ten to fifteen years to prove oneself to the point where the family and members of the clan accept a person enough to call them "my son" or "my daughter."

This exclusiveness by the extended family or clan people carries over into the conduct of traditional ceremonies. For instance, let's say that a woman is having an Enemyway ceremony performed for her. She will have a house built for her and her clan members, but if it was a man's ritual, he would not have one built for him. The reason for this is that she has children and the man does not. Her extended family would be very involved in preparing and paying for the entire ceremony, including two structures. One will be a long, rectangular shade house while the other shade house is much smaller. The long one is where much of the food is prepared and the extended family members or clan relatives gather. This gives spiritual and emotional support for the woman having the ceremony. The smaller structure is for members of the other clan—the in-laws—and they are not supposed to come over to the other building. If there is no second building, the people who are "outsiders" may even have to leave the area—"chased out"—until the ritual is completed. This is done to maintain the spiritual purity of the ceremony according to clan teachings. There has to be a space, whether the separation is done through the two structures or with the other people leaving. Her husband may have to just mount his horse and ride out of the camp. The couple who are having the ceremony, as well as people from different clans, cannot even visit each other during that time. Even though they are all in the ceremonial place together, opposing clan members are not supposed to look at each other but rather turn away and stay on their separate sides. Spouses are not to talk with each other.

I am not aware of any particular traditional story that teaches about the action of in-laws and what they can and cannot do. But it seems to me that

Coyote, the trickster, is close to providing the view of how in-laws act and should be treated. He wanted to be an in-law to people, but he was always acting foolishly or clumsily and never seemed to handle social situations well. Consequently, he was always on the outside, accepted by no one, killed or trashed because of his behavior. I think a lot of the thinking about in-laws is like, "We are going to have an in-law" with the response, "What kind of coyote is it going to be?" People never liked the way he acted or presented himself, and that is the way in-laws are viewed, but there is no story linked to that role that I am aware of. He was always trying to have relationships with other animals, acting stupid, and was one of the first to display those unacceptable human tendencies.

The perfect metaphor to describe an in-law who has come to investigate how things are going in a married couple's home. Interestingly, owls are also associated with members of the Ute tribe, traditional enemies of the Navajo. (Photo by Kay Shumway)

There is also a mother-in-law taboo where she and her son-in-law are not supposed to see or interact with each other. She is given the name The One You Cannot See (Dooish'íinii) or Owl (Né'éshjaa'). The young man is to avoid her presence, but if he accidentally comes into a room where she is, the mother-in-law needs to cover herself so that he can come in. Once he leaves, she can uncover. I asked my mother what this was all about, but she never really answered me. Rather than get into a discussion on the topic, she just said that to avoid that problem, on the wedding day, the boy's father has to light some tobacco and stick it through the cloth hanging in the doorway. He would burn a hole in it and pass the burning tobacco through the hole so that the people inside can take it. The mother-in-law and son-in-law would then enter. The mother-in-law and the boy's father first smoke the tobacco and then pass it over to the boy who is getting married, and then he would puff it. Next, the mother-in-law would get an ear of white corn and the son-in-law's mother one of yellow corn, and the two would exchange them and then shake hands. Now the son-in-law and mother-in-law can see each other without any type of problem.

CHAPTER SIX

Healing the Sick

A Spiritual Look at the Physical Body

A Navajo medicine man, like an Anglo doctor, must have a systematic way of understanding the functioning of the human body. Rather than depending solely on aspects based in biology, chemistry, physiology, and related fields that analyze then explain in totally material terms what might be happening to a patient, the medicine man works with holistic medicine rooted in traditional teachings to interpret why the person is sick. These beliefs provide spiritual explanations that combine with physical remedies and ceremonial practices to give a broad understanding of how the body functions and how the holy people provide healing. While some cures are purely physical—for instance setting a broken bone, providing herbal potions, and prescribing rest and certain foods—there are many others that depend on cures that were set in motion at the beginning of the world, when the first humans were created and different illnesses began. In this chapter, Navajo organizing principles combined with the understanding of how the body functions join with physical remedies derived from Navajo perception to heal a patient.

As the holy people sat in council during the creation of the first earth surface beings, they shared a strong desire to assist by providing helpful qualities to this new creature being formed. Each wanted to do its part. Earth Woman was the first to speak and offered to provide the feet and ankles, everything in pairs. Mountain Woman joined in furnishing the shins, calves, and knees while the waters offered to create the thighs and hips. The Male and Female Deer along with Blue Corn Boy and Black-and-White Corn Girl formed the torso with all of its internal organs because this is the place where meat and plants are digested. Male Lightning (zigzag) furnished the arms while Sun Bearer added the hands. A host of other holy people wanted to have a part in creating the face and voice, each bringing their unique view of how these two humans should look and sound. But it was Sun Bearer and Moon Bearer who created the eyes, since in order to see, their light must be present. Dark Sky added the hair.

The two forms lay inert. Something had to get them moving. The holy people needed to add two more qualities. Lightning again took his turn.

> Radiating from the tip of the feet, a person runs by means of zigzag lightning. Radiating from the tip of the fingers, a person moves and works by means of the zigzag lightning, that is how it was created. Then the Holy Wind was placed standing inside; it extends out at the toe tips, at the knee tips, from the shoulder tips, from the finger tips, from the tip of the voice, from the tips of the eyes, it moves the eyelashes. Then the spirit extending out from the top of the head was created. We move by it and it moves us and by means of it we talk. Long Life and Holy, it is that way. It was like that when they created a person . . . and it went on that way until the person stood up.[1]

The Navajo were now ready to assume their role in the Fifth World.

Anthropologist Maureen Trudelle Schwarz has written extensively on health issues and modern medicine affecting the Navajo. In the course of her work, she collected information on how the body is viewed and of what it is comprised. Not all medicine men agree on every aspect, but the general consensus is that much of a person is related to the sacred stones (ntł'iz) associated with the four directions. Schwarz explains:

> Azooł, the windpipe, alizh—urine, ajóozh—the vagina, and íígháátsiighąą'—the spinal cord, all consist of white shell, the precious shell of the east. Azid, the liver, acho' the penis, and the blue blood traveling to the heart all consist of turquoise, the precious stone of the south. Acázis, the pleurae, are abalone, the hard good most commonly associated with the west. In addition, ajéí, the heart and lungs and adátsoo, the clitoris, are said to be red coral, a material often associated with the west. Anáá, the eyes, are composed of jet, the precious stone of the north.[2]

This description of how the human body was formed is particularly helpful in understanding what Perry offers in discussing its creation and how the ceremonies are designed to work against illness. For example, when identifying different body parts, duality in gender, function, and forms of power are apparent. They are also viewed as "independent" in that they have a leader and so may demand a different cure than some other aspect of an individual. The forces that initially helped design that body part have different qualities and characteristics and so require a different kind of ceremony and medicine. What that might be, goes back to when the sickness was first introduced and how it was cured. The division of the body also explains the reason, in part, for the seven healing points (ałhą dazh dit'áagóó) outlined in the Lifeway ceremony. Why a prayer starts at the feet and moves upward, how each area is blessed, and whether to bless with pollen both parts (feet, hands, etc.) simultaneously or separately are all an extension of the teaching. Gladys Reichard, conversely, points out that when cursing an enemy, the "good way" is reversed. "The prayers are like this: the warrior starts with the enemy's head and mentions all the different parts of his body down to the ground and ends his prayer in the ground. This is just the same as burying the man."[3] Upward-moving toward the heavens or downward-casting to the grave are reversed elements in the prayers.

The Navajo believe that the human body, as explained here, is specific to their people. Not only is this how they think about it, but there is also the feeling that it is distinct for a purpose. Beyond the noticeable physical differences, it is also believed that their body, spirit, and intellect are particular to this people. One time while I was attending a ceremony, a Navajo acquaintance decided to inform me about an aspect of his culture concerning the creation. He had started talking about problems and eventually made reference to an incident involving witchcraft. I asked him why this form of evil did not seem to bother white men but was of great concern to Navajos. His reply took us back to creation or the "palm of time." He pointed to his hand, then to mine, and asked what the difference was. Size and texture were not the concern but rather the color. Next, he pointed to the reddish-brown sand at our feet and let me know that the Navajo people had come from the soil and the worlds beneath, their skin color being proof of their origin. Next, he asked where my people had come from. Across the ocean, a different soil was the reply. His answer to my question eventually led us to the belief that the problems particular to this race were engendered in the origin, the soil, the very essence of Navajo spiritual and physical being, and that the problems that were faced by my race, derived from its own creation, which had not involved emerging from the ground. Along this same line of thinking, Mother Earth is made of the same things that humans are, but which part of the earth also makes a difference. The land encompassed by the Four Sacred Mountains is the building material for the Navajo people.

As one reads Perry's thoughts below, it becomes apparent that each appendage, organ, or vessel is its own powerful entity. Take the hand as a good example of how the body provides fertile soil for metaphorical teaching. Navajos refer to all humans as either earth surface beings or the five-fingered ones. The five main posts of the Navajo sweat lodge, a male structure designed by the gods, are referred to as "fingers." When people are in the sweat lodge, it is said that they are in the hands of the gods. Sacred thoughts and prayers remain in the structure, creating a holy place where people can return to be renewed, suggesting that great peace is found when one is removed from the "world" and placed in the hands of the gods. Four fingers used in traditional thought can serve as a mnemonic device that represents: earth, wind, water, and fire; birth, puberty, marriage, and old age; physical, emotional, mental, spiritual; a person's four clans with the thumb as the individual; or corn, squash, beans, and tobacco, the four most sacred plants of the Navajo. Four fingers can teach profound concepts concerning life.

Hand trembling, discussed in volume 1, chapter 5, offers a number of examples of how the hand, when influenced by the Gila monster spirit, takes on its own personality. Some practitioners become afraid of their hand during this type of divination because it cannot be controlled. John Holiday explained, "Sometimes the hand trembler cannot find the answer or understand the impression, so the sacred spirit will let the hand and fingers grab the diviner's nose or ear, or poke his or her ribs, as if to say, 'Here's the answer, can't you see it? Are you stupid? You can't even guess the answer!'"[4] If a hand has been bitten by an animal like a jackrabbit or prairie dog, it cannot be used to transfer the spiritual impressions that would otherwise feed into it. The opposite is true when a person is receiving images through the hand. It may draw a picture of the answer being sought that needs to be guessed, and it may tap in agreement or disagreement with the diviner's interpretation. Literally, the hand has a mind of its own and works on its own spiritual level in conjunction with the brain.

The last part of this chapter and the next one is concerned with sickness. Serious physical ills are often viewed as manifestations of something that is spiritually wrong and so not surprisingly, the origin of the sickness can be traced back to the time of creation. According to Gishin Biye' who practiced the Upward Movement and Emergenceway (Ha'neełnéehee) ceremony, First Man and First Woman are credited with getting the process started. In the Black World, as the creatures were beginning to learn about this dark and different place, First Man placed a colored basket in the cardinal directions, each one containing the appropriate material—white shell, turquoise, abalone, and jet. He also placed a basket in the center with small red and white stones. He and eight other beings were wicked and wished to bring sickness and pain to people in the future. "The basket in the center contained smallpox, whooping cough, nervousness, paleness or pulmonary diseases and every fatal disease. Indeed, First Man and his companions were evil people who practiced witchcraft. Their wish alone was sufficient to inflict these diseases and to cause death through them."[5]

As other creatures joined them, none suspected that First Man and his friends had harmful intent. But by the time these beings had traveled to the

Yellow World, there were many who had obtained some of this power in various forms to hurt people. The spider ant, rattlesnake, bumblebee, cactus, yucca, and different types of winds and storms, along with other plants and animals, received a portion of the "dark medicine" to inflict pain and death. Witchcraft, evil wishing, shooting projectiles into the body, stinging, poking, and insanity were different ways to afflict someone.

> All of these, being evil, cause sickness and death among the Navajos. Each has its own prescribed prayerstick for sacrifice. Some require prayersticks in white, others in blue, yellow, and black. White bead, turquoise, abalone shell, and jet jewels are required, as well as iron ore, harebell pollen, and flag pollen for their sacrifices. The Holy Ones inhale this sacrifice and thereby sickness is removed. According to this version, then, there are thirty-two different ways of injuring us, although there may be more than this. For these there are just as many remedies, consisting of stones and lichens, of plants, their seeds, flowers, leaves and roots, trees with their limbs and bark, many of which may be used as medicine. . . . Step by step, the evil is removed and the patient restored to his former healthy condition. This accounts for the name "to pray it out." Pollen is then placed on the tongue and head of the patient and otherwise is used freely by the singer.[6]

Two examples from the life of Tall Woman illustrate Navajo thoughts concerning some of this sickness. The first event occurred during her midlife. Some time before, she had been bitten two separate times by rattlesnakes and so had participated in a Navajo Windway ceremony. For a long time there was no problem, as good health ensued. Then her face started to hurt and became increasingly twisted. Her husband noticed in her mouth a thin piece of yellow bone that had mysteriously appeared. He removed it with tweezers but the facial distortion continued. Over time, her face became increasingly paralyzed, twisting into a "lopsided" grimace. Her husband, Frank Mitchell, called upon a number of hand tremblers to determine the cause and paid for a five-night Chiricahua Windway ceremony, but to no avail. Another singer, a series of Windways, and finally a Shootingway ceremony were brought forth, all in an effort to correct the problem. Eventually her face returned to normal, but even by the end of the sickness, she was unable to identify a specific cause. Was it the two snake bites, witchcraft, some broken taboo—she just did not know, although she felt like she had lived as she should. Somehow, the evil created at the beginning of the world had succeeded; it took a Shootingway ceremony to remove it.[7]

The second incident occurred much later in life, after she had spent years assisting expectant mothers as a midwife. Her joints began to swell and created problems walking. This time she identified the cause. "During childbirth, both the one who catches the baby and the woman who stays behind like I did are exposed to blood, and it's hard not to get it on yourself. We believe contact with blood like that is damaging; it causes your bones to swell; it makes them all crooked and it blows up your joints. The only kind of blood that isn't dangerous in that way is the blood from the first two menstrual periods, when a girl becomes a kinaaldá."[8] Interestingly, there is an antidote called chííh dik'ǫ́ǫ́zh comprised of red ochre, rock salt, berries, herbs, and other substances for a woman who is menstruating. The mixture can either be ingested by people affected by her condition or sprayed about the room as a protection.[9] Tall Woman left the practice of delivering babies; her understanding of the problem was based in the perception of what causes illness and ill-effect in the Navajo world, but she does not mention taking the remedy. For an Anglo person approaching the issue solely from a physiological perspective, the diagnosis would be at odds with their understanding of sickness; for a Navajo person who mixes the physical with the spiritual world, it was time for this midwife to retire.

How the Body Is Put Together

As with every aspect of the Navajo world, different parts of the body need to be shown respect; the chief organ that is in charge of one of the body systems—for example the heart for the circulation system—is representative and can be approached by the medicine man if that part is injured. In other chapters I told of when a tree or plant stands for all of the trees or plants to which we pray. The same principle of speaking to a leader is extended to each part of the body. By giving it the respect that it deserves, that organ will work with the medicine man to bring about a cure. At times, this leader might get boastful, but it is still addressed and helped to understand what is needed. In the medicine way, when a person offers a prayer, it always sits with the leader or representative that is being spoken to directly.

The teaching that accompanies the thought about the inner workings of the body and how to heal it goes back to the story of how Monster Slayer and Born for Water were badly crushed and dismembered by a rock slide from the side of a mountain. This was triggered by jealous evil people (see volume 1, chapter 6, under "Performing 'The Two Skulls That Came Back'"). Once the remains of the Twins were found, Talking God scolded the ground and mountain, saying that they must work together for the good of the people and should be part of the healing process that now needed to take place. This is why today, when a ceremony is going to be performed for a woman, prayers and offerings are given to the San Francisco Peaks (female) or the Chuska Mountains (male) if a man. Through the different animals, insects, and other helpers, the mountains were able to direct the curing process and became leaders in doing so. The medicine man calls upon these healing powers for assistance. For instance, Mother Earth would help with the body, the heavens would help with the head, rain would put the hair back on, and the ants would restore the blood. As each part of the Twins was placed back into their bodies, each helper also held the power to make it better and function properly. Soon after this, the holy people left the earth surface beings and went to their appointed places located throughout Navajo land. They remain there today in rock formations, rivers, mountains, and other physical phenomena, waiting for a medicine man to use the sacred, magical words that will summon them and their powers to assist him.

Medicine men talk about how the two different areas of a body—the inside and outside—are often at odds with each other. The outside is known to do foolish things because of its wishes, which are tied to external senses. Drinking alcohol, sex, thrills, eating bad foods that taste good but are harmful, and physical pleasures are tied to the exterior and encourage the body to do things that are not good for it. These outside "people" make a lot of mistakes, lead to temptation, and cause harm because they are at odds with the inner organs and senses. The heart, lungs, intestines, and so forth, are holy and encourage right living and health. The outside does whatever it wants, the inside is filled with self-control and sound judgment, approving what is right and warning against trouble. For example, a person may be curious about what it is like to stand on the very edge of a cliff. The outside spurs on this curiosity and allows the person to walk ever closer, but the inside warns them away from the danger. An individual who is participating in a ceremony is to avoid sex during this healing process; the physical desire (outer) may be strong, but inside where deep thoughts reside, are the organs of the body warning against any such thing; bad food and strong drink may bring momentary pleasure, but it comes at a price—poor health, excess weight, and vomiting—where the internal organs reject what they are given.

This dialogue is an ongoing process, and when a person is sick, it becomes even more important. Navajo medicine does a lot with herbal remedies, casting out that which is bad, and putting troubled parts of the body back in harmony. There are strict teachings that warn of the role the internal organs play in the healing process. None of the medication given to a person has any effect—in fact the patient may become worse—if it is not accompanied by meditation and correct thinking. The inside is holy with strong beliefs, and so must be treated with respect in a proper atmosphere, otherwise the organs reject what is given to them to cure the illness. The two cannot work against each other. Only when they are compatible can there be

Care for the body through cleansing is an important aspect of both daily and ceremonial life. Traditionally, yucca was one of the most favored plants because it not only provided soap for bathing and shampoo for the hair, but also cordage and food. Many ceremonies require some sort of washing with yucca as part of the healing process.

real healing through a "holy moment." This ability for the organs to think and pass their messages through the right brain came at the time of creation when the holy people knew that they would no longer walk each day with the earth surface beings. It was part of the warning system given to humans to keep them out of trouble. If they needed further spiritual assistance, then medicine men were given higher powers to summon the gods to make corrections through ceremonies. To the holy beings at this time, "From here on, you will walk with your body."

Feet, Hands, and the Seven Healing Points

The Lifeway ceremony teaches about the seven healing points of the body. In a physiological sense, these are located at the joints that allow for movement of major parts and associated functions of human anatomy. In nature, most living things grow upward, which is also true of the human body. This is why in ceremonies, hand trembling, and blessings, the medicine person often starts with the feet, then proceeds to the ankles, knees, hips, shoulders, elbows, wrists, and neck in that order. These are places on an individual that are subject to pain but are also important for healing and critical to motion. Just as a person may twist the wrong way or not walk on a "straight path," the pain felt in a particular spot may indicate that one is not acting in an appropriate fashion. Each one of these sites, as well as others, sends messages as to what that individual is doing wrong, which triggers a possible cure. If a person is able to undo the cause of the pain, it will go away. These seven places talk to a person and indicate what went wrong and how to fix it. The medicine man, like a doctor, interprets the cause of the illness and what is the best way to enact a cure. Healing is a complex activity that depends upon many different parts of the body to be effective. Each element of the system has a physical and spiritual function that is necessary for the furtherance of life. Navajo traditional teachings identify how each part works and the role each plays, but all are necessary for a long and happy existence.

Each of these seven points has its own leader. The ankle is number one, the knees two, hips three, shoulders four, elbows five, wrists six, and neck seven. When a medicine man is working with a patient, he will bless through prayers and pollen these spots because they are where the healing must occur. The prayer follows this upward direction through the body and helps determine what a person did wrong and what is causing the pain. Perhaps an individual twisted the wrong way, picked up something too heavy, or pushed a bone out of alignment. It is said that if that person is not living a straight life or doing things correctly, the joints will tell him by hurting in different places. Another example of how things can go wrong is when a person has visited a grave site and their knees begin to ache. They know that they should not have been there, and so now the event must be reversed. Whatever was done incorrectly physically or spiritually has to be fixed by unraveling and returning to the beginning when things were in order. The prayers go back, redo, and replenish whatever was damaged or is causing pain.

The foot has a lot of important teachings, and like its close neighbor the ankle, has a leader. But unlike the seven healing points of the joints, the foot's leader is a snake. This creature crawls along the ground with all of its body in contact with Mother Earth. This is why the snake is called The Leader Who Knows the Noise from the Ground through Its Body (Bits'íís Yeedigáhii Tsííłkéí Naat'áanii). If a blessing is needed for the feet, the prayers go to the snake (bullsnake) because both are in contact with the earth. The snake becomes the lead person to effect the cure, and so by showing it the proper respect, it and the feet can heal that part of the body. As the master of the ground, it can learn what has happened but also anticipate things in the future. During the Fearing Time and Long Walk Period (1859–68) at a place called Kits'iilí, there was a large rock slide (Tsé Náázhoozhí) that warned of difficult times ahead for the Navajo. The people had not been praying at many of the sacred sites, and so the earth warned them to return to the old ways and become more spiritual. The earth spoke again during the 1918 influenza epidemic and again more recently at Big Mountain, saying that the Navajos there would be removed if they did not return to the old ways of praying to the land. By the end of the 1970s, the government had given that area to the Hopi. In the early 1990s at Rocky Ridge, part of a mountain nearby opened up a big crack in the earth in which a large collection of mice was found. This was the start of the hantavirus disease that killed and sickened a lot of Navajo people. All of these warnings from the ground were given because the people had lost contact with their ceremonies and were not visiting the sacred places that could keep them safe. The feet and the ground communicate together to provide warnings.

There are other parts of the body that have important teachings—the hands, head, legs, heart, stomach, and other organs—are all treated individually as separate leaders and are spoken of as people who live inside of a person. The heart, liver, and kidneys all have a job to do, and so the one praying says, "I have a sickness in me so I am asking the people inside of my body to accept the medicine I am taking. I am going to eat it and put it in there, so that you will heal me inside and help me to feel good again. Help me in this way." Medicine men talk about these different internal people just as they recognize external powers. Those things that are outside are able to help, but it is the people on the inside that give life. Both need to be cared for. In the prayers, one talks to both sides, which is the only way that true healing takes place.

The feet are two of the most sensitive parts of the body. Medicine men talk about this by acknowledging that feet are always connected to the ground and through this, information can be communicated. The earth trembles when something happens on it, which then tells our feet a story. The ground can also indicate what will occur in the future or when something bad has taken place. This is made known by an uncomfortable feeling beneath the feet and by a person sensing that something is not right. For example, when a person walks on a grave, even unintentionally, the feet are so sensitive that they are the first to swell and feel the pain before it moves to the legs. They are the first to get sick. This is another reason that when the medicine man begins to diagnose what is wrong with a patient, he places corn pollen on the soles of the feet before moving to the seven healing points and finishing with the top of the head. The blessing makes clear where the patient has been and what happened there. When washing a person, it also starts with the feet.

The toenails on a foot are said to be made of abalone shell, which have seven rainbow colors on them. The feet carry these colors as one walks the Rainbow Path or Road (Nááts'íílid bee hada'iiztiin). Even when a man goes to war and the outcome is unsure, he carries with him peace and harmony because of these rainbows. Somewhere there will be peace again, and his toenails show that. There will be comfort in his feet, and he will feel good walking. If he is injured, his recovery will include walking, indicating that peace and happiness are achievable ahead. Even though a person may be able to ride, real healing takes place with walking because every step connects a foot to Mother Earth and is on the Rainbow Trail. The more the patient walks, the more thinking there is, which connects more things to the eyes, which then is connected back down to the ground. There may be a flower or beautiful view that helps the healing process as one's feet with their rainbows take that person on to recovery that in Navajo is called the Corn Pollen Road (Tádidíín atiin).

The male rain that forms a rainbow has seven colors, and the female rainbow has five. On the male rainbow, the top color is red and is where the patient walks and sits. That is why it is sung, "I stand on top, on top of the red rainbow." If it was a female rainbow, then the red band would be on the bottom where the medicines are placed, and the person would say, "I stand on the bottom of this one" and would be able to see that everything from there is good. Once the patient moves to the top, they are beyond the colors. This explains why the color red is used in sandpaintings. All of this connects back to the feet, to the abalone shell, and to the toes that make it happen.

Prayers also speak of following in the steps of the holy people. Because we are the children of White Shell Woman, we follow in her footsteps. Her footing is my footing, where she sits, I will sit, and where she places her handprint, I will leave mine. These are three sacred areas that are mentioned in the songs that have to be addressed before moving to the actual healing songs and prayers. It singles out three parts of the body—the feet, buttocks, and hand (akék'ehashchíín, asdá k'ehashchíín, alá k'ehashchíín)—that all touch the ground. The first one—the foot—represents travel and walking on the earth. For example, I might pray, "Just as White Shell Woman moves about on this earth, so will I. Her sitting stands for meditation, which I will do, and whatever she touches and brings to her with her hand, I will also take. My children, my work, my money, whatever it is that comes to my hand through the ten-fingered people will be mine as well as the goods that I grasp in my hand. I will be stable and sit straight when I say my prayers and not walk around, but I will walk to wherever my goals take me, leaving footprints all the time."

Navajo moccasins (kélchí) that cover the foot are part of this travel. They are described as the dawn because of the white bottom or sole, which represents the east. The red upper part is considered to be the ground that we stand on as well as the west where the sun sets. Our traveling leaves footprints that are either going to meet the dawn and then go in a clockwise half-circle, or they will go directly to the yellow sunset in the evening. A person who is wearing these moccasins is walking on the white dawn and red sunset. This is one of the means by which the holy people recognize that individual and will walk with him. Nowadays, people do not wear these moccasins, and so the holy people do not know who they are.

The ankles are also about one's journey and where a person is going to go. They receive four directions (cardinal) from the toes on the foot, but the large toe is the one that really steers a person on a particular path. Like the thumb on a hand, the large toe has a special mission to guide the others. Elders say that this is similar to the Four Sacred Mountains with a fifth one guiding—each one has its own direction, but it is the feet that will take one there.

The knees are often a good indicator if something is wrong with a person. They are close to the ground—when one kneels or is picking themselves up after a fall—it is the knees that do the work. People say that if there is any place in the body that is having problems, the knees will be the first to know and show it. This is because the knee brings one closest to the ground. In a ceremony, it is important to wash them so that anything bad on the ground does not stick to the knees to be carried off and bother that person later. The washing is done from a basket that has water in it. Four pinches of sacred corn pollen are spaced on the ground so that each knee is placed first on one then on a second spot, which renews the blessing on each knee. More than any other joint, they determine what that person is doing— sitting, standing, getting up or down—it represents the body most of all.

There are a number of short teachings that I am aware of for the shoulders, elbows, and wrists. The shoulder is spoken of as the top of a hill or mountain where one can see far away. There are many things to view, and it is the resting place for the head, which is the focal point for many spiritual teachings. The elbows and wrists hold the markings for the Evilway or Lightningway ceremonies. These lines run down from the shoulder, down the inside of the arm, and encircle the wrist, but the lines are never closed so that the bad power can depart. A flint arrowhead is placed in the palm that helps drive out anything that is evil. This is the only time that the wrist is talked about as a healing place.

There are many different teachings about the hand. For instance, if one spreads their fingers, each of the spaces between stand for something. The large opening between the thumb and the index finger represents the time from birth to young adulthood. The area between the index and longest finger symbolizes the time when a person reaches puberty, while the next space over is married life, with the last one becoming a grandparent with grandchildren. The thumb always represents you, the index finger the mother, the tallest finger the father, the next the grandfather, and the smallest finger the grandmother. The two longest fingers are male and the two shortest ones (index and pinky) female. When one says prayers, the thumb covers the other ones, representing the person praying and protecting the family.

On the outside of a clenched fist, there are the Four Sacred Mountains sitting on top. The veins found beside and between the knuckles carry the water running off these mountains to the heart. The hand is one of the holy ones, so it is called The Five Finger Holy One (yódí ałhą'ánáyoołiłí tsékę' naat'áanii). The gods there bring good things together as gifts when they are respected. The fingers are there to receive them and are called The Ones That Collect Good Things (yáyee'áha'ánéyoodliiłii tsíłkéí naat'áanii). In the same respect, if a person balls his fists and strikes someone, the person who hits will destroy everything those fingers have worked for. It is like taking the Four Sacred Mountains and abusing them so that you will never get those good things back. Everything in life that you lived for will be destroyed right in front of your eyes. Remember that each of the mountains has a sacred stone associated with it, and so when these four stones that are used as an offering are abused, their powers are turned on the abuser. The person who is hit may never heal, but the person doing the hitting is hurting themselves and becoming an evil one. He is cursing himself.

The palm of the hand holds one's life story and tracks into the future. Each person's palm lines or "roads" are different. The flat of the palm is the earth, and the lines across it are the trails that the individual travels. Everybody has a different set. This takes a person into the future, but no one really knows how it is going to turn out, the places one will go, and what lies ahead. Elders say that the hand is one of the holiest places on the body because it breathes, sweats, and gets hot. Like the heart, it is a sensitive aspect of the body system. If my hand were to take something, even if it was just a small thing, and hold it in my palm, and I prayed with it, it will come to life. The hand is the one that really holds on to spiritual things. If I pick up a baby and hold it in my hands and then put it on my heart, the infant will quiet down because it knows it is safe; if I hold my family with my hand, they also will know they are secure. Everything that the hand touches becomes holy.

I really believe this is true because medicine bundles are put in the hand when the prayers are completed for the one who is sick. The medicine man says, "With this hand, today, we will heal." Even Christianity has spiritual ways where people put their hand on a person and pray in the name of Christ to heal. If a Christian picks up the Bible and puts his hand on it and prays, their prayers will be answered. This is the same as Native Americans using a medicine bundle and praying with it, making it holy. Anything with the hand is very spiritual and is important in the Navajo way. They say to really take good care of your hand. If you make your hand bleed, then you have to make an offering again because the holy ones got injured. I was told that the hand is one of the holiest of all the body parts.

Like the toes with their toenails, the same is true with fingernails, which are said to be made of abalone shell with its many colors that are part of a rainbow. There is red, white, and yellow that sit on top. The rainbow is part of the Blessingway of life and is an important aspect of being a family man, but there is also the Protectionway, where the hand holds the bow and another releases the arrow. This is the opposite of Blessingway because the hand can also be about shooting and killing, while also bringing good things in.

Head and Spine: Connectors to the Heavens

Moving up the body to the neck, the spine ties all of the parts of the body that deal with the physical world to the spiritual part of the body—the head—which connects to the heavens. The neck has a lot to do with meditation. My father talked about this as a very vital part because of the spine, which goes from the tailbone all the way to the head. Inside is the spinal cord, which connects all parts of the body and is one of the most important places when it comes to healing. This is where the healing takes place, inside that cord in your backbone. He said that it is the most important part of life. On the very top of the head in the middle is the connecting point of the body to the heavens where communication takes place. This is always about identity between a baby and the holy people. When an individual is born, there is a big opening on top of the skull, because unlike an adult who can think for themselves, an infant cannot. The holy ones are allowed to go through that soft spot on the head before it comes together and heals, giving time for the child to grow. Even for a man and woman, this is a sacred place.

If one stands in the darkness or early morning light and closes their eyes, they will feel something fly on top of them. That is sacredness passing through the holy feather (ats'os diyinii) that sits on top of one's head. Everyone has an invisible holy feather that is unique and is their identifying mark with the holy people. Just like fingerprints, no two feathers are alike. What people call a cowlick (atáá'ha'noots'eeí), that swirling spot of hair usually found on the crown of the head is the entrance place for the spirit and the attachment location of this spiritual feather. When praying, this is the last spot where the corn pollen offering is placed. The gods recognize the feather, accept the pollen, and hear one say "I am your child." Every time one identifies themselves spiritually, this feather is part of the process. It is all about meditation and the belief system. Prayers go from the nails of the toes to the tip of one's holy feather. In sandpaintings they are pictured differently for men and women. For instance, if it is a Male Lightningway or a Female Lightningway, the male will have longer feathers and the female shorter ones, but all of them will have tips that point to the right.

Hair and one's head are connecting links to good thoughts, traditional practices, and the pathway to communicating with the holy people. A wife who cares for her husband's hair is expressing deep devotion and commitment to his well-being.

Hair has many different teachings already discussed in chapter 2. The health of an individual, the cleansing of oneself for ceremonial purposes, and its use are all part of personal care. Hair can also be used as a sacrifice in thanksgiving. Heat, in Navajo thought, is associated with cleansing oneself. A sweat lodge, for instance, is heated to a high temperature, burning away the sickness or bad things that are causing distress. Extreme heat removes it from the system. Sometimes it may take years to enact a cure as the person goes through many difficult times. The elders had a way of giving thanks for this type of healing. They would undo their hair bun, measure four inches using the tips of their fingers from the end of their hair, cut it off, and then burn it as a sacrifice in appreciation. In this way the cured individual recognizes that the sickness has gone and will not return, because it has been given to the fire people. Next, the hair bun is tied back up, restoring traditional thoughts represented by the hair bun being put back in its normal fashion. My sister went through four years of intense sickness. Finally, she began to recuperate after receiving the right medicine. She listened to the old teachings of my grandmother and decided to cut her hair to her shoulders. As the hair regrew, she healed and became a new person, as did her hair. This is how she thought of it.

An individual's head, hair, and holy feather are important at another time—when a person is having their puberty ceremony. On the top of the head a turquoise shell is tied for the girl and a white shell for a boy. This is done on the first day and will remain there for the entire four-day period. Each day, the power of the medicine is renewed—four times total. This is to remain there without being untied. At that time, it belongs only to that individual and is a part of their spiritual identity. Because the head is considered one of the holiest parts of a person's body, the bead goes with it. This cannot be shared with family members, and if someone takes it and puts it on themselves or plays with it, both that individual and the person having the ceremony will become sick. After the four-day ritual is finished, the bead is removed. It is still part of an individual's identity—they are still considered to have it and an eagle feather on their head as part of their spiritual protection. Later, when a person gets sick, they will tie the bead back into their hair until that curing ceremony is completed. When a medicine man performs a ceremony, he will put a bandana on his head. This is like the bead. The holy people recognize that person by their bead and holy feather, and for the medicine man, they recognize him as having certain powers and the ability to work with them when he dons that headpiece. The kerchief helps hold the powers in and identifies that person as a medicine man.

Before he starts praying, a medicine man offers a three-part blessing. After taking a pinch of corn pollen, he will place some on his tongue so that he can say the prayer correctly and in a spiritual way that will be acceptable to the holy people. Next, he puts some on top of his head where the holy feather, blue bead, and point of communication with the holy people exists. This provides the identity of who is praying. The last of the pollen is held out at arm's length and scattered as an offering with words to the effect of, "I am going to talk directly to this person." The patient will either repeat what the medicine man is saying or they may do their own prayers. This is up to the individual, but usually medicine men prefer the patient repeating after them.

The head and face have another healing power as represented in the clay pot water drum (ásaa' dádeestł'ónígíí). These drums are very sacred and are thought of as a heart. It is in the shape of a heart, and when beat upon with a drumstick, its rhythm is connected to the heartbeat of the patient. The clay pot has two live coals—one to represent a male, the other a female—taken from the fire and put into it, before filling the container about halfway with water. This brings all four of the sacred elements—air, water, earth, and fire—together. Next, a piece of buckskin is stretched over the top and fastened tightly around the edge of the pottery. In the hide, a pin is pushed through to make small holes that represent two eyes, a nose, and mouth. This face is to acknowledge that the holy ones are joining in with the singing. The patient is now blessed with the drum, starting with the feet to the knees to the hand to the heart to the back, shoulder, mouth, and head, in that order. The drum is hit as the different parts are blessed, the tone going from it to the body areas and joints being addressed. With each strike of the drum, that part of the body is "awakened" to the blessing that is taking place. The eyes, nose, and mouth, marked by pinpricks, let the air and water out of the pot. The sacred song and the drumbeat announce that the holy ones are there with the patient and will remain until the ceremony is finished. At that point, the drum and patient become one as the healing song cures the patient.

Thinking about Illness

Another way of understanding how the Navajo view the body is through the categorization of sickness, its name, and diagnosis. For instance, diabetes (ats'íístah áshįįh łikan nanit'ą' silįį'—body sugar is bothering you) is translated as "sugar disease." It just appeared among the Navajo fairly recently and is hard to describe because it was caused by the food people ate. Anglo doctors just kept using the words "sugar" and "sweet" and so it became the sugar disease and is considered more of a white man's sickness than something controlled by the holy people. One illness that really bothered Navajos until the 1960s was trachoma (anáziz bii' diwozhí—eyelids inside are bumpy), which really affected their eyes. The people said that it had something to do with the clouds and their interaction with thunderstorms. This disease would affect a person's eyes if they kept them open in a sweat lodge. The heat burned the eyes, so that one day they would have clouds in them. A second explanation is that when lightning strikes too close in a blinding flash near a house, the lightning, as it disappeared, captured the person's eyesight. A third explanation comes from looking directly into the sun, not that it burns out one's sight, but that the person doing it is not showing proper respect. In Navajo, the first being who tried to look at the sun could not do it directly because Sun Bearer was too bright. The man had to use his hand to shield his eyes like a visor or a military hand salute. They also should never look directly, but rather off to one side, in order to catch a partial glimpse. This is the respectful way to do it, showing that the person does not want to look into the holy being's eyes. This is true for both adults and children and is quite similar to the proper behavior that is shown during an eclipse in order to protect the eyes and show respect. One is not supposed to look at them when the sun and moon cross their paths. People are strictly warned to stay inside, not to eat or drink, and to be quiet. This is a holy thing that is happening and so is not to be watched. Today, people use all kinds of shaded objects, dark glasses, and other devices to observe an eclipse, but soon they will have eye problems.

A final explanation for trachoma is connected with looking at a tornado as it whirls about nearby. One may see lightning coming out of it and all of the things that are getting swept up and tossed around. This also has something to do with clouds as they connect back to the sun with wind and lightning. All of this is crossing over, creating film and cataracts in the eyes. A lot of people have their own explanations of why their eyes become cloudy—some say that if one sees a naked person or a couple having sexual intercourse, that could be a cause of blindness. All of these different reasons boil down to showing proper respect. Each one of them centers on seeing things that are inappropriate or watching the holy people without being polite. Much of Navajo medicine is based on correctives that get a person back in harmony and acting appropriately.

A lot of contemporary diseases are considered to have been introduced by the white man. The heart is called ajéídishjoo (heart that is smaller) and the lungs are ajéídilzólii, or that which sits beside the heart. Heart disease is called jéí'ádįįh, which means the heart is fading; it is said to have come from the east and is connected to alcohol and other man-made processed foods. The name for tuberculosis is very similar to that of heart disease because the heart and lungs work together. Tuberculosis, like chicken pox and measles, is looked at as another illness that was not a problem until the white man arrived. Navajos tried to burn clothes and blankets that might be contaminated by these diseases. If someone had the measles or chicken pox, the medicine man might do a Blackening ceremony to drive the sickness away. Sometimes it worked, most of the time it did not. Disease often acts like humans that can be chased away by things that they do not like.

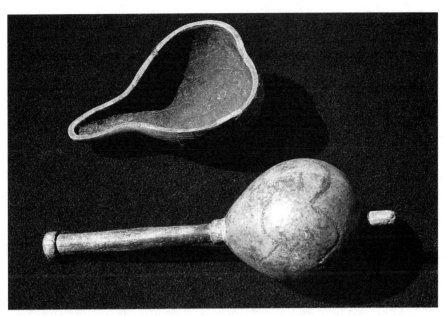

The gourd rattle used for Windway ceremonies has "sacred stones" (ntł'iz) inside to summon the holy people. It is used differently than a rattle made from skin—this one deals with illnesses connected to air, wind, and water; the half gourd is used for drinking herbal medicine and is part of the healing process for allergies, headaches, and stomachaches. (Photo by Kay Shumway)

Cancer is called The Sore that Cannot Be Cured (łóód doo nádziihii) and is described as a bump or bones that are deteriorating. In the old days when someone came in contact with an Anasazi or Ancestral Puebloan bone, it could cause cancer. This is true not only of bones but also antlers as discussed in a previous chapter. When the bone or antler starts decaying, the process is transferred to the person who picked it up or is near it. The individual's bones start to become like it, as the aging process accelerates. The Navajo name for a cold is tahoniigáá meaning The Body Is Getting Hotter. Accompanying that cold may be a headache (tsiits'iindiniih—The Head Hurts). Navajos associate that with something that an individual has done that was silly or improper or a misdeed. It is often considered a big thing—"What are you thinking or worrying about?" The cause always has to do with thoughts, while the general cure comes through talking and counseling with others.

In 1918 the very destructive influenza epidemic (dikos ntsaa—big cough, pneumonia) killed many people on the Navajo Reservation. This disease was called Sickness That Came but Is Unknown (naałniih). When medicine men talk about it, they say that the holy people allowed it to happen as a punishment because we were not following them and had forgotten the traditional ways. The sickness, just like chicken pox, German measles, and other illnesses introduced by the dominant culture, was in the air and could not be cured. The elders prayed and talked about it and went to the mountains to meet and discuss the problem, but they still could not figure it out. Some just decided that it was a punishment from the holy ones and that it had to take its course. To them, it was "the enemy that you can't see, feel, or touch, is here now" so named it naayéí doo yit'íinii—Enemy That Cannot Be Seen or Felt. The medicine men told the people that they had to reevaluate themselves and try to remember what they had done wrong. They say that even the holy beings were surprised that it came and were just as lost as the people were. Surely whoever brought it would also have the remedy. The Navajos felt that the white man had introduced it so must be able to heal it as well. This is in keeping with the thought that the holy person who controls the disease also has the cure.

The medicine men said that the white person in the east who brought it was also a sacred being and would be able to cure things in the future. This white person would be able to heal things that our people could not cure or figure out. Even though there are negative elements that native people will never try to look at, there is still good healing that will also become available. Medicine, surgery, and other health practices are now here, and the Navajo are taking advantage of these other ways of curing that we have never before considered. We are now just starting to understand these things that come from the white men. When I hear medicine people talk about this, the white person who is said to have started all of it is described as a single being like a man or woman, but it could also be a holy person. I think that the elders are referring to the first doctors who had the cure as the holy one and are not talking about the white community as a whole. In the medicine way, you think of the individual who cured it, not all of the other people. He becomes the representation of what happened.

In the beginning, some of the Navajo medicines were selected and asked, "Can you stabilize this type of sickness?" The answer will have to come from the holy people and will be found when the diagnosis of the illness is made. The medicine man has to ask Talking God and the spirit people what the medicine would be and where it will be found. He will sit down and pray, "Beauty from the different directions, Dark Gila Monster lying in the way of the sun. I am asking you where this medicine will be found to cure this sickness (Kodéé' hózhǫǫ doogo át'éí adahaas'éí tiniléí t'áá shá bik'ehgo dasínítínii). There is a situation where the body has a rash and the pustules are split and bleeding. Where will I find its medicine? How will I recognize it?" Then the spirits will talk to him and say something like,

"Go to the place called Durango; go up into the mountains, and there you will pray again. You will see flowers of this color. Look for the root, pull it up, and put it in your mouth. Do not bring back the entire plant, just cut off the top. Replant the top and put corn pollen on it, and bring home the bottom part or root." This is how new medicine is given to the medicine people. The plant may have a bitter taste and sting the right eye or maybe the left. Close both of them and decide which side is best suited for this medicine.

There are two ways that this works. Each person has both a male and a female side to their body. When a medicine man starts to test new medicine, either the male (left) or female (right) side will react more strongly. Sometimes it will not work on one side but will on the other. When one chews the plant, it will tell the nerves which one is correct for the person being treated. The female (yellow) or the male (white) side may be more dominant in the healing process based upon if the medicine man's mother or father were healers before. If he is trying to discover a new medicine on the male or left side of the body, there will be a stronger reaction. This does not always work with me because my mother practiced the Windway while my father conducted five different major ceremonies. Some medicine will speak to one side while another may communicate to the other. When I am doing this ritual, I close both eyes, take the root in my mouth, and then see if my mother's side will tell me more than my father's. At first, I concentrate on my right side because this ties in with my mother's clan people, while the other side I am just born for. But, if I am involved with the Enemyway (male) side of treatment, then my father's side will be much stronger than my mother's. It all depends on the heritage of the medicine man. Most people do not have both parents practicing medicine, so they rely just on one side. That is how it works.

CHAPTER SEVEN

Contemporary Navajo and Western Medicine

Two Views

Traditional medicine practices over the years have been flexible enough to work alongside differing Anglo interpretations of illness and treatment of a patient. The holy people provided Navajo teachings rooted in song, prayer, and narrative that continue to assure those who follow their guidelines. Today, western medicine, although fundamentally different in its dependence on science, observation, and physical remedies, is also used by the Navajo people. The differences between the two—even though they share the same goal of healing a person—present two varying approaches that could eliminate use of the other. Religion and science make strange bedfellows. Fortunately, the Navajo people are able to see the benefits of both and call upon remedies and procedures from either side. At the same time, the use of one may raise ethical or physical questions as to its appropriateness when compared to the teachings and perspective of the other. Both provide solutions to illness not found in or at odds with the other accepted way of healing. In this chapter, we will explore both ends of the dynamic, changing spectrum of healthcare in the shifting world of medicine.

The introduction of western medicine to the Navajo has been well documented. An excellent overview is provided in Robert A. Trennert's *White Man's Medicine*, which takes a historical approach, ending in 1955. For a more personal glimpse of healthcare by sympathetic physicians who made a real effort to understand and help the People in the 1940s, see Alexander and Dorothea Leighton's *The Navaho Door*.[1] By their time, the germ theory of disease, internal and external medicine, and a growing sophistication of life-saving measures derived from the World War II experience, offered a series of established practices for dealing with the physical world and its sickness. This was in sharp contrast to what Clyde Kluckhohn described as the Navajo theory of disease: "Although the People distinguish between naałniih, 'disease' (mostly contagious infections like measles, small pox, diphtheria, syphilis, gonorrhea) and the more generalized tah honeesgai, 'body fever' or 'body ache' (often translated by English-speaking Navahos as 'sick all over'), still all ailments, mental or physical, are of supernatural origin. The notion of locating the cause of a disease in physiological processes is foreign to Navaho thought."[2] The Native American response is our primary focus here.

Traditional Navajos practiced two primary ways of curing a sick person. The first was through the use of herbs and other natural elements accompanied with songs and prayers provided by the holy people during and following the creation of the world. A previous example of this was the healing of a burn victim by using the tips of a piñon tree and sacred words that pushed the pain away and healed the damaged flesh. In this instance, the world was a pharmacy waiting to dispense medicine, but it was dependent on spiritual knowledge and the gods to actually unlock the curative power. Equally significant are the primarily religious ceremonies that may require as many as nine days or nights to call upon spiritual beings to effect a remedy. Based in events from the past, sacred names, formulas, songs, prayers, paraphernalia, sand paintings, birds, animals, lesser creatures, and other elements of the physical world, these ceremonies invoke invisible powers to work on behalf of a patient. Central to this is establishing a harmonious relationship with everything involved.

That is why Perry starts with a discussion of "sa'ąh naagháii bik'eh hózhǫ́" ("long life, happiness"). This is a phrase, complex in meaning, that hits at the heart of Navajo perception and healing. For those interested in pursuing its teachings and ramifications in depth, there is an entire book, *The Main Stalk* by John Farella, that wrestles with its implications.[3] A much simplified version is offered here. As discussed previously, qualities like Old Age and Hunger are personified in Navajo thought. The same is true of Long Life (male) and Happiness (female), the two beings represented in the phrase "sa'ąh naagháii [and] bik'eh hózhǫ́." Made from corn tassel pollen during the creation, the male was dressed in white shell and the female in turquoise. They received their assignment from Talking God, who directed,

> "Of all these various kinds of holy ones that have been made, you the first one will be their thought, you will be called Long Life," he was told. "And you who are the second one, of all the Holy People that are put to use first, you will be their speech, you will be called Happiness," she was told. . . .
> "You will be found among everything without exception, exactly all will

be long life by means of you two, and exactly all will be happiness by means of you two."[4]

Thus, when Perry speaks of two holy people sitting in front of him, they are the ones who guide the way to obtaining the qualities they represent.

Since most songs and prayers in the ceremonial system include this phrase at its conclusion, a short explanation based on anthropologist Gary Witherspoon's linguistic analysis follows. Sa'ąh refers to obtaining old age as a lifetime goal, while naagháii means that it will be a continuing part of the life stages. Hózhǫ́ is that perfect state of being where everything is ideal and without turmoil. Achieving this level of happiness and beauty, the inner being (spiritual) of an individual, needs to harmonize with the outer physical state and environment of that being. All must be in peace and settled, functioning in unison. Through speech (physical) the thoughts (spiritual) of a person work together to heal. Thus, songs and prayers are the agents through which both physical and spiritual health are achieved.[5] This is part of the reason why traditional medicine works on two levels—tangible and intangible.

Medicine man Frank Mitchell and his wife, Tall Woman, provide good examples of this thinking. He explains that the holy people are very aware of what is going on with the earth surface beings. Comparing their awareness and involvement to a radio, he felt that even though they may not be seen visually, they certainly know what people are doing regardless of whether their actions are intentional or unintentional. The gods are there to protect a person, know when an individual has been asked to perform a ceremony, and assist when called upon. They also know when something has gone wrong.[6] Tall Woman tells of when two of her daughters became ill, and so she called in a hand trembler for a diagnosis. The cause became evident— the two girls had been burning weeds near the family alfalfa field and had inadvertently destroyed some prayersticks that had been placed there as part of a ceremony. Even though the young women had no idea that the offerings were present, the holy beings did. The cost: two five-night Shootingway ceremonies to provide a cure. Both daughters returned to health.[7]

Matching illness to cause in the Navajo world may be bewildering to those not aware of perceived origins. Gladys Reichard took an encyclopedic approach, reporting that sickness such as head diseases, boils and sores, throat irritation, swollen legs, itching, lack of appetite, and vomiting were contracted through shake-offs from supernatural birds. Their effects could be healed by the Chiricahua Windway, Eagleway, and Awlway ceremonies. Snakebite, rheumatism, stomach, kidney, and bladder issues are handled by the Beautyway, while venereal disease, pelvic pain, gallstones, and kidney problems by the Shootingway, Red Antway, and Eagleway.[8] Also, as an astute observer of the physical world that she and her Navajo friends and adopted "family" lived in, Gladys recognized, from a white perspective, other causes of ailments.

> Their manner of living is conducive to bronchial and lung troubles— frequent exposure to marked changes of temperature, sudden downpours, heavy snowstorms combined with low living standards and ignorance of sanitation—that bring on and foster pulmonary diseases. Spitting is so habitual as to be a vice. During a ceremony there is not an inch of floor space in the hogan free from sputum. Everyone sits on the floor and becomes the potential carrier of the germs on it. The women particularly disseminate bacteria with their rippling cotton skirts, twelve or fifteen yards in fullness, and the Pendleton blankets laid on the floor and subsequently used for bedding.[9]

Dorothea Leighton also recognized this problem and worked toward a solution that mixed medical practices from the two worlds. Medicine men often used chewed substances as part of the healing process, spitting or blowing the material on the sick person, while the patient and other participants continued to expectorate. Anglo practitioners, concerned with the germ theory of disease, saw this as spreading the illness. Both types of "healthcare workers" agreed that there was power in the saliva—one from bacteria, the other from evil causing the sickness. Schoolteachers also observed continuous spitting and so introduced the idea of doing it in a can with a little dirt in the bottom or into a small pile of sand on the floor of a hogan that could be carried outside with a shovel. Many Navajo people accepted the practice.[10]

With the adoption of more and more white culture on the reservation, government clinics, hospitals, and missionary services exposed an increasing number of Navajos to Anglo medicine. For years, Tall Woman suffered from pains that she thought were caused by indigestion. Finally, they got so bad that she went to a hospital to consult with a doctor, who determined the problem was her gallbladder. She talked to Frank who, even though a medicine man, told her that she should have it removed. Tall Woman felt she was too old at this point in her life, but he reasoned the malady was going to kill her anyway if she did not have it taken out. She agreed. Following a one-night protection prayer (ach'ááh sodizin), she had the operation and felt much relieved. The doctor, understanding traditional practices, offered to show the gallbladder that had been removed. Tall Woman reacted. "He brought that thing to my room and asked me if I wanted to see it. But right there, I said No and I told him to throw that thing out and let me go home! But Augusta [daughter] looked at it; she told me it was huge, like a lemon."[11] Her reaction to discarding the small organ was not as typical as some might think. Navajo doctor Lori Arviso Alvord, MD, recorded that, "Such requests from Navajo patients who have had their appendix, gallbladder, or other body tissue surgically removed by now seemed normal to me. They even wanted infected tissue back. It was commonplace for patients to leave the hospital with a line of new black stitches sewn on their abdomen and a small paper bag in hand, the contents of which had resided inside them several days earlier. It was the same for any body part: hair, skin, nails, even the skin from a circumcision—all are carefully protected."[12] As Perry explains, fear of witchcraft and exposure to other influences gives reason for this reaction. This practice raises new questions on both sides of the cultural gap discussed later.

Frank Mitchell, as a medicine man, was initially wary of hospitals. Although he knew other practitioners who were using their powers to bless the facility and assist enrolled patients, he was not sure this was acceptable to the holy people—no hogan, an overall foreign environment, nontraditional practices, far different procedures, opposing worldview— there was a lot to overcome. By the end of his life and a number of experiences, his thoughts had changed. "Taking everything into consideration, we are being planned for by leaders and white people. We now have better hospitals than before. When you go to them, you get all kinds of treatment for different kinds of diseases. I don't know what those sicknesses are; maybe some of them are dangerous. But the young men who take care of you in the hospitals still do not think of you as a stranger or think of that sickness as ugly. Instead, they just go ahead and care for you as if you were their relative."[13]

One might think that with those kinds of sentiments coming from a medicine man, that traditional healing might lose relevance. Not so. There are many examples where Navajo medicine healed people long after white doctors had given up. One singer of the Shootingway Chant had been sick for years. He went to a physician who diagnosed fatal cancer with no hope of recovery. His travel home was too much to complete in one day, and so he visited with friends, who sang over him for many days. By the time they finished, he was restored; he went on for many years to sing over others.[14] John Holiday healed the daughter of a woman who had flown all the way from Washington, D.C., after hearing about him from a group of healthcare workers he had instructed. The Anglo mother was desperate, offering $1,000 for her daughter's cure from recurring nightmares that were so frightening the girl had to be physically restrained. John performed the Evilway for his patient and provided additional materials for use once they arrived home. A short time later, the mother wrote a letter, indicating that they had followed all of his directions and that her daughter was totally healed.[15]

John also had to be healed. As a young man, he had worked on a railroad crew. During that time, there had been a serious accident where some of the workers had been killed, and John, as one of the survivors, had to pick up the dead flesh and other remains. Years later, he felt the effects, his feet and ankles turned black and grew extremely painful, while walking slowed to a minimum. He had "many different kinds of sings" including a nine-day Enemyway but without results. John went to a hand trembler who diagnosed the problem and then recommended an Evilway ceremony. He next went to some white doctors who determined that amputation was the only solution. The patient strongly disagreed, even though walking by this time had become increasingly difficult. Once the Evilway began, he listened intently but eventually fell asleep, only to awake at dawn to find the medicine man still singing, but now the pain was gone. The swelling was still present, but he could walk without crutches and before long returned to normal. He later said, "I believe this is what causes a lot of amputations among our people, even the white man, but they do not realize it. These people make mistakes, and they do not get any ceremonies done, so their lives are shortened and amputations are performed. This is how I was healed about eleven years ago."[16]

The last part of this chapter presents a discussion of new Anglo procedures, technology, and thought that challenges traditional views. For readers who are in the medical profession, Maureen Trudelle Schwarz's *"I Choose Life"* is highly recommended.[17] There is a wide range of thinking about specific diseases and practices that have been recently introduced and gained ground in affecting the Navajo. For instance, up until the 1960s, trachoma was a scourge that greatly affected Navajo health of young and old. There was no ceremony for the disease specifically, and so a patient could be involved in someone else's ritual and as part of that, would have their eyes anointed with tallow, which was then returned to the practitioner's medicine pouch for use with another patient.[18] Diabetes is considered a white man's sickness and so, like cancer, there is no ceremony for it.[19] Tuberculosis, another foreign disease, on the other hand, responds to Navajo Windway ceremonies, according to Tall Woman. Frank Mitchell's brother had a severe case of TB when he went to the Fort Defiance Hospital. Later, following a ceremony, the doctors "took another picture of his insides" and found no trace of the illness. Tall Woman's daughter Isabel had a similar situation, but after the ritual, "they took a picture of her [and] that spot had disappeared."[20] While Tall Woman appreciated these pictures, she later bemoaned the fact that almost all of her daughters were now having their babies in hospitals where they had pictures (ultrasound) taken to determine the position of the infant. Her long-practiced art of midwifery was getting lost.

One procedure that has become increasingly more common on the reservation is abortion. Perry obviously has strong feelings against it, viewing it as an affront to the holy beings as well as the Navajo people. Those who follow traditional teachings faithfully can find no acceptable reason for taking an unborn human life, which is in direct opposition to White Shell Woman and all of the guidance provided during the kinaaldá. Ruth Roessel, a Navajo traditionalist, reported that in 1979 she and others met with a group of medicine men working for the Navajo Health Authority. Their response to the "widespread use of abortion" was that it would cause mental health problems for the mother. "As a result, evil will return and harm the mother at some point in the life of that individual."[21]

Time moves on, healing practices evolve. Dennis L. Fransted, an anthropologist who studied application of past experience to modern trends, summarized nicely the future of Navajo and western healthcare. "There is today in the Navajo Nation a genuine wish among many in the health care field, and most in political leadership, to construct a uniquely Navajo health care system, incorporating what are usually called 'the best elements' of the traditional Navajo and Western approaches."[22] The challenge will be to integrate the two before too much is lost.

"Long Life, Happiness"

The ultimate goal in healing the patient is not just the removal of the illness, since most of the physical problems are really just symptoms of an underlying spiritual issue. The person in need of help has, in some way, disturbed and harmed a relationship and so now needs to restore or mend what has been broken or offended. The desired outcome is found in two phrases that sound quite similar but are different in meaning. The first is "sa'ąh naagháii bik'eh hózhǫ́," often translated as "long life, happiness," but which is generally misunderstood by many people. This phrase does not refer to a human being. It is not "us." Instead it teaches about the qualities of light, water, air, and the ground we walk on. They are like gods who sit opposite me and hold happiness for me to use. Each of those elements has their own joy, and from them I can find pleasure and the things necessary to live a good life. The sun is going to make the plants grow, the water is going to nourish them, the wind is going to blow, and the ground is going to enrich them, making life as beautiful as it is in springtime. This makes a person happy. That is what is being described. Those elements are the ones that

These medicine men working on a sandpainting from the Windway are assisting a person to return to the pollen path and eventually achieve "Long Life, Happiness." They are specialists ordained to be intermediaries between the patient and the holy beings to remove an evil affliction.

make it possible for us to walk in beauty. These are the things that make the Blessingway or living a fulfilled life possible; we walk into that beauty.

Medicine men are more concerned with a second phrase—"yísah naagáii bik'eh hózhóní doo atíhanéhé"—referring to someone who will live a long life without problems and who will be a happy person. This phrase almost sounds the same as "sa'ah naagháii bik'eh hózhǫ bikék'eh naasháá dooleeł"—I want to walk and I shall walk in beauty. That is what my goal is and what I say. In the medicine way, this says who I am and that I will live a long life and be happy while the other says these qualities sit before me. It is as if the individual and happiness are facing each other and the person is trying to obtain those good feelings. When one gives a prayer, they say, "I am going to walk in beauty; that is my goal." Unlike when Christians pray about being with God, having eternal life, and receiving heavenly rewards—

Navajo thought is for the present. This is something that will be achieved today. Being healed, receiving a gift, getting a job are all possible ways of obtaining happiness. It is something that sits there in front of us that we can obtain today. "I'm going to have you; I want to get a job and be happy. I want to achieve good things today." There is nothing eternal; ceremonies and prayers are being done here and now, and good things need to be accomplished soon. Help me walk through my problems, give me direction, or arrive at my home, so that I can grab on to those things that are helpful. These experiences are the ultimate purpose of a ceremony—to restore a person to happiness by correcting something that has gone wrong.

Specialists Ordained to Serve

Western medicine has doctors, nurses, and technicians, some of whom are general practitioners while others are specialists for a specific illness. Their cures are dependent upon understanding the physical laws of health that have in some way broken down and caused sickness. Sometimes through trial and error, sometimes by shifting medicines, and sometimes by exploratory surgery, these doctors will identify and remove the cause of the problem. From the Navajo perspective, Anglo doctors, just like medicine men, who heal others and discover miraculous cures, are believed to be doing the work of the holy people. They were sent to this earth with a responsibility to use their gifts to help others. These people receive praise and offerings as ones chosen by the gods to serve a very specific purpose. There is no difference between a medicine man and a doctor in having a talent or power to perform an operation or a ceremony. For example, hand trembling can only be performed by someone who is given that gift. The holy people are the ones who make the choice, not the individual, who then can only accept or refuse the gift. If the person takes on the responsibility, then they have to follow the rules set by the gods in order to be successful, just as a doctor has to follow the physical rules of anatomy, medicine, and his profession.

In Navajo practice, following a diagnosis through divination, a medicine man who understands the cure for the identified illness will be asked for treatment. There are some ceremonies like the Blessingway/Beautyway that address more general needs, while others such as the Evilway, Enemyway, Mountainway, and Windway are much more specific in treating the symptoms and causes for particular problems. A medicine man may know up to a half dozen, and in some exceptional instances even more, but no one will know all of the ceremonies past and present. Even within the ranks of those who practice a particular ceremony, there are varying levels of expertise and an informal hierarchy. For instance, those who conduct the Evilway have their own people; the Lightningway have their own, and the Windway theirs. Each is a specialist and has been ordained to perform this service or ceremony.

While western doctors are constantly learning about the latest theories and cures for a disease, the medicine man goes in the opposite direction to learn about how and why the holy people instituted a particular practice in the past. Ultimately, it goes back to the beginning, when all of the gods, plants, animals, and other creatures gathered together in council to determine how many things in this world would work. All creatures and elements were in human form, ready to discuss the powers and opportunities each had to offer to the earth surface beings. Talking God, Black God, the Yé'ii Bicheii, and many others from the four directions sat in a circle with the plants and animals to select and approve who would be in charge of certain aspects of medicine. The holy ones listened to each one, then said, "This young man will represent this; his name is this; he comes from here; he takes care of this aspect of medicine; he will be represented by this." Then those present questioned the individual who came from a certain species or type. This is why today, when a medicine person picks a plant, he prays to one of that species but leaves it alone and gathers others around it. After all questions were answered, everyone present agreed that this was the way it should be and that a certain plant or element would have the powers agreed upon. As mentioned in volume 2, chapter 5, Peyote was the only one who refused to accept the council's decision and so, although it is a medicine plant, it did not receive approval and a blessing from the holy people in this council. If he had just chosen to sit down and go through the process like everyone else, he could have been, but he refused and so is not recognized. He went to the Plains Indians instead and received his blessings from them. As of today, he is a visitor, an outsider, even though he wants to be part of Navajo medicine. As for the rest in attendance, they were ordained to serve future generations with their medicine powers.

Songs and prayers are the means by which these powers are summoned and asked to help in curing people. Most medicine songs used to address medication for people are very similar. There may be slight variations coming from different clan teachings, but generally there is not much difference. My aunts have all of the Edgewater songs that they use to heal people. While some of their medicines may differ, the songs are close to identical to those found in other clans. Sometimes a medicine man encounters a problem and is unsure where to turn for help. Just as with a doctor in western medicine, he needs something new or different to correct the situation. To get this information he calls upon the "Creator," which unlike the Christian use of this term, is more general and is not referring to a single, powerful being. Instead, when the medicine man uses this term, he is addressing the entire medicine world with the hope that the one who holds the power to heal will make itself known to him through thoughts, dreams, or experiences as to what plant, animal, element, or holy being will have the answer and cure. This is an unknown god; I do not know its name so I am asking for direction. I could say Haashch'ééyáłti'í (Talking God) or Haashch'ééwoon (Calling God) but they are in a different level with different abilities. If I were doing a ceremony and I knew that they could help, then I would use their name.

At this point I am talking to plants and animals in a spiritual way, but I do not know which one. I use my sacred name then say, "I might not know your name but you are the holy ones. Tell me. Talk to me. You know who I am. I'm your grandchild. You know me, so tell me, talk to me, show which one of these plants work for you. I am going to start mentioning names and you can make yourself known to me. You recognize who you are and so please help." In respect, I do not use the holy people's names unless I know exactly who I am going to for help. When I say "Creator," I say it as a means of finding out—I do not have my medicine with me, I am not performing a ceremony, I am just exploring for answers for a cure. I am asking for someone to respond to me.

Nowadays, many Navajo people turn to the North American Native American Church (NAC) to provide ceremonies for healing and blessing. Much like western medicine, there are certifications and legal procedures that need to be followed for licensure to obtain peyote buttons, and so a brief explanation is offered here. A medicine man can belong to either the Navajo Nation Medicine Men Association or Diné Hataałii Association. They also have to be a member in good standing with the Native American Church in order to purchase and use peyote. Failure to follow the law can land a person in jail, just as with an unlicensed doctor practicing western medicine. One's home of reference is the chapter the person votes in. Even though an individual is an Indian and can vote on the reservation, if he or she does not have a card showing membership in the NAC when carrying peyote, they can be arrested. The police will hold them until they contact their chapter, who then sends a representative from Window Rock to sign affidavits before the jailed person can be released.

Still, there are a lot of people who sell peyote for other than ceremonial purposes. New Mexico and Arizona have strict laws and enforcement for its use and sale. In the past, I provided mental health counseling in Shiprock, New Mexico, and was licensed to purchase and carry peyote. Behavioral health wanted to hire some medicine people to use peyote when counseling, but the state licensure board for New Mexico and Arizona does not allow the use of any drugs when advising patients. Since peyote is a hallucinogen and plays with the mind, its use in that setting is forbidden. A lot of people who were doing NAC ceremonies mixed with traditional counseling bumped heads with the state and lost their licenses as behavioral health workers. Both the state and federal governments forbid it even though the Navajo Nation approved it. Nevertheless, the counselors had their licenses suspended and were told not to practice. That happened about ten years ago. So when people came to me and asked if I was a peyote runner, I told them no and that I was just a straight medicine man. This allowed me to maintain my license. I thought that because of the American Indian Religious Freedom Act (1978) that peyote would be allowed, but not so. The licensure board for counseling had its own regulations. The Utah Navajo Health Systems allows the use of peyote except when counseling as a licensed individual.

Western Medicine: Conflict and Consensus

While the Native American Church has had a great impact on people who practice Navajo traditional medicine, there has been an even greater impact on them with western medicine. The two systems of healing are polar opposites in many respects, with one dealing primarily in the physical world with tangible processes and the other mainly in the spiritual, religious world. The old way with its ceremonies, prayers, songs, and herbs was how Navajos dealt with sickness going back to the time of creation. Now our world has changed, and many people do not use medicine men the way they used to. People live by or in border towns, have access to hospitals and clinics both on and off the reservation, are losing the Navajo language and so struggle with what is being said in the ceremonies, do not understand the stories from which traditional practices come, and are pressed for time to hold lengthy rituals. Parents are raising their children according to the dominant society's values, do not speak our language in the home allowing English to come first, and think about the world through western values. They go to clinics, get flu shots, pick up their medications, and receive the latest medical procedures, which often remove the illness or its symptoms.

I tell the people much of what is received in western medicine has been researched and proved. For the past one hundred years, it has provided some of the best practices and it continues to improve. It really works. We know this because the headache is gone after taking an aspirin and we do not get the flu after the shot. A lot of diseases that used to be around are cured or at least prevented. Look at tuberculosis, hepatitis, and trachoma, to name a few. Accepting western ways has caused this. Being Navajo or native does not prevent it from working on us. Many of the cures are solidly proved through

The Native American Church uses symbols derived from a variety of Plains Indian cultures such as the tepee, gourd rattle, beaded staff, eagle feather fan, and ceremonial altar. A full night ceremony involves intense prayer, singing, and visions assisted by ingesting peyote, considered a sacrament by participants. (Courtesy of Samuel Holiday)

tests with facts and a lot of history to back them up. Today people check their blood work to see how their enzymes are doing, the status of their white and red blood cell count, and current level of cholesterol. It is a modern world in which physical proof dominates.

At the same time, we are native people. Even though we stabilize diabetes, lower high blood pressure, and get pills with a certain number of milligrams of something to lower cholesterol, there are still traditional practices that need to be performed. The results from a ceremony cannot be tested or evaluated in the same way as much of western medicine. We have meditation and the spiritual aspect that is part of a cure but works in a different way. I tell people it is important to take their medication and that these doctors are well-trained, well-educated helpers working to assist them. Their type of medicine is important and cannot be put down and walked away from. This is how I explain western medicine to traditional Navajo people who are familiar only with the ceremonies.

While many people are very comfortable with modern medicine, there are many places where traditional Navajo practices help in ways that physical cures cannot. Illnesses like post-traumatic stress disorder (PTSD), depression, fits of anger and rage, suicidal thoughts, and an excessive lifestyle are just a few of the illnesses that through counseling and ceremonies can place a patient back on the right path. A lot of times these feelings are pushed upon a person by outside forces, other times they come from within, but many people do not know how to understand and handle them. Navajo teachings are very effective for this type of sickness. Ceremonies help people to accept their situation, forgive, and understand themselves, while at the same time they involve greater spiritual powers in the healing process. Ceremonies clean a person, both physically and spiritually. For example, if a woman feels deep regret over something she did, she may be convinced that there is no hope for a good life. This becomes the cause of her sickness. The ceremony unravels the problem, brings her back to the beginning of the world, builds her self-esteem and understanding through being "remade," and prepares her for life in the future. This is possible as she exercises faith and belief, plus takes care of herself physically, including medication.

Traditional Navajo teachings and medicine practices like the girl's and boy's puberty ceremonies stress the importance of fitness for life and taking care of oneself. I once heard a person, speaking of another, say, "This man was only allowed to live up to this point. The gods gave him life up to this point." I disagreed. "The only reason this man passed on is because he never took care of himself. If he had, he would have been just as healthy as the next person and lived longer. But he did not want to see a doctor, did not take his pills, so like his father, he had high blood pressure. He ate a lot of fat and excused his excesses by saying, 'Natural people live naturally,' meaning there was no consequence to his lifestyle because he was living the old way and not paying attention to modern understanding." He never practiced anything to do with western medicine or a healthy lifestyle. Exercise, drinking a lot of water, getting enough sleep, watching his diet, was just not part of his routine. He died young, but could have lived a lot longer if he had done what the doctors told him. What he considered his traditional way was not enough to save him. Much older people have outlived him because they use both traditional and western medicine. This young man ignored all of the signs and fell back on, "Well, you know, I'm the natural Navajo. I don't need that," and that is why he died the way he did. That is why I take care of myself, take my pills, drink lots of water, exercise every day, and watch what food I eat. I do this for my grandchildren. I feel good. It is not all about the Indian ways.

Life is given to a person to think about and learn from. That is why everyone has a male and female side to their brain, so that they can teach each other and reason through issues. The mind is a gift that helps one to look and think about things from different perspectives. Traditional practices are always good because they form a belief system that is spiritual, but so do Anglo ways. When combined properly, these can help one to live a long life. My mother is a good example. She is now 103 years old. Her life is built upon positive behavior that keeps her in her kitchen cooking and around the home working. One time I asked her, "What is it that you do and what kinds of things do you eat to have allowed you to live so long?" She surprised me. "Nothing. I just eat regular food." She then clenched her fist and said, "My Son. This is the amount of food you should eat three times a day. If you do, you'll be okay. The size of a balled fist; don't eat too much more than that and you'll be okay. Also, be holy, respect other people, and you will go far." I believe her. She cautioned, "Listen to yourself. Listen to what you are saying. Do you walk in the same manner as you say you do? If not, you need to shut up, because it is very easy to talk and not do what you say you're going to do. Talk is cheap." This is what I was told.

Another reason there are so many problems with cancer, diabetes, and illness is because of the diet we now have. Some of these sicknesses can be inherited, but most of it has to do with stress, depression, and eating. People today go into depression that was rarely seen in the 1920s. One never heard of a young man or woman being depressed. Life was too busy building a home, caring for livestock, planting gardens, participating in ceremonies, and many other activities. There were not enough hours in a day to get all of the work done. All of this exercise kept diseases like diabetes and high blood pressure away. They were never really talked about, and no one ever heard

The contents of a medicine man's jish are just as specialized as what is found in a doctor's black satchel carried in the old days. The reader, by now, should be able to look at each of the items placed in this wedding basket, and tie it to a particular ceremony or practice. (Photo by Kay Shumway)

of people dying from them. Starting in the 1970s and 1980s, health issues really started to escalate. I think it was the beginning of food stamps and general assistance when Navajo people really began to suffer from these diseases. Many of them no longer needed to work, the type of food and how it was processed changed, and they received extra money that could be spent on "luxury items" like sweets and sodas. The people slowed down and began turning into "couch potatoes." Stress and depression built up, fostering these diseases. Today, children and adults are floating in junk food that causes more sickness and, when coupled with less physical activity, create the conditions for mental and physical disorders. When I was growing up, I never saw a candy bar. The first candy I saw was when I was nine years old when one of my sisters cooked some sugar and turned it into something like caramel. We ate it as candy, but other than that, I never had any professionally produced candy until much later, although the trading posts did carry it.

Evaluating Anglo Forms of Healing

Once a Navajo steps into the arena of western medicine, he or she is confronted with a vast array of machines and procedures that are foreign in function and may oppose traditional understanding. Here is, starting with the least invasive—technology represented by the x-ray machine—and progressing from CPR to abortion—a basic understanding of how Navajo thought deals with the bewildering array of innovative techniques present in the twenty-first-century clinics and hospitals found on or near the reservation. This is an area ripe for further investigation, and one that Navajo medicine men are still discussing as to what is acceptable and how to deal with the change.

The x-ray machine in Navajo is known as The Unknown Light that Goes through the Body (nighá'diildlaad). I think a lot of times people never really sit down and think about its cause and effect. The machine is part of the white doctor's world, and it is up to them to know how it can help and harm as part of their procedures. Patients never challenge its use. In Navajo thought, x-rays are connected to lightning and so have part of those qualities that can be harmful. When lightning strikes, just as in a fire, there are a series of colors that appear—a bright white light that goes over a person followed by blue then yellow colors. People say that the blue light is the bad part of the lightning and is connected to getting cancer. The light or color from the lightning goes through one's body like an x-ray, and having once been exposed can lead to cancer. It is just like having an x-ray without any kind of protection for the radioactivity that goes through the body. These two kinds of lights are similar and can kill a person. The Lightningway ceremony teaches about twelve different gods, paired as males and females, who sit with the lightning and have their ways of making the colors when they want to. The medicine used in this ceremony removes the effects of the lightning, as the six male-female pairs work to remove the harm. This is how it is talked about. These holy people are only mentioned within the sacred words of the songs at special times. Only medicine men who specialize in this ceremony know these things. At the beginning of this ceremony and in others as well, there are opening songs called bee atsá̱łééh (chant introduction of any song) that introduce and summon those holy people to participate. This is when the singers start saying "eh, heh, neh, heh, no, huh," then follow it with the names of specific holy people, who in this case, enter into the hogan in male/female, male/female, male/female pairs in six different ways. This is according to the Lightningway, but it is not necessarily associated with any kind of x-ray procedure.

When one comes upon an accident and a person is not breathing, Anglos are taught to provide CPR (cardiopulmonary resuscitation), a part of which says that following thirty compressions with the hands, two breaths are given to the victim. In Navajo thought, putting one's breath into another person is exchanging part of the helper's life force into someone where it will remain. This can also transfer that person's qualities as well as connect the two individuals so that if something happens to the patient, it can also influence the person who gave help. I have recently had a situation with this problem. There was a mother who found her son lying on the floor unconscious and not breathing. She went into action providing CPR including the breaths, but he died. In addition to her grieving over the loss, she began to have pains in her chest and other illness that seemed to indicate that what she had done was now harming her. She visited different medicine people on two separate occasions, but there was no clear path for her to take to correct the problem. Later when I sat down with her, we talked about how, as a first responder, she had done what she had been taught, followed correct procedures, and that it was part of her job. In a larger sense, the death of her son was also a loss for her during which part of her died. He had come from her body and was still connected to her. The CPR, in this case, can be looked upon as this woman breathing into herself. Now part of her body had died, but she was still alive. She came to understand that although part of her body, the son, had died, she had taken the proper action and could still feel good about herself. When she arrived for the next session, she was a different woman and told me that she understood what I had said. It was comforting for her. All of the pains that she had been suffering were now gone. The woman had taken a step forward, away from the guilt and worry about having done something wrong, and was entering a more comfortable time in her life.

What if the person receiving CPR is not a family member? Younger Navajo people do not have a big problem with this procedure, but some elders would. For those following strict traditional beliefs, even being touched by a person considered evil can have bad consequences, not to mention their blowing their breath inside of the body. That is a major concern because it transfers anything negative into the recipient. The evil must be removed, which means one of two ceremonies, either of which can be very expensive. If the person providing CPR is a Navajo treating another Navajo, then the Evilway ceremony can be used; if it was an Anglo or non-Navajo providing the resuscitation, then an Enemyway ceremony is recommended. As a medicine man, I am able to deal with these things because I have been ordained to touch and handle these situations, which will not bother me. I had the ritual, the medicine, and carry a medicine bundle, so I am protected. But if a non–medicine person gets involved in

Anglo medicine and traditional Navajo practices meet, opening a new world for each side of the cultural divide to consider. Imagine the thoughts of the woman peering into a microscope at the small realm of bacteria, how the translator (center) struggled to describe in Navajo what she is seeing, and how oblivious the doctor is to the rich heritage of healing that his patients understand.

these kinds of activities, then they will need a ceremony to give them the peace of mind they are looking for. Crystal gazing or hand trembling will help determine what needs to be done. The Evilway ceremony is particularly effective in cleansing a person from ill effects because the herbs one drinks force the evil to be vomited out.

Blood transfusions raise similar issues. When a patient enters a hospital and needs a transfusion, the blood comes from a centralized bank made possible by many different donations. Race, personality, moral standards (good and evil), and circumstance are all swept aside; the blood recipient does not know whose fluid is entering their body. Whoever and whatever are now a part of that person and can have an influence. Those characteristics are embedded in the recipient. This does not bother me personally, but for the older people who have not been educated in western ways, it can be an issue. They will attribute their thinking, walking, or acting differently to the transfusion. I try to explain that this was all part of saving their life and that there will not be any side effects. Sometimes I give them herbs to help clean their blood and put their minds at rest. For the Navajo, there are three types of blood medicine that come from plants. One of them cleans the blood, another maintains the flow, and another removes cholesterol. These three medicines are used in the Lifeway ceremony after being boiled. The patient drinks this mixture for two weeks. It cleans the blood and is what I prescribe for someone who is concerned about blood transfusions. All of those negative feelings leave them, and life gets back to normal.

The issue with amputations creates more problems. Again, for the younger generation, there is no concern, but for older Navajos, there needs to be a way of securely controlling who has access to the removed part. This goes back to the time when something from an individual, no matter how small—hair from a comb, sweat on a shirt, fingernail clippings, blood, anything that has elements from a person—can be used against them through witchcraft. Whatever it is becomes a proxy for the targeted individual so that evil is projected against them. When a foot or hand or some other body part is removed, if it falls into possession of someone working against that person, real harm can be done.

I have not encountered much of this, and so I talked to a friend who is a medicine man to learn his thoughts. We agreed that the problem exists and that for some people it needs to be handled carefully. He felt strongly that the amputated part—let's say a foot—should not be buried. One cannot go out and bury himself. If a person did that, it would be like saying they are only part there, part alive. He had actually counseled a person not to do that. On the other hand, that foot cannot be kept around and constantly guarded. From the practical standpoint of housing decayed flesh and denying access to it, there needs to be a better way of disposing of the problem. We both agreed that the answer lay in burning the body part. This is not to suggest that cremation of a body is in keeping with traditional Navajo values. This will be discussed in the next chapter, but to dispose of part of the body with fire is the safest and most practical thing to do. Once the task is completed, then the ashes are scattered over the ground, not buried, so that they are taken by the wind. This way nobody has to deal with it.

One issue that traditional Navajo medicine and the Indian Health Service (IHS) agree strongly about is abortion. Since IHS is a federal entity, and the government will not directly fund abortion, it is in complete keeping with Navajo values that see this practice as murder. Some women may go off reservation to border towns; for the Navajo in the Four Corners region this means Colorado, since Arizona, New Mexico, and Utah have very restrictive laws. The Navajo people for the most part are always against abortion for a number of reasons. First, we prize human life and see the killing of innocent children as wrong. Second, the child has a right to live and is both a physical and spiritual being. Third, it has a really harmful impact on the woman who has it done. Finally, it tears away at the fabric of a family and what they should be about. This was true in our past and is true today. A person cannot choose abortion over life. Navajo medicine men counsel women who are considering it, that from the day they have the operation performed, they will never receive the good things of life or any kind of help and blessings from the holy ones in the spirit world. Instead, the woman will be poor, struggling to exist for the rest of her days. She will never know success because she took a life. These are the teachings concerning abortion.

Today, I see a lot of women who have had this procedure and how they struggle with problems because of it. They are loaded with debt, never finish school, have low paying jobs, and live in troubled families with lots of unsolved issues. Navajos are told not to talk about abortion, not even mention it. Some people will even chase you off if you bring up the subject. This is true within the family as well as with others outside. The topic is taboo because it is considered to be like preparing someone to kill an individual. Nothing makes this clearer than a personal experience I had many years ago.

One of the families I knew very well had a woman who was a good friend of mine. They came to me often for help, and so I understood how they thought and acted, something I had learned over many years. Sometime ago, this woman, whom I will just call Jane, asked me to conduct a Native American Church ceremony to put some of her problems behind. I started to wonder. It seemed like she was trying to hide something but I could not put my finger on it right away. She had been telling people that she needed to have a growth removed from her body and so everyone assumed she was talking about a cancerous tumor. Her family had never had a problem with cancer, in fact, they generally had good health and lived a long time, having a grandmother who had lived to be 103, with Jane's mother fast approaching that age also. The suggestion of cancer just did not make sense. I first received this news just as I was beginning to practice medicine, and so it fell back to me to decide what actions needed to be taken, including which ceremony to perform.

Jane was anxious to get the medical procedure underway, hinting that the sooner this problem was resolved, the better the recovery. I approached her about the situation saying, "One thing that I know is that you don't have cancer in your family. I know the members of your family too well; I can also tell if you're doing something wrong. I believe what is taking place is that you are trying to get rid of a child you are carrying. The issue has nothing to do with cancer. You say you want to go to Durango to have this tumor removed, but why go there when there are IHS hospitals a lot closer that can perform that operation? I think it's because none of these hospitals give abortions unless there are very serious concerns about the mother's life." She just looked at me, then asked how I knew all of this. I replied, "I'm not stupid and can put two and two together. You are making up these stories about cancer to cover your real reason. You have never had cancer in your family. Then you started talking about Durango, where Navajo people run for an abortion because it is legal in Colorado. I'm not going to be part of this. I don't want to do the ceremony that you're asking for. Go find somebody else that will do it for you, but not me."

She confessed that everything I had said was true, but in spite of the counsel she received, she went ahead and had the procedure performed. I felt awful because I could have stopped this terrible loss of life. Instead, she ended its existence before the child even had a chance to move. What kind of person does that? We should not be like that; no family should do such things. Jane tried to explain that there were lots of other people who do it, but I told her that no one should use abortion for those reasons. "Your family comes from a long line of medicine people. Your mother is a medicine woman, father a nine-night and Yé'ii Bicheii singer, as well as your two brothers who are medicine men. They perform some of the most sacred ceremonies; they would never allow this. It's scary even to think about." I refused to perform the ceremony that she requested and told her to get someone else to do it because I would not have any part of what she did.

During all of this discussion—from the time she claimed it was a tumor to her finally admitting her real intent—she complained about suffering. After she had the abortion, that is when the real suffering began. Her eyes were injured and within ten years she was blind. People understood that her blindness was a punishment for her having an abortion and was directly connected to breaking the spiritual law that forbids such an act. She still struggles with the handicap of blindness every day of her life. This is what happens when one does not follow the teachings of the holy people.

CHAPTER EIGHT

Aging and Death

Walking the Old People's Road to the End

T he ideal in traditional beliefs takes a person through the final stage of life, old age, in preparation for the new spiritual beginning when death arrives. Both experiences have their drawbacks and limitations, but each, if lived appropriately, ends in fulfilling the goal of "sa'ąh naagháii bik'eh hózhǫ́" ("long life, happiness"). There are various views of death and what it means to those about to experience it, where that next spiritual world is located, and what it is like when one gets there. Here, Perry shares his understanding from both a personal and teaching perspective, to which is added an extended excerpt from Father Berard Haile's study on the topic. While one can compare these beliefs with those of other cultures, those followed by the Navajo are distinctly integrated through its mythology, theology, ceremonial performances, and daily life. They form a unique system that encapsulates many of the People's teachings: relationships, respect, spirituality, patterns of the holy people, and familial responsibility to name a few. This topic of old age and death offers a fitting conclusion to the preceding material found in this trilogy.

We first encountered Old Age living on the San Juan River near Navajo Mountain. Monster Slayer and Born for Water went to destroy some of these last remaining monsters, but softened when they saw this couple (volume 1, chapter 8). There walked an old woman with white hair and wrinkled face, hunched over, slowly hobbling along with the help of a cane, with a man known as Old-Age-Lying-in-a-Heap, so ancient he could not move, curled up in a fetal position grasping a stone ax. The Twins listened to the old ones' reasoning about appreciating youthful health and making room for the next generation, and so decided to let them live.[1] Today, however, embedded in the phrase "long life, happiness" is also the belief that once one lives through the difficult years of old age, there will be a rejuvenation or restoration to youth that is experienced in both life and death.[2]

Elderly people should be respected for all of the things they have survived to reach old age. John Holiday warns not to make fun of their carelessness or helplessness, failing personal hygiene, or forgetfulness. In fact, "It is said that you could pick up their spit and swallow it; this will make you live as long, or longer than this elderly person. That's how respectfully we should think of them."[3] Even in death, often forewarned by one's skin peeling and flaking off too easily, the elder brings good things to the living. Leland Wyman wrote,

> It was customary to observe the number of deaths of old age occurring in certain families and if one after another died of old age in the family, there was said to be one "old-age generation," i.e., repeated death of old age. If this happened twelve times it was said the inner form of the earth would rise to stretch itself and then lie down again in a different position. It used to be said that this has occurred eight times and is still to occur four times more. Old age and repeated deaths of old age are desirable.[4]

This positive view is diametrically opposed to what one hears about Navajos and their fear of passing. The literature is filled with examples of avoiding the deceased, asking white men to bury a body, or medicine men performing a ceremony to prevent ill effects. Perry points out that there is a large difference between the deaths of those who die young and those who are old. Navajos consistently refer to the handling and burial of the dead as "very sacred" regardless of age, but when a younger person died unexpectedly, special restrictions and practices went into effect. The hogan in which the person died was permanently abandoned. Women and children could not go near the body; those who were burying the corpse had to follow ritually prescribed restrictions. (See volume 1, chapter 8) Underlying this behavior was the concern that those who had died early still held a desire to linger, to continue on in this world, and to take some of their associates with them.

Compare that to the death of an old person. Many of the restrictions are lifted and the death is celebrated. Father Berard Haile, when speaking of the abandonment of the hogan, noted,

> Those reaching old age in it have nothing to fear. Not even death. They remain in the hogan to the very end. Their children need not destroy the hogan which harbored one or more inmates that reached a ripe old age. You pray in Blessingway for the blessing of a death of old age. The hogan in which such a death has occurred is not destroyed. It has been blessed by

a "generation of old age." The family may witness such a death. The four days of mourning, otherwise customary, are not observed. Family life continues on in the same hogan.[5]

The origin of death goes back to the time when the holy people were organizing this world and Sun Bearer demanded a life each day for the work he did in crossing the sky. Then it happened—someone came up missing. Two of the gods called ni'hwiididlídí and ni'hwii'a'á searched in the four directions to find the dead body and where the spirit had gone but without success. They were about to return to the Yellow World beneath when each suddenly felt the flesh in their knees pinch. Moving on, they experienced a rattle in their throat, then a strong odor, and a strange eerie feeling. When they reached the place of emergence, the two holy people looked down into the hole and saw a man combing his hair. This was the person they had been looking for, but now when he glanced up and whistled to the two above, they felt strong, frightening impressions. The two gods went back to their group, warning everyone not to return to the "Country of the Past." If any of them experienced such sensations, heard a mysterious whistling, or saw a deceased relative in a vision, they should have a ceremony or prayers to ward off impending problems.

First Man and First Woman had planned to have everyone live forever, had never experienced death, and were not sure how often people would die. They were confused. The couple made a smooth pole with a point on it and brought it to a lake to see, after they cast it into the water, if it would return to shore. If it did, there would be no more deaths; if it sank, there would be. Just as they cast it into the water, Coyote appeared with a stone ax, declaring that if his item did not float, dying would be frequent and a normal part of life. Naturally, the stick came back and the ax remained submerged. "So it was decided that, although there would be death among the people of the earth, sometimes the very ill would recover because the log had floated back to the shore."[6] The presence of death was assured.

From this point two different realms were recognized—that of the living and that of the dead—both of which have their ways of either avoiding or interacting with the other. For the living, beyond the funeral and four days of mourning, there are rules to be followed by those grieving for a lost one. Tears, a natural part of Navajo expression of joy or sadness, are a very acceptable way of showing unity. During the four days of recognizing the initial loss, crying profusely is accepted and expected, but after that it is to stop. Continuing to do so would indicate that the person is anticipating another death.[7] Objects important to the deceased during life may be buried with them or destroyed on top of the grave, but the rest of their possessions are burned unless given away before passing. No one should ever wear the clothing of someone who is gone. Even the shovels used to dig the grave should not be used again and so are broken and left at the site. This or three small poles slanted to a peak indicate a burial and should be avoided. Following the funeral, a bowl of water with needles from a special cedar (gadni'eełii) are mixed together for the participants to wash in to prevent harm from the deceased who longs to be with them.[8] The pungent odor of the solution keeps evil away. The full name of the dead person should not be spoken as it was in life. If family members wish to discuss something about the individual, then either a kinship term is used or some type of circumlocution such as "he who was my father" is appropriate. Great care is taken to respect the deceased.[9]

Where the departing spirit goes raises other questions. Beyond what Perry and Haile call the "Old People's Home" and "ghostland," there are further possibilities. John Holiday taught that the Holy Wind received at birth is eternal and that when it leaves the body at death it "goes back to a beautiful place down below the earth somewhere, and when another baby is born, a pair of Holy Winds will go there again. It could be the same pair or another. That is what I was told by the elders."[10] To John, as we move through life, we do things that are wrong and that we regret. They slow down the ability of the spirit to reach the good place where one wants to be.

> Therefore, when we bury a person, we have to hold sacred the death and burial for four days. If it is kept sacred, the person will be able to go to the other world where the good people enter. Our keeping of the four days changes the deceased and makes a bad person worthy to enter the good world. That is why it is so important to observe this after burial. Those who commit suicide have their own world. It is chaotic and wild. But for those who die a normal death and were good, there is a beautiful place.[11]

The finality of death in the Navajo world may not be so final. Take Navajo Oshley's experiences as an example, then multiply them numerous times for other people. By midlife, he was happily married, had a child, and was well respected in his community. Tragedy struck, first with the loss of his wife and then his son, both to tuberculosis. As a hand trembler, he tried to divine what was wrong with his wife, receiving impressions that made his lungs burn as if "an eagle was sitting on my chest." Ceremonies had no effect, the doctors could do nothing, and another hand trembler told him that she was going to die. Within a short time, she passed away, her last words were of love and respect for her husband.[12] For well over a year, he grieved.

Oshley continued through life, walked the Old People's Road, achieved the age of around 102 (birth dates vary), and was preparing to die. (Note: he remained mentally sharp to the end.) Starting about three months before he passed away, he began to have an increasing number of dreams or visions.

He said that a young Navajo girl, who knew him but whom he did not recognize, came to visit. She stood before him about four feet tall, wore a yellow dress, held a matching flower, and told him that he should prepare to go. His daughter believed this was her daughter, who had died seven and a half years before at the age of six months. The baby, when laid to rest in her coffin, was clothed in a yellow dress with a daffodil in her hand. A grandson, who had also died and whom Oshley recognized, also came to visit. He, too, urged the old man to go.

The most dramatic manifestation came in a vision. A spiritual world opened to Oshley's gaze in which he saw a beautiful land with trees and a lake. In front of him he observed deceased members of his family—his brother, daughters, his former wives, a man he believed was his father (although he had never seen him before), and the girl in the yellow dress. A black horse he had once owned as a young man was also there, along with some other people he named but the listener did not recognize. These individuals waited behind a line in front of which stood three men. Oshley did not recognize the three except to say that they were not Navajos. Their job seemed to be to block his way, saying that it was not yet time. When the vision ended, he told his family that there were people waiting for him and that he would be going to them soon. A few weeks later, he made that journey. I have personally had many Navajo friends tell of similar visitations from beyond. The worlds of both living and dead are close by.

Old Age: Reaching Full Circle

Navajo elders have earned the respect that younger people give them because of their long life of hard work and learning. As Monster Slayer cleared the world of angry, destructive creatures, he decided to let four types of monsters remain because they would be helpful as a reminder of important things. One of the four was the Old Age People. They told Monster Slayer to spare them, arguing that men and women should not remain young forever, but rather should mature each day to the point where they will need to pass away to make space for the next generation. By becoming older, they will return full circle to the point when they were first born, helpless and dependent on others. Ideally, 102 years will mark the time when their life has finished and they return to the earth. Until then, they will walk the Old People's Road.

It begins halfway through life around the age of fifty. The body starts to slow down, not every part works as well as it used to, white hair grows on the crown of the head, and people notice that they are now stepping onto a different path—the Old People's Road. It is Old Age's way of showing that they are becoming elders. They are not used to being this way, and at a certain point a person realizes they are a grandmother or grandfather now, and this is how they are going to be for the rest of their life; the old days of youth are gone. At the end of the road is the Old People's Home, not like a nursing home in today's society, but a place of peace and rest in a spiritual realm. Until that time, however, there are things to do and ways to act. Prayers change as one asks, "Be good to me to the last day. Let me have my eyes. Let me have my ears to the end. May I continue to walk until life is over. I am praying for all of these good things. Help me to continue to walk until I go to the Old People's Home in the heavens." That is how one talks and prays about this stage in life.

The Twins encounter Old Age as she walks upon the Old People's Road, while her husband rests quietly. Traditional society held elders in high respect, in spite of their increasing frailty and loss of acuity. Young people sometimes find it hard to believe that they may be in a similar condition in the future, which is one of the reasons the Twins allowed these monsters to exist. (Courtesy of San Juan School District Media Center)

However, people also understand that you will only walk on the Old People's Road and go to their home if you are a good person and learn to take care of yourself. If not, you will die young with black hair, never to know what it is to be an elder. The foolishness and chance-taking of a young person must be left behind. As a person matures, they have to use both their male and female thinking to avoid situations that will lead them to death or injury. If a young person fails to take care of themselves and does foolish things that cause them to be injured, like breaking their back, drinking and driving, or causing trouble, these things will catch them and hasten their days of inability.

To be on the Old People's Road, one must plan and be careful. It is always caring about where you are and knowing what could happen. Think twice before doing something and have a backup plan. A cane, like a fire poker for a young woman, becomes an object that gives honor and respect to the elder using it. Life is lived step by step. As with the physical body, there are also changes in attitude. An elder acts with love and caring; everything is gradual, more gentle, and kinder. This is a good thing as one moves toward peace and rejects things that are harmful. A young person, on the other hand, has power and energy and is anxious about aspects of life. His spirit is different. It is all about attitude, about challenges, and life's adventures, which can sometimes be fierce and new and powerful. When an elder who is old and has had a good life dies, people are not as afraid of being around that person, whereas if a younger man or woman dies, there's power and energy that still wants to live and interact with people. That is why there is a big difference between a natural death after a long life and one who dies prematurely under difficult circumstances.

My grandfather talked about the cane. He said, "Sometime it will come to you. There will be a cane, which just like the staff that Moses carried in the Bible, you can talk to, and magical things will happen with it during difficult times." The old people talk about a cane having the same pattern for old people as a fire poker does for newlyweds. Each serves as a helper or doorway for the young couple or elders. For the young marrieds, the fire pokers bless them to have grandchildren on the father's side and grandchildren on the mother's side, while the pokers become their teachers. The cane does the same for the old man and woman, providing guidance to those younger than them. It steadies an old person as they walk through the remainder of their life, guiding them down the Old People's Road. The elder becomes more holy than a young person, whose spirit is different. For them it is all about attitude, challenges, and being powerful. The old person, on the other hand, becomes kinder, gentler, more loving, and less concerned about the challenges of life. Things happen gradually and with less force.

That is why when a young person dies, there are sacred "Mourning Prayers" to help the family bid farewell to their loved one.

To grandchildren their grandparents become the holy ones, helping and leading the young along a path of safety. They share wisdom and teachings that keep youth away from trouble, and when the elders speak, it is like the Holy Wind, warning of danger and guiding them to things that are good. Elders should take the opportunity to do this, but youth must have a desire to listen. Rather than dwelling upon the problems of old age—and there can be many—elders now look at it as a chance to share their experiences and help those who have questions or face difficulties. Family members who have respect, one for another, find peace along the Old People's Road.

One of the abilities really affected by age is loss of memory. Forgetfulness, dementia, and amnesia are three different forms that medicine men can work with to bring the patient back into the circle. I have dealt with a person who had amnesia after he went into a coma; he came out of it following a miraculous cure. This happened to a medicine man living in Piñon. He had been drinking and was going up a flight of stairs when he missed a step, fell five feet, and landed face-first on a hard surface, sending him into a coma. Following a long drive, he entered the hospital and eventually awoke, but he did not recognize his wife and children, had forgotten all of his ceremonial songs and prayers, and had lost his general memory. The hospital provided therapy, but nothing seemed to help. There was little recognition of anything. It was total amnesia.

At the time, I was working in Page when I received a call asking me to provide a ceremony to mentally bring him back. I had never performed anything like this before and was unsure of the procedure, but I agreed to try, although I felt uncomfortable and insecure. This was my first time to address this kind of illness. I returned to Piñon and prepared for the ritual. We got together and used herbs, medicine, and washing before starting the ceremony. I then conducted an all-night ritual until about five o'clock in the morning, when the first white light of dawn broke over the horizon. We both went outside of the hogan and faced the east, while I sang the songs of Talking God. As I did, I took a feather representing the east and put it on his head; suddenly he began to accompany me as I continued to hold the feather in place. Then he really began singing by himself and I just let him go. As a medicine man, he knew those songs, so I just got him started, then we turned around and together reentered the hogan. He was singing all by himself. I sat down and he joined me, taking up the right position as he finished the song. He looked around and then greeted me with "Yá'át'ééh" (hello). One of his sons sitting across from him and a daughter nearby watched with amazement as he started to cry. He greeted them as his babies and asked how they were doing, then turned to his wife and told her that he loved her. Now he recognized everybody. This was still early in the morning so we all took corn pollen and prayed, thanking Talking God for bringing him back. It was his song, one of the male Morning People songs, that worked.

Life's Purpose, Life's Length

This brings us to the purpose of life. We are here because of the holy people who want us to have experiences and finish the things we are to accomplish while on this earth. We did not choose to be here, but everyone is given the opportunity to make a difference. This medicine man was restored because there were still things that he needed to complete. If we do not like the life that we are living, then it is up to us to change it and continue to learn. My grandfather talked about this a lot. At one point I had a cousin who was trying to hang himself. Grandfather was supposed to talk to him about why he did not like himself and why he wanted to leave this life before doing many good things. This cousin was convinced that he did not want to live because he felt no desire to be a part of the family and did not even like his name. He had totally ignored the purpose of life. He eventually changed his mind, but not until there had been a long struggle.

My understanding is that everybody is given as long a life as possible by the holy people, and then it is up to us to live it as carefully and as well as we can. Problems arise and events may occur that might shorten a life, but it is the individual who makes those things happen, not the gods. If you do not take care of yourself, then you will have a short life. But if you say your prayers, live well from day to day, appreciate the things in this world, eat right, and exercise, you will have a long life. There is no limit to its potential until one reaches around 102. Grandfather explained that life is just like a planted seed in the ground. Each seed has the possibility of growing and gaining its full fruit, but there are also things that can cause it to die before ever reaching its full promise. Navajo teaching is always about complete potential. No one, not even the holy beings, know when a person is going to die. Navajos never talk about this.

Sickness and death for humans began at the separation of sexes in the Yellow World. When the men and women came back together, they agreed to forgive and behave themselves. The gods felt that this was good, but they still sensed that there should be some lessons learned from this experience, and so there were many rules established at this time to remind humans about life and its frailties and to respect one another. Some of the men and women did not want to go through this process and so jumped into the River of Death and perished. One of the rules created to remember these incidents was that there would be life and death so that people would know that not everything continues forever, that circumstances change. There might be a husband who dies before his time, leaving a widow to struggle; perhaps there is a child who is killed or a teenager involved with drugs. All of these events alter life. Drinking, drugs, murder, and many other actions can result in a person's death, just as those people who threw themselves in the river perished. Whether slowly like binge drinking or quickly like a car accident, there are many things that can kill you. This is the lesson brought to this world. As a man or woman, there are decisions that you will make each day, and there is an enemy that you cannot see waiting to snatch you. It may be alcohol, disease, drugs, sexual addiction, gambling, or many other vices that will pull you into trouble and destroy or kill you. The choice is yours, but it all leads back to the teaching of the river.

Each man and woman is given the opportunity to choose. The holy people agreed to the plan and gave the five-fingered beings solutions to some of the issues, but those problems were created by humans. For instance, people introduced venereal disease, but there were two nádleeh who worked with the gods to develop cures. Still there was no guarantee of being healed. Pain and death can also result. Often the patient is the only one who can really heal himself. People first have to want to be cured. This is how life is going to be—it will not be the doctors, medicine, medicine men, or anybody else who can really heal you, only yourself. That is what our ancestors were told. Man was given this understanding so that he will be responsible for his own death; it is not chosen for him by the holy people.

Heading North

Once death had been established and people started to realize that there was an end to life and substance, the holy people identified the north as the place where expended things would go. This is the direction where things are put back when their use is over and where medicines once spent are placed, never to live or grow again. Ashes from a fire, cold rocks from a sweat lodge, or sand from a destroyed sandpainting are sent to the north. People asked why this was done, and so the holy people explained: "The reason is that there has to be a place where we can put these things away and the sun does not go. The sun travels from the east to a little south before ending up in the west. All year long from winter to summer and back there are 102 trails it travels, which is the same number of years that a person can live and the amount of travel they can perform. So the sun's pattern always comes from the east, south, to west but it does not travel to the north. This is one reason

Whether it was the River of Death in the Yellow World, the trench carved by Monster Slayer's knife to ensure Big God remained dead, or contemporary practices concerning the deceased, Navajos have institutionalized ways of handling death. In addition to the protective blades (white female and dark male), there are the feathers of the eagle, which kills directly and is the Holy One, and those from a flicker, who has blood on its feathers. These are tied into the hair of the patient, who dons small spruce branches on their head, then prays with this object. For a short time, the patient becomes a god (holy). The practice is tied into three Evilway ceremonies—the Antway and Big Starway, which are on the same level, and the "Something is Lifeless" (used for abortion and similar life-taking issues), which is the most powerful. All three are becoming extinct. (Photo by Kay Shumway)

why things that grow from the east to the west are used in ceremonies about growth, change, and development. Those medicines used for chronic diseases, death, killing, and that are harsh and unforgiving come from the north."

The teachings about the black bow, flint, arrow, and mustache have been touched upon elsewhere, but a short reminder puts the importance of the north with death in perspective. All of these powerful tools for killing were developed or placed there. Many of these objects were on the dark side and were used to destroy monsters. They are not to be handled by an immature person, but usually only by a medicine man who understands how to control their powers and has the right to display or carry them.

Responsibilities follow the ability to have them. Take the mustache as an example, given as a gift to men as they grow to maturity. Referred to as a black bow, the person wearing it was taught that he had to tell the truth and could not curse. If that man does not have something good to say or speaks with a foul mouth, he has to remove it. This came from the elders, who insisted that an individual act like a mature adult in order to use some of these things that came from the north. This was also the place where holy people developed the bullroarer (nitsidi'ni'—Stick with the Lightning) used in the Enemyway and Evilway ceremonies. The bullroarer is made from an eight-inch piece of lightning-struck wood that is painted with black charcoal, covered with hot pine pitch, and has two turquoise eyes and a mouth inset on one side. The object is attached to a two-to-four-foot cord, which when twirled about the head chases ghosts away. "Twirlers" or "spinners" were developed in the north, the place where the souls of the dead go. This "black" lightning stick frightens and kills the spirits of the enemy when put in motion.

Death and Visitation

Navajo people have a strong respect, sometimes bordering on fear, for death. We do not speak openly about death to children or within the family unless there is a special occasion that makes it necessary. The loss of a close friend or family member, when people are gathered together, is considered an appropriate time to discuss these things. This helps those mourning the loss. The person who died is said to linger around their grave and near the family for four days before departing for the spirit world. After this time of mourning, the deceased leaves with a sign, showing he or she is going. On the last night, those who are mourning talk and listen for an indication that the spirit is departing. It may be the appearance of a bird or its song or some other event that lets the family know that the dead is leaving.

The loss of a loved one is hard to bear. I shared part of my experience in volume 1, chapter 8 when my father passed away and my world seemed hopeless, but there is more to the story. We had spent many days and nights together performing ceremonies and living through daily experiences before I went to college. Just as I finished my degree, he died, shattering my world and what I had hoped for my future. Devastated, I entered a period of life where sadness and my own death seemed to be the only way to remove the pain of this loss. The brightness of the Glittering World held nothing of comfort or interest. Perhaps joining the marines and getting into combat would be a good way to end it, but my grandfather thought otherwise.

I had asked him to perform a Protectionway ceremony for me before I entered the service. He had agreed to do it, but the more he watched me, the more he realized that I was doing things for the wrong reason and with an incomplete understanding. Grandfather cornered me before the ceremony and asked why I was entering the military. My answer was confused, based in grief over a loss, and a desire to end my life, fed by my father's death and my lack of hope for the future. He lost no time challenging my attitude. "I know you loved your father and you believe you cannot live without him, but that is not true. All of this crying needs to stop. Don't do it. Let me tell you a story of how you are and what is happening to you." He taught that half of me came from my mother and the other half from my father, and although he is gone physically, his teaching still rests inside of me. "He's part of you. He's living. You are carrying his blood line. Why do you want to harm yourself?" When he explained it to me this way, I began to feel better. My father and I had been inseparable, and now I felt that he was with me as I continued his work and teachings. Death is not the end for us. Whether one's relatives are physically here or not, they are still part of you as you live your life. You will carry their lineage on to the next level, as you pass through to your children that part of you. A grandfather's bloodline never ends but continues to grow in other people and in different ways. It never stops.

I began to realize that I had been trapped in a negative web that had "no life to it." Instead of thinking about the good things that had filled our father-son relationship, there was only sorrow and loss that overwhelmed the happiness that needed to be remembered. I now understood that the things that we shared together I needed to save and keep alive to pass on to others. These good things needed to be celebrated. Grandfather's teaching had changed my view of loss through death, but it was not until later that this truth was confirmed. Early one morning, as an all-night ceremony moved toward conclusion, I felt my father's presence. The songs were strong with everyone putting all their energy into singing, but there was more than just those visible in the hogan. An unseen presence sat beside me, assisting with the words and energy that seemed so abundant. I became aware of this helper and at times intentionally paused just to see what would happen, but the lyrics and song continued to roll forth. There was no denying that my father was there, participating with me. I heard that familiar voice singing beside me, so I stopped a number of times to listen and finally just did not sing a whole part of the song, but he just kept on chanting. I didn't say anything, just smiled and told myself, "I know you are here with me."

After this experience, I never returned to my father's grave and stopped mourning. I believe that my work as a medicine man is not just in my hands but that others in the spirit world are at times involved. Today, the teaching, counseling, and ceremonies I perform come from my father. What is inside of me is my father who talks continually of important things, which makes me feel complete again. That is why I say "I am my father." My mother, brother, and sister are also a part of me. They may be gone, but they live within. Everyone should do something good with their teachings and experience shared by their family before it is too late. We can't just let it sit there, but rather we have to use it to explore and help each other.

As mentioned previously, the stars are also connected to the dead who have left this earth. Grandfather continued to link my deceased father to my life when he taught, "Yes, your father is gone because he is not on this earth. He has joined others in the spirit world and can be seen only at night when the stars come out. These spirits are in the constellations and unrelated stars. One day when you really miss your father or another loved one, go outside and watch the stars. Think about the person you miss. Suddenly in the sky there will be a star that is going to move, sparkle, and breathe like you. This is where that loved one is located. Once you have found them, then you are ready to talk. They will answer you through your dreams. This is how you can become connected." Grandfather taught that those spirits become part of what is called The Holy One That Lives Beyond at Night (Asázígo haz'á). When the name is looked at closely, it actually translates as The Ancient Ones (Iizází), suggesting our relatives who have gone before. The stars are where they reside. The spirits may become new stars at night that will guide you and assist in a night ceremony. They become the holy ones.

The Body and Burial

One of my grandfathers lived to be 103 years old when he died in 1968. As a young boy, he had been at Fort Sumner and remembered many of the things that had happened to him and his family. When he passed away, he quickly started to deteriorate. He was found sitting in his hogan, and when people went to move him, his head fell off and his body started to break up. Family members put him in a wagon to bring him to the nearest missionaries for burial. Covered only by a blanket, his body began the journey with my mother guiding the team over the rough roads. All of the jostling and shaking caused his body to fall apart even more. The journey proved to be too much, and so my mother turned the wagon around and returned home, then sent for the missionaries to come to us. They brought a zippered plastic bag to put the body in so that they could bring him to a cemetery. At that point, my father, who had been away at work, returned and took charge of the situation.

Father ordered that my grandfather not be buried in the white man's way. Instead, he took the body and put it underneath a rock overhang, then placed a few sticks on top of him, and said, "Let him soak back into the ground like that. You don't bury people like this. He has finished his life. His death is like a graduation from life. This is how people are buried in the old way. You don't put them into the ground, but just let them sit on top of it like he is doing here." Father said that we should not mourn or cry for him but rather celebrate. The same day, my father made a hogan-type shelter from cut piñon and juniper trees. We all went in and sat down, he lit a small fire and added some herbs and plants for purification, then later he led us outside to walk and sing. We sang my grandfather's song as we moved around; that was his celebration. The next day we had a big feast. There was no four days of mourning. Instead it was our way of saying thank you for letting him live this long, full life.

Another type of burial that does not take place in the ground is the tree burial. There are three different kinds of death during the birthing process. The first kind is from miscarriage. This can happen any time before the child is actually brought forth from the mother. If there is tissue beyond just the loss of blood, then the remains are wrapped and placed in a tree. If the baby is born but is dead—stillborn—then its body is placed in a tree and the Bird People take care of the physical aspects and bring the child's spirit to the Second World. This kind of baby is often referred to as "the bloody body child," or "the unspoken baby," or "the one who never made a sound or noise." A miscarriage or stillborn are treated the same. But if the baby has had a chance to nurse or cry or receive a name, then its remains are buried in the ground or in the crevice of a rock. This is because the child, who has lived for a couple of weeks or more, "has no blood on them," has become one of the earth surface people, and belongs to the ground, not the tree, which belongs to the birds.

As the Navajo world changes and more and more practices of the dominant culture become accepted, there are things that challenge our traditional ways. One of those concerning death is cremation. In the last chapter I talked about cremating a body part that has been removed from a person who is still living. This is acceptable because the amputated appendage has to be destroyed. The important point is that the individual who had that surgery is still alive. Fire destroys the part, whose ashes are given back to the earth through the wind. But cremation of an entire being is disrespectful to the earth and the holy beings. A person who lives on this earth is a part of the entire creation. The holy people expect a person to be buried in the ground and to return all that belongs to it. An individual uses vegetation from the plant people and animal people, and these holy elements need to be deposited back into the earth. This is part of the replanting. One cannot burn what was life itself. During our life we talked, laughed, and cried. Our spirit has a lot of memories in other people's minds and thoughts. It has grandchildren and relatives. This cannot be burned or just put away. If a body is placed in the ground, then there will be new flowers in the springtime, and this creation will sprout forth with new existence. This is where life turns into a cycle with new generations and should be part of our teachings. Cremation stops all of this.

Anything that is destroyed by fire belongs to the Lightning People because that is where fire came from. It was born with lightning, and water is its brother. These two elements are the ones who determine how life is lived in the end. The spirit goes back with the water because the fire and water are brother and sister. They are the same. This is why when a person is struck by lightning, burned by lightning, or dies by lighting, people think of the spirit of that individual returning in an approaching thunderstorm. He is making noise, coming in, and he knows where his land is located. Those watching expect that person to sprinkle water in their area, and so they call his name and the rain comes. This is an old story from an elder who has his own teachings about the Lightningway ceremony. It is said to happen to anybody who dies by fire, whether in a fiery crash or in a burning building. Rain comes to the land. Since cremation is a choice, this is different; that choice is not considered good because that person does not respect the elements. They bring no rain with it.

In the old days, when a person was approaching death, they would be moved outside of their home so that they would not die inside. As long as they passed away outside, then the hogan could still be used by the family, who would bury the body away from the homestead. If a person did die in the home, this "death hogan" had to be abandoned. Usually, family members would leave the structure standing and let nature work its power, leading to its eventual deterioration and collapse. No wood from it could be used for anything, including as firewood, once it was associated with death. A second practice was for the family to disassemble the structure and stack the wood in a pile, then leave it to nature.

Even if these two elders have not yet reached the ripe old age of 102, they are well on their way. When their time comes, their body will return to Mother Earth and their spirit will go to the north, joining relatives and friends.

Once the body was buried and the four days of mourning completed, the family packed its possessions—those that had been moved outside before the death occurred—and traveled to the south. This might be a short distance of a few hundred yards or a long distance going miles before they stopped and set up a new camp. The reason for this is the sun's pattern. As mentioned previously, the sun's 102 trails include moving from the east to south to west during a year. When a death occurs, the spirit travels north, away from the sun, allowing the family to move in the opposite direction away from the dead. Once they have gone to the south, they can also travel to the east or west. After a year they can move back to the north, when everything is settled. They continue to live with the sun.

Notes from Father Berard Haile, O.F.M.

ROBERT MCPHERSON

Father Berard Haile, a Franciscan missionary who for sixty-one years lived at Saint Michaels Mission in Arizona, is one of the foremost Anglo authorities on Navajo culture. At his prime in 1943, he published a short tract entitled *Soul Concepts of the Navaho*, in which informants discussed pre-mortal, mortal, and post-mortal beliefs about the human soul or spirit.[13] This work provides one of the most complete studies on Navajo views of life after death, confirming many of the teachings discussed in this chapter. We have decided to include part of it here to build upon what Perry has said. Following a lengthy discussion on the inner soul (the being that stands within) of humans, plants, and animals and the origin of the human spirit with accompanying influences, Haile offers thoughts on death and burial. What follows are excerpts (pp. 88–94) from his report. Today's standardized Navajo spelling is used to replace the archaic form the author employed at that time.

> The dread of the dead is universal. Preferably the person is permitted to die outside of the hogan. But if death occurs inside the hogan, some cover the corpse with sticks or brushwork, securely bar the entrance, vacate the hogan, and allow it to decay and collapse in time. Others appoint two or four men to put the corpse away. They strip to the breechcloth, untie their hair bundles, bathe the corpse in silence, dress it in new or best clothes, beads and silver jewelry, then make an opening in the north wall of the hogan, through which the corpse is passed, as it is considered improper to carry it out through the regular entrance. It is then carried to the place of burial, which is either in the ground, or it is placed under a stone ledge, and

then securely covered with sticks and stones to protect it from scavengers. After interment shovels and other tools are broken and left on the grave, and the men skip and hop over brush and stones lest they disturb the soul on its return journey. After bathing themselves they join the mourning family, and remain in mourning for four days. Meanwhile, vessels and pots used in bathing the corpse are broken while the hogan is set afire and burned to the ground. The spot is avoided and called "nobody's home." The purpose of dressing the corpse in good clothes and ornaments, of shooting the owner's best saddle horse fully rigged, of removing sharp edged tools and arrowheads from the corpse is to ensure the person a peaceful entry into "ghostland" (ch'įįdiitah), and to avoid cause for fear to the inhabitants of that region.

This ghostland is somewhere. One suspects that it is in the north. The stillborn are placed in tree branches which point northward. The opening through which the corpse is passed out of the hogan is preferably made in the north wall. Many insist that the corpse should face northward or, at least, lie with the head pointing northward. But wherever this ghostland may be, one wonders just what the native term of ch'įįdii conveys? . . . Mortuary customs strongly suggest that the corpse alone is not defined by this word. It appears to be an ethereal, shadowy, palpable something which manifests itself, even after the "wind soul" has left the human body, either to make its report, or to simply return to the realm of winds as popular notion conceives it. . . .

While there may be some confusion on the post-mortem status of the soul, there is a general consensus concerning a person's soul "whom old age has killed" or who had died of old age. One taken in death by old age is not to be feared and is not ch'įįdii. A definite number of years do not appear to have been required for "death of old age." The individual's rugged constitution might well carry him or her to a ripe old age of 80 and 90 years or more. But when senility set in and the person became unable to walk, simply wasted away, and had to be carried around and generally taken care of, without indication of a known sickness, that was taken as safe evidence of having reached old age. Nothing was, and still is more desirable than this great fortune. The person himself is happy over the event, and his family and relatives share his happiness and contentment. Should death approach, people go about their daily chores as usual, without a thought of fear, much less with a thought of removing such a person from their midst. Even actual death did not disturb the daily routine, and preparations for proper interment were made by the family as just another piece of ordinary work. Any member of the family could perform the burial and, when completed, no thought of observing the customary four days mourning was entertained.

Such behavior indicates the native feeling that "death of old age" cannot be equated with "ghost," as the latter are always avoided and feared. Furthermore a definite place is assigned to old age, meaning that these persons live on, though no mention is made of their soul. This "old age home" is the opposite of "ghostland." It was customary, therefore to correct children by holding out prospects of reaching the "old age home." On the other hand, it is a common cussword today to tell a person, "Go to ghostland!" The inference is, that the one: "old age home" is more desirable, the other: "ghostland" is a place, which most people detest and, in the language of an impassioned human being, a detestable person belongs there and should never reach "old age home," which well-minded persons desire. "You certainly should stay in that detestable ghostland" well expresses the sentiment of the angry native. But nothing in native ideology, as expressed in custom and language, allows us to equate these concepts of "old age home" with the Christian heaven and the "ghostland" with the Christian hell. But there is much in this ideology which allows the inference that the ego, in some manner, lives again, either in "old age home" or "ghostland."

In the case of "death of old age," for instance, we can truthfully say that the older generation at least, gave much thought to it. For instance, songs of Blessingway, as well as any number of songs of chantways, conclude with the refrain: "sa'ah naagháii bik'eh hózhǫ," or "long life, happiness," which older natives, at least, believe has reference to old age, and the happiness and contentment it brings with it. Accordingly, the ultimate end sought in every native ceremonial is a renewed lease on life, a new opportunity to reach "death of old age" and its concomitant contentment. And because old age continues in "old age home," restored health through a ceremonial, in reality, prepares for that future place. Undoubtedly, natives have good grounds for linking the song refrain of "long life, happiness" with "where old age exists." . . . Nevertheless the meaning of "long life, happiness" is none too clear, and among natives we find frequent inquiries about its true meaning. Perhaps as a result of this uncertainty, older natives feel justified in connecting "long life" of song and prayer with "old age home" of their tradition.

HAILE'S SUMMARY

Our study of Navajo soul concepts reveals the following prominent tenets:
Supernaturals of the Navajo pantheon are conceived as manlike in shape, having a body and a wind soul "standing within them." Animals have a soul, which manifests its presence in their movements and utterances. Plants, too, are animated. Plants and animals were man-like in pre-emergence times, and some evidence points to a belief that they continue so in post-emergence times. Natural phenomena, also are believed to be inhabited and controlled by beings which "lie within them." In popular opinion this "in lying person" is identical with the soul of the natural phenomenon. But, more probably, these "in-lying ones" have a soul, or "wind standing within them" of their own.

While a dispatcher of wind souls is mentioned in the case of some supernaturals, the existence of a wind soul is usually taken for granted in other instances, as those of animals, and perhaps of plants. Much of the knowledge concerning the life principle, or soul, of supernaturals, natural phenomena, plants and animals, is considered esoteric knowledge.

Every human being (in the Navajo sense) is equipped with a wind soul, which enters the body at birth, controls every action and movement of a human being, and leaves the body at death.

Many kinds of winds may be differentiated. These do not multiply themselves, but many of the same kind are distributed as wind souls among human beings.

There is good evidence for the belief that a wind soul enters the fetus, which leaves in the event of a stillbirth. This belief is not general, as popular belief prefers to have the wind soul enter the body at the child's birth. Yet the custom of depositing the stillborn in tree branches suggests a belief in the independent life of the fetus.

A supernatural, or at least, a non-human being is said to dispatch the wind soul into the body of the child to be born. No consensus of opinion exists on the identity of this being. Nor is there consensus of opinion on the exact point at which this soul enters the body. But all are agreed that, in lifetime, this soul is accountable for the actions of the composite soul and body, known as a human being.

This soul is corporeal and takes the shape of the body. In fact, it seems to account for the size and shape of the body.

Society always charged the individual for untoward actions, not the soul within. The language, too, appears to consider the soul as something foreign to the person known in society by a certain name.

This foreign wind soul does not die, but leaves the body in which it "stood," and this departure appears to cause death. Whichever report it may make to its original dispatcher does not, apparently, affect the status of the individual in a hereafter.

Apparently, too, there is a belief in a partial transmigration of souls, at least from one human body into another, especially of the souls of those individuals, whose good fortune allowed them to die of old age.

Death of old age is accepted as a blessing by general consent. Oppositely, death in childhood, youth, early and mature man and womanhood, which does not approach old age, is undesirable, because popular opinion assigns such dead to "ghostland," which the living eschew.

At times, some of these tenets on the hereafter are interpreted at their true value, namely, that the Navajo as a whole expects his life or soul to continue, either in the "old age home," or in "ghostland," or someplace where they will live again.

CHAPTER NINE

Conclusion

Pleas of the Holy People

At the beginning of this trilogy, Perry expressed his concern at the loss of traditional teachings with the passing of each generation. The information he has shared has a cumulative history of over one hundred years when including that from his great-grandparents, grandparents, parents, and his own generation. To summarize seven hundred fifty plus pages, with the variety and complexity of teachings and experience that Perry has provided, demands a broad, sweeping account of traditional Navajo beliefs, some of which are centuries old and others more recently derived. On the broadest level, the Navajo Way springs from the patterns, rules, and interaction established by the holy people. Their guidance, from the beginning, centers on relationships with all elements of the physical and spiritual world in which the Navajo dwell. The people's responsibility is to follow what has been outlined and work toward achieving the goal of total hózhǫ́. Perry, by sharing his teachings, has pointed the way through a multiplicity of examples, sharing what it means to be an earth surface being with all of its pitfalls and corrective remedies to keep a person walking on the pollen path. Everything from mountains to mice, trees to táchééh, lakes to lightning, and family to femur are enlivened by an inner being that holds power that can help or harm. Respect or lack of it underlies all interaction.

Another way to summarize what has been discussed, while pointing to the past, present, and future, is to look at what has evolved in Navajo medicine over the last one hundred years or roughly four generations. Whether looking at the shift from horses to cars, from weaving to purchasing clothing, gardening to shopping at Walmart, or wind listening to x-rays—dramatic change has occurred throughout. Perry's concern about culture loss is real and shared by many older Navajos. The amount of loss, the strength

189

of traditional teachings, and the direction that both are going, perhaps can best be summarized by looking at three different illnesses and how response to them has changed but also remained constant.

The Spanish Influenza epidemic (1918), the hantavirus outbreak (1993), and the coronavirus pandemic (2020) provide mileposts in the shifting terrain of medical care in the dominant culture as well as in Navajo medicine. These three events provide a good overview to evaluate change. The influenza epidemic occurred at a time when traditional medicine was in full practice on the reservation and before major inroads by the dominant culture in healthcare took place. This pandemic serves as a baseline for presenting traditional practices. Seventy-five years later, the hantavirus appeared in a very different era in terms of medical possibilities, but still evoked a traditional explanation and response. The coronavirus, roughly twenty-five years later, elicited an even more complex reaction, with muted cultural undertones. Each example adds to understanding future trends by suggesting changing views of healthcare. In this brief survey, particular emphasis is placed in the Navajo reaction to each of these diseases as opposed to providing a full-blown discussion of the pandemics. Within this survey of events sits the medicine man rooted in traditional teachings and practices obtained in the past yet challenged with adopting and adapting to new diseases and contemporary Anglo procedures. To best understand their reaction, one must return to the time of creation.

Origin of the Pandemics

In the palm of time, as First Man, First Woman, and Changing Woman sat around the cooking fire, they thought of the earth surface people and how life should unfold in their new world. Changing Woman, true to her nature, pulled the stirring sticks out of the cornmeal mush simmering in a pot, raised them above in prayer, and offered a blessing, pronouncing all of the good things that she would do and bring to the Navajo people. Rain and mist, fine fabric and jewels, plants and animals, pollen and collected waters— everything was for the benefit of others. She offered the way to long life and happiness. Across the fire on the north side sat First Man. First Woman had her own pot in which simmered mush made from red-white stones. She removed her stirring sticks and handed them to her husband, who immediately raised them above and prayed, "From here may it always happen whichever way I may think! May epidemics come time and again, and may fatal events happen time and again! By no means should people live comfortably! May I be in control of disease! May I be in control of fever! May I be in control of everything that kills time and again! May death occur regularly as I wish!"[1] His prayer has come true. While other holy people worked to provide cures for the known illnesses that the Navajo would suffer, when the Anglo culture entered upon the scene, there arrived three different diseases for which the holy beings had not planned. Spanish Influenza, hantavirus, and coronavirus stalked the land and killed the people. They are part of First Man's wish.

Influenza of 1918

The Spanish Influenza (dikos ntsaa—Big Cough—pneumonia; or Sickness That Goes Around but Is Unknown—naałniih—general term for a virus) raged across the United States and much of the world primarily during the fall of 1918 through the spring of 1919. Just in the last week of October alone, it killed over 21,000 Americans.[2] According to the statistics of the Office of Indian Affairs, 24 percent of reservation Indians caught the flu between October 1, 1918, to March 31, 1919, with a mortality rate of 9 percent, about four times as high as that in the nation's big cities.[3] For the Navajo, recently revised figures suggest that within a population of 28,802 there were 3,377 deaths or a 12 percent mortality rate, while in the United States, in general, 548,452 people died with a mortality rate of roughly 2.5 percent.[4] The disease, with an incubation period of from twenty-four to seventy-two hours, attacked the respiratory system and acted as a gateway to other forms of illness, primarily pneumonia, by lowering an individual's resistance. Symptoms included severe headaches, chills, fever, leg and back pains, intense sore throat, labored breathing, and total lassitude. Once infected, a person had little desire to do anything but rest and avoid exertion. Almost half of its victims were healthy young people.

In understanding the higher mortality rates among the Navajo, one has to consider the physical and cultural circumstances found on the reservation at the time. Oral tradition has kept alive the trauma that accompanied the "Great Sickness," and though much of what was done to prevent it may appear to an outsider as ineffective, the main issue for the Navajo was a religious one. Events do not just happen, as indicated by omens appearing before hand. On June 8, 1918, a solar eclipse occurred, presaging misfortune. Sun Bearer, an important Navajo deity, hid his light from his people because of anger, warning that a catastrophe would soon take place.[5] During the summer and fall, dawns and sunsets had pronounced reddish hues that bathed the landscape in an ominous red.[6] The tips of piñon and juniper trees started to die, a sign indicating that sickness was in the area and would be visiting humans, while some Navajos had bad dreams portending disaster. Informants indicated that the holy people sent the disease in order to make room for a growing population of the younger generation; still others suggested that poison gas or the smoke and fumes from artillery rounds fired in World War I somehow infected the Navajo.[7]

Once it struck, the disease was devastating. A few examples illustrate how quickly people died. Some Navajos tell of a Yé'ii Bicheii ceremony held in late October at Blue Canyon, approximately eighteen miles east of Tuba City. Large numbers of people congregated for the performance and contracted the disease, but showed no symptoms until suddenly they were gone. Navajos in the Monument Valley region claimed to have received the sickness from Paiutes and Utes as they moved through their area.[8] Gilmore Graymountain, a local resident, encountered a man, four women, and some children who asked the Navajo for assistance in building a fire and constructing a shelter. "They were just under a tree and it was very cold, with the wind breezing through the spot."[9] By the time Graymountain returned with a wagon load of wood, two of the women were dead.

Hosteen Klah, a famous medicine man, also appeared sick after a visit to Durango when he arrived at the Blue Mesa Trading Post run by Arthur and Franc Newcomb. He was the first in the area to contract the disease, so he self-medicated with herbal teas and fumigants burned in his isolated hogan. He healed himself during this initial wave of influenza, which proved mild compared to what struck three months later in February, the "Hunger Moon." Food was scarce and cold intense, with sleet and snowstorms frequent. Whole families died, while the living barricaded the doors and blocked the smoke holes from the outside to keep wild animals from entering and eating the corpses. Later, Indian agents sent teams around to burn the hogans and bury the dead, but in the meantime, those who survived fled to other people's homes for refuge, thus spreading the disease.[10] Even those who remained at home were often deprived of their warm winter hogans, abandoning them once a person had died inside, in keeping with Navajo tradition. In other instances, those who were about to die were sometimes placed outside, hastening death but allowing the other occupants to have shelter.

Response to the illness came in two forms—spiritual and physical. Since the roots of the epidemic were thought to lie in religious beliefs, it was on this level that the most emphatic acts of prevention and treatment were found. There were two types of ceremonies to cure or prevent this illness, the Blessingway and Evilway. Ada Black from Monument Valley tells just how dependent her family was on prayer. Her maternal grandmother used them to "shield" off the sickness. "At the break of dawn she offered white corn meal, at noon she offered mixed (multicolored) corn meal, then at twilight before the golden glow passed she offered yellow corn meal, and at midnight she offered blue cornmeal."[11] Ada recalled how red skies in the morning or evening portended the approach of the disease, so her parents told her to get up and offer cornmeal and pollen with prayer to stem the tide of death. Her grandfather had the sweat lodge ready for the women to enter to cleanse themselves with intense heat three or four times while drinking specially prepared herbs to fend off the illness. By the time the sun had risen, the women were finished and ready for the day's chores so that the men could then have their turn. No one in this group caught the disease.

From an Anglo perspective, some of these cures created more problems. While sweat baths provided both an external cleansing and a spiritual preparation for prayer, the cramped space and intense heat put those infected in extremely close quarters. Since influenza was primarily a respiratory disease, the sweat bath, like healing ceremonies held in a hogan, encouraged its spread by those infected. To the Navajo, they were divinely inspired means for countering the illness, as were the bitter plant remedies made from boiled sagebrush or juniper trees to wash the body and cleanse internally. Sagebrush tea soothed sore throats, while juniper pitch mixed with a red ochre was plastered on the outside of the neck, forcing pus from the infected area.[12] Well-known protective symbols such as arrowheads and fire pokers also embodied defensive values to fend off the disease as it worked against the people.

Hilda Faunce, a trader living at the Covered Water Trading Post, recalled when Hastiin Tso first entered the store following the pandemic. In his account, he reminds the reader of Perry's search for medicine during times when it is not clear how a patient should be treated.

> In those first days when the rains were cold and the Diné were sick and died everywhere, two of my boys had very hot bodies and could not get up. I went for a medicine man, and another, and another, many of them, but they were sick themselves or were singing the chants for others who had the sickness. All of two days I rode but could find no one to go to my hogan to save my boys. At home I found the women and all of the other children, nine altogether, were very, very sick too. . . . I rode away again, seeking a medicine man. Where the cedar trees grow thick on the hill that stops suddenly, I got off my horse to pray. I prayed to several Diné gods that know me; then I knew I must be the doctor for my family and I took berries from the cedar trees and gathered plants here and there. It was slow work in the rain, but there were those nine sick ones in my hogan. The plants and the berries I boiled with water in the coffeepots and gave each of my family a drink. I sang one of the songs for healing and gave another a drink. I timed the doses until the medicine was gone, and I rode out and got more plants and made medicine and the sick ones drank. There were

days when no one came to my hogan. I did not sleep but sang the prayers
and gave the medicine until all of my family was well.[13]

Perhaps the best individual account given by a Navajo person who
became sick and survived is provided by Tall Woman, who tells of mixing
both physical and spiritual procedures. Approximately forty-four years old
at the time, she recalled how whole families perished overnight while hand-
tremblers and star gazers could not determine what was wrong. Navajo
families buried live babies with dead mothers because there was no one to
care for them, many graves having multiple occupants. Tall Woman felt that
the sickness was like measles or chicken pox but that the characteristic
pustules actually turned inward instead of erupting on the skin's surface.
Once she became ill her body swelled to the point that she could not open
her eyes or talk, sores covered her, and she became so weak that people had
to carry her outside in a blanket. She lost all awareness of time and
surroundings, a state of being that lasted for days.[14]

Her father, Man Who Shouts (Hastiin Dilwoshí) a Blessingway singer
and community leader, sprang into action. He told the people to move
together so that they could help each other, then prepared herbal remedies to
be taken internally as a drink and applied externally as a healing paste or a
compact. He also processed medicinal plants to apply in the sweat house but
warned the people not to wash themselves because it would lower their
temperature and open the door to sickness. Man Who Shouts had many of
his horses killed, providing meat to make broth and the fat to render into a
paste mixed with herbs and red ochre. He encouraged all to use the
Blessingway prayers for protection, since none of the other ceremonies were
effective against this disease, while he and others who were not sick buried
the dead. Weather and health conditions combined so that Man Who Shouts
determined that his people's annual move to Black Mountain should be
cancelled and they should remain where they were.[15] But above all, "he
believed that the Blessingway was our main guide, and where we could get
strength to withstand all the hardships we would face every day and also, in
the future. . . . He really stressed those things to his grandchildren, the ones
who had not passed away during the flu."[16] Tall Woman attributes his efforts
to saving many lives of family and neighbors.

In summarizing the response to the influenza epidemic, it is clear that
the Navajo at this point were totally responding to the pandemic in
traditional terms. From divining its origin, classifying it as a new illness—
one not covered by traditional medicine—to praying for and testing new
remedies, to reacting to circumstances for both the dead and the living, and
to accepting the traumatic consequences, the People defined the experience
according to their time-tested teachings. Except in a few isolated incidents,

such as Navajo children in boarding schools, Anglo medicine was not a factor. Gathering together for ceremonies and sweat baths, inhabiting isolated camps, living in difficult conditions, hauling water and firewood, obtaining food, and battling winter weather all worked against those needing help. In the dominant culture, those who did the best were able to self-isolate yet still be under the care of either family, neighbors, or medical professionals who could render aid; for those in the Navajo community who did so, with some exceptions, it often led to more death. This time was particularly hard on medicine men, who were sought after for cures against this invisible unknown enemy killing the people.

Hantavirus Outbreak of 1992–93

Jumping ahead seventy-five years, the hantavirus reared its head to confront the Navajo people. As in 1918, the summer of 1992 through the spring of 1993 had seen much higher averages of rainfall in parts of the Four Corners area due to a four-year El Niño weather pattern.[17] In a high-country desert environment like this, the abundant moisture gave rise to increased vegetation, and in particular, large crops of piñon nuts. Ordinarily considered a boon to the region, in this case, the plentiful food fostered an accompanying bumper crop of rodents—ten times the number in May 1993 than in the previous year.[18] The biggest culprit for the spread of the hantavirus, newly named Sin Nombre Virus (SNV), was the deer mouse (*Peromyscus maniculatus*), a frequent visitor to homes and barns looking for food and shelter. Based on extensive trapping and studying of these animals, 30 percent of them at this time were carrying the disease. Not until November 1993 was this vector determined to be the culprit.[19] In the meantime, the cause of the disease was a mystery waiting to be solved. To Navajo medicine men, it was not as much of a mystery after considering regional history.

On April 29, 1993, Florena Woody, an energetic twenty-one-year-old new mother living in Littlewater, New Mexico, began feeling sick. Aching muscles soon progressed into flu-like symptoms that worsened into a raging fever and a struggle for breath. Her lungs quickly filled with fluid, and she died on May 9, despite all the efforts made by doctors in the Crownpoint Indian Health Services Hospital. Her nineteen-year-old fiancé, Merrill Bahe, father of their six-month-old son and a former high school track star, fared no better. On May 11, he visited the same hospital suffering from similar symptoms; three days later he died on his way to the larger Gallup Indian Medical Center (GIMC). These first two cases of what was then called a "mystery disease" and later misleadingly dubbed the "Navajo flu," "Navajo plague," or "Navajo epidemic" sent doctors and epidemiologists on a hunt to identify the cause. With both families' permission, the young, normally healthy bodies of the couple received autopsies in spite of traditional beliefs to the contrary, even to the point of postponing Florena's burial, another breech of custom.[20]

Other fatalities soon followed, most of whom were relatively young. Navajo doctor Lori Arviso Alvord, MD, was at that time working at the GIMC facility and reported the anxiety felt by her patients and the other doctors. Within a few weeks eleven more people had died, with seven others exhibiting similar symptoms. Geographically they ranged from Farmington, New Mexico, to Phoenix, Arizona, with a number of places in between. Speculation as to the cause ran wild. Alvord wrote,

> The explanatory theories were spreading with a speed almost as rapid [as the disease], among them that the deaths were caused when the government sprayed peyote plants in order to deter Navajos from eating their hallucinogenic buttons; an unidentified bacterium was secreting "lethal proteins" in people's lungs; it was a version of the Epstein-Barr syndrome, AIDS, streptococcus, or staphylococcus pneumonia, anthrax, or bubonic plague. My favorite explanation was the one about Fort Wingate, a storage facility for missiles near Gallup. Some people were saying that radioactive materials had leaked from the weapons there and sunk into the groundwater, and that was what was making people sick. The illness was a conspiracy theorist's field day.[21]

Beyond the obvious problems of sickness and fear, there was a decidedly derogatory slant against the Navajo in the media. Since they were the ones being affected by the disease, outsiders concluded it was their fault. Stereotypes about living in dirt and poverty, backward traditions, and other racial slurs placed the blame squarely on their shoulders. Some off-reservation restaurants refused to serve Navajo customers or threw away their plates once they were finished eating; a number of universities demanded physical screening of students before attending classes on campus; and an estimated 34 percent of the media coverage about Navajos during that first year was negative.[22] Tourism on the reservation plummeted. Although tribal spokesmen such as Chairman Peterson Zah went on the offensive to paint a brighter picture, there were many who would not buy it.

Yet it was the Navajo who provided the key to unlocking the mystery. In May 1993, fifteen medicine people met in Window Rock to discuss the problem. Many of the elders testified that there had been forewarnings, that the excessive rain received was the earth illustrating that behavior was out of balance, that the abundance of mice really was what needed to be investigated by the Centers for Disease Control (CDC), and that previously in 1918 and again in 1933, the People had encountered similar situations. Given the traditional attitudes against mice and their presence in a home, it appeared that they were the ones causing the problem. As Perry mentioned in a previous chapter, "In the early 1990s at Rocky Ridge, part of a mountain nearby opened up a big crack in the earth in which a large collection of mice was found. This was the start of the hantavirus disease that killed and sickened a lot of Navajo people. All of these warnings from the ground were given because the people had lost contact with their ceremonies and were not visiting the sacred places that could keep them safe."

Maureen Trudelle Schwarz in *Navajo Lifeways: Contemporary Issues, Ancient Knowledge* discusses exactly what Perry was talking about.[23] Sunny Dooley in 1992 compared the sickness to monsters created by the earth surface people, just as in the past in the Yellow World: "The monsters that you probably read about were created by us. They were not sicked on us by somebody from the outside. But we created those monsters ourselves, because first of all they manifested themselves with us. The monsters like selfishness, greediness, envy, hate, jealousy. All of those things that we don't like about ourselves came out." Another person believed, "We were warned by Changing Woman that the time would come when our clan system will be tampered with and then chaos would reign and giants will once again walk the earth."[24] Other missteps included being out of balance with life, not offering prayers and generally ignoring the holy people, sharing sacred knowledge inappropriately, adopting white man ways, giving up things that are culturally precious, an improper relationship with Mother Earth, not making offerings, and general disregard for the teachings of traditional culture. The result of excess and imbalance was now visible as seen through the snow and rain that brought the mice.

While this perspective was far different from that held by the doctors, scientists, and epidemiologists, they were wise enough to pursue the lead offered by the Navajo. Following the fastidious research required in the physical realms of science, the disease hunters trapped 1,700 rodents of all different types and in all different circumstances, dissected them, and examined their tissue to determine the exact cause.[25] Among the answers they found was that the disease was in fact hantavirus, an illness found in many different parts of the world—even its name derived from American troops encountering it overseas during the Korean War. The scientists also realized that it was not transmissible from human-to-human, but rather came from contact with mice urine and feces either through touch or when the dried virus became airborne in disturbed dust. Those infected had, at that time, a 30 percent chance of survival; that has since raised to 64 percent.[26] The disease is now found in thirty-one states in America with the preponderance in western states. Approximately five hundred cases have been reported to present.[27] There is still no vaccine developed to target hantavirus, and so the best defense against it is prevention by sealing mice entrances into the home, trapping and disposing of the invaders, wearing self-protection (rubber gloves and face masks), hand washing, and cleaning surfaces with disinfectants.

Visit from the Holy People, 1996

Three years after the outbreak of hantavirus, on May 3, 1996, there was an incident at Rocky Ridge, Arizona, that confirmed the previous message encountered during the disease's eruption. Two holy beings visited Sarah Begay with her ninety-six-year-old mother, Irene Yazzie, and gave a warning for the Navajo people. "In the view of these Diyin Dine'é, Navajo people have been negligent in their responsibilities regarding prayer and offerings; *k'éí*, 'relatives and others with whom one has peaceful relations'; language and culture; and nature."[28] While this event takes us beyond the topic of medical change, it highlights the explanation given by many Navajos for the hantavirus, while underscoring the power of traditional beliefs.

Within two weeks of the sighting, an estimated 6,000 people had made their way over rough roads with difficult travel to the spot that the event occurred. They left offerings and prayers, expressing heartfelt desire to adhere to more traditional practices. Navajo Nation president Albert Hale made the visit and requested that the place be designated a shrine; on May 16, he issued a directive allowing all 5,000 tribal government employees a four-hour leave to go to Rocky Ridge to give prayers and make offerings. By mid-July, an estimated 20,000 visitors had made the pilgrimage to the extent that an official slowing of the surge had to be enacted for the sake of the residents.[29] Speaker Kelsey Begaye of the tribal council inaugurated the first annual Navajo Nation Unity Day of Prayer on June 20 where a half day was set aside to give prayers and offerings. Proof of its validity came the next day, when rain ended a year-long drought.

Navajo elders strongly emphasized to their family members the need to return to the old ways, while younger Navajos translated this advice into actions they could take in their modern setting. Sarah and Irene had a Blessingway ceremony performed for them at their home. How it was carried out strongly supports what Perry discussed about requesting, organizing, and conducting a ritual.

Many medicine men and elders had come to visit her [Sarah]. As instructed by others, she made four loaves of kneel-down bread. The loaves of kneel-down bread were made as an offering to the medicine man to conduct the Blessing Way. The medicine man himself requested the four loaves of kneel-down bread as a payment to him, too. Nothing was to be offered. No fabric or material cloths were to be put on the ground where the medicine man's "tools" generally are placed. The medicine man offered only a sprinkle of corn pollen in place of it, and then he placed his tools on top. The loaves of kneel-down bread, offered to the medicine man as payment, were eaten by the attendees on the final night of the Blessing Way. The water used to soften the kneel-down bread was even consumed at the Blessing Way, too.[30]

Back on the pollen path, holiness was being restored. Mother Earth and Father Sky soon shared the rain and restoration of plant life.

Coronavirus 2020

There would be other pleas from the holy people to retain traditional values, the most prominent one being the introduction of COVID-19 or coronavirus (Dikos ntsaaígíí náhást'éíts'áadah—Big Cough 19) in 2020. At the time of this writing, the complete story has not yet unfolded as it has for the other two illnesses, but enough has taken place to illustrate the trend. In this instance, the Navajo Nation has posted on its official website a history of the disease's spread, the Nation's reaction to it including formal executive orders and directives, and newspaper and journal commentary for those who wish to track the progress in fighting the disease.[31]

Like the pandemic of 1918, the spread of the virus occurred quickly, but the response toward it, for the most part, was quite different. In short, on March 3, 2020, there were only two confirmed cases of the disease in Arizona. Even though there were no known cases on the reservation, Navajo Nation president Jonathan Nez declared it to be in a state of public health emergency. A week later the first positive test emerged from Kayenta, two days later the entire community of Chilchinbeto was quarantined because of seven infected people, and two days after that the first stay-at-home order for the entire Navajo Nation went into effect. The tribe restricted travel of on-and-off reservation traffic; a series of lockdowns on weekends closed the entire Nation; tourism at tribal parks and in general was cut off; the nine grocery stores servicing a reservation land mass larger than the state of Rhode Island were open only for necessities and at times even shut down, pushing people into border-town communities; residents were commanded to "shelter-in-place" and self-quarantine or else suffer a fine of up to $1,000

Traditional elders and medicine people understand the holy ones and how they can bless the lives of earth surface beings. The life feather from an eagle transmits the prayers and offerings, when given with sincerity. This grandmother understands the past, prays for the present, and hopes for the future.

and thirty days in jail; the police also enforced the mandatory wearing of face masks.[32] By the end of April there were 2,141 identified cases with 71 deaths; by August 27, 2020, the tribe reported 9,601 positive COVID-19 cases and 499 deaths, receiving the undesirable reputation of "having the highest per-capita infection rate in the country, surpassing even New York State."[33] The thirteen health facilities on tribal lands had their hands filled meeting local needs, which were exacerbated by the general living conditions of the population, many of whom had to haul water and wood, had no electricity or indoor plumbing, and lived in relative isolation.

What is immediately apparent is that a traditional response such as that which occurred in the 1918 pandemic was far from what was now occurring. Indeed, the Navajo Nation, in an effort to maintain social distancing and keep groups of people to ten or less or even better none, banned any type of ceremonies that involved gathering. I decided to call Perry to get his perspective.[34] As expected, he started at the time of creation with the story about when the rain was taken from the earth. Frog went to the realms of the Water People to find out what was wrong and learned that the earth surface people had not shown respect, had forgotten their prayers and offerings, and so were being taught a lesson. Then he explained in his own words exactly what Gladys Reichard had said seventy-five years before—that because of incomplete knowledge or carelessness, "evil rushes in where goodness weakens or when it leaves. Evil must be driven out before holiness can have a place."[35] To Perry, the virus was a warning that people needed to "get back on track," in other words, on the pollen path, and start practicing the old teachings.

He recognized that the tribe's approach stressed individual protection instead of collective defense. The four elements of life—fire, water, air, and earth—along with their associated colors and powers, needed to receive offerings and prayers in their respective directions. "If we lose our focus and way, all of these powers will be taken away from us." He then mentioned that when the hantavirus outbreak occurred, the tribal council contacted the Medicine Men Association to appear before it. Council members selected five representatives to provide a communal response to the holy people. Perry and his uncle were two of those chosen. These medicine men went individually to the Six Sacred Mountains, where they set up tepees, made offerings of "sacred stones," and performed the Blessingway (Hózhǫ́ǫ́jí) and Protectionway (Naayéé'jí). Perry's assignment was Gobernador Knob and Huerfano Mesa, the two doorposts of the reservation hogan. He explained that this was just like a soldier going off to war to destroy the enemy and return in peace, free from any negative effect. "Go out to fight, but return in beauty." It took a week to complete the visits, but at the end, "the illness suddenly stopped and people were cured." Now, Perry longs for a reinstatement of this cooperative attitude instead of people today being so busy "doing their own thing" and not working together. This is the root of the problem—too many Navajos have forgotten to call—individually and collectively—on the holy people.

Perry is not alone in this belief. On March 19, the *Navajo Times* ran an article "Surviving the Coronavirus Crisis: Diné Perspectives," in which traditionalists shared similar views.[36] Their responses should feel very familiar. For example, Clayson Benally expressed gratitude for his 102-year-old grandmother, Zonnie Benally, who received two omens during the 1918 pandemic when a saddle unaccountably burst into flames and a large meteor shower occurred. Her family strengthened themselves by eating horsemeat and riding throughout the region warning people that something bad would soon come. To Clayson, the warning of the approaching coronavirus came from the World Health Organization, who recommended many of the same actions taken in 1918 of isolating and washing hands. "This is everything that our elders prepared us for." Eugenia Charles-Newton noted that there were a lot of ceremonies going on, that her family burned cedar at home to accompany family prayer, that blue cornmeal mush had healing properties, and that her husband was going to start hunting. Emery Denny cautioned that the People needed to take better care of the earth, plant gardens with traditional foods, treat others as friends and relatives, arise early, run, and get the most from life. Nathanial Brown tied events directly to deity. "Mother Nature is responding to us. When she is stressed, she wants to cleanse herself. . . . There's a reason why oil, coal, and uranium are buried. We are earth surface people. Everything we have on the surface is more than enough for us to live. The truth is that we've been hurting that which feeds and shelters us. . . . Mother Earth is telling us we need to change. Maybe this coronavirus is a blessing in disguise." Other forgotten practices include not visiting or praying to the sacred mountains; ignoring previous warning signs of fire, earthquake, and weather extremes (drought, hurricanes, tornadoes); language loss and disuse; and forsaking traditional values. As one Navajo elder commented, "Perhaps the pandemic is the great discipline whip of the Earth, from having irretrievably damaged the earth. This virus is a force to be reckoned with. It is alive with death."[37] The earth (earthquakes), wind/air (tornadoes and hurricanes), fire (forest fires), and water (floods) are all part of that whip.

Closing Thoughts

In addressing Perry's concern established at the beginning of this trilogy and the outset of this chapter, there are two final points to be made. The first concerning the decline of traditional teachings is straightforward. Since the baseline pandemic of 1918, there has been a significant loss of traditional understanding, especially with today's younger generation. Loss of language, ceremonial knowledge, and practices, as well as the insistence on obtaining an Anglo education, a decrease in traditional teachings in the home, and the attractiveness of all that glitters in this Glittering World all become counterproductive in strengthening traditions. There are, of course, exceptions to this trend, but generally, studies, anecdotal information, and observation indicate that many of the cherished beliefs and practices are disappearing. Ask the Navajo medicine man who has to hire a translator for a young patient so that what is being performed in a ceremony can be understood. Parents have a need to be concerned. While reaction to the coronavirus indicates that cultural loss is the reason for the pandemic according to traditionalists, the response—from forbidding ceremonies to enforcing lockdowns, and from executive orders to healthcare practices— illustrates the latest in contemporary practices, often at odds with those from the past.

From the second question—should there be concern about this loss and are traditional practices worth preserving—comes a resounding yes. Here is one final example to illustrate why. In 1954, a young college student named Barre Toelken was prospecting in Montezuma Creek Canyon in southeastern Utah when he became helplessly sick. A Navajo elder, Little Wagon, went to the white man's camp, placed his almost lifeless body in his wagon, brought him to his hogan, hired a hand trembler to determine the necessary ceremony, then paid for a six-day Red Antway to be performed as the patient drifted in and out of consciousness, only able to drink herbal liquids. A short Protectionway followed, and each day during both ceremonies the illness receded. Sandpaintings, passage through a series of hoops, and smoking mountain tobacco accompanied with songs and prayers restored hózhǫ. Barre returned to good health, ended up living with Little Wagon's extended family for two full years, went on to obtain his PhD, and became a folklorist of world renown while still maintaining his strong bonds with his adopted Navajo family until he died in 2018.

Toelken was well-aware of the power and value of Navajo medicine. Having followed a lifetime interest in the teachings and practices, he offered a number of thoughts about their efficacy. He was old enough to remember the introduction of medicine men on the full-time staffs of hospitals. At first these healers were brought in to be a "familiar voice" for Navajo patients, but as the two different "medicine men" worked side by side, the Anglo doctors began to realize that the chants could bring patients out of comas, that there was a greatly improved chance of healing their afflictions, and that recovery times improved. No formal study existed at that time of this phenomena, but one of his friends, who was a doctor working at the Tuba City Indian Health Service Hospital, suggested an 80 percent success rate.[38] The Anglo doctors had no explanation for these results, but to the medicine man, as long as niłch'ih existed within the patient, there was an "inner form" that could respond. The songs and prayers encouraged it to re-animate the patient's body. Even while asleep or in a coma, the mind processed and remembered upon waking what had been said. Toelken closed these thoughts by affirming, "We can help to foster the idea that cultural diversity in thinking is neither a virtuous political exercise nor a threat to science but a rich and underestimated source of insight for humankind in general."[39]

Notes

Introduction

1. River Junction Curly, "Version III" in *Blessingway: With Three Versions of the Myth Recorded and Translated from the Navajo by Father Berard Haile, O.F.M.*, ed. Leland C. Wyman (Tucson: University of Arizona Press, 1970), 619–21.

2. Navajo Nation 2016 Census, accessed March 18, 2020, https://en.wikipedia.org/wiki/Navajo_Nation.

3. Evon Z. Vogt and Ethel M. Albert, eds., *People of Rimrock: A Study of Values in Five Cultures* (New York: Atheneum Press, 1966, 1970).

4. Clyde Kluckhohn, "A Navaho Personal Document with a Brief Paretian Analysis," *Southwestern Journal of Anthropology* 1, no. 2 (Summer 1945): 260–83.

5. Robert S. McPherson, ed., *The Journey of Navajo Oshley: An Autobiography and Life History* (Logan: Utah State University Press, 2000).

6. Gary Witherspoon, *Navajo Kinship and Marriage* (Chicago: University of Chicago Press, 1975), 119–20.

7. Ibid., 120.

8. Katherine Spencer, *Reflection of Social Life in the Navaho Origin Myth* (Albuquerque: University of New Mexico Press, 1947).

9. Kluckhohn, "Navaho Personal Document," 267. Further quotations from Mustache's life history are found on pages 267–73 and so will not be given an endnote.

10. McPherson, *Journey of Navajo Oshley*, 30, 32.

11. Kluckhohn, "Navaho Personal Document," 274.

12. Charlotte J. Frisbie, ed., with Rose Mitchell, *Tall Woman: The Life Story of Rose Mitchell, A Navajo Woman, c. 1874–1977* (Albuquerque: University of New Mexico Press, 2001); Kay Bennett, *Kaibah: Recollection of a Navajo Girlhood* (Self-published, 1975).

13. Richard Hobson, *Navaho Acquisitive Values*, Reports of the Rimrock Project Values Series No. 5 (Cambridge, MA: Harvard Museum, 1954, 1973).

14. Ibid., 4.

15. McPherson, *Journey of Navajo Oshley*, 142.

16. Hobson, *Navaho Acquisitive Values*, 8.

17. McPherson, *Journey of Navajo Oshley*, 80–82.

18. Clyde Kluckhohn, *Navaho Witchcraft* (Boston, MA: Beacon Press, 1944, 1970).

19. Kluckhohn, "Navaho Personal Document," 275–76.

20. Ibid., 275.

21. See Robert S. McPherson, *Viewing the Ancestors: Perceptions of the Anaasází, Mokwič, and Hisatsinom* (Norman: University of Oklahoma Press, 2014).

22. Robert W. Rhodes, *Nurturing Learning in Native American Students* (Hotevilla, AZ: Sonwai Books, 1994). The following information is found on pp. 25–27.

Chapter One

1. Gary Witherspoon, *Navajo Kinship and Marriage* (Chicago: University of Chicago Press, 1975), 15.

2. Charlotte J. Frisbie, ed., with Rose Mitchell, *Tall Woman: The Life Story of Rose Mitchell, A Navajo Woman, c. 1874–1977* (Albuquerque: University of New Mexico Press, 2001), 83.

3. Maureen Trudelle Schwarz, *Molded in the Image of Changing Woman: Navajo Views on the Human Body and Personhood* (Tucson: University of Arizona Press, 1997).

4. Ibid., 69.

5. Charlotte J. Frisbie and David P. McAllester, *Navajo Blessingway Singer: The Autobiography of Frank Mitchell, 1881–1967* (Tucson: University of Arizona Press, 1978), 324–25; Franc Johnson Newcomb, *Navajo Omens and Taboos* (Santa Fe: Rydal Press, 1940), 27; Frisbie, *Tall Woman*, 388, 438; Ernest L. Bulow, *Navajo Taboos* (Gallup, NM: Southwesterner Books, 1982), 27–31.

6. Ruth Roessel, *Women in Navajo Society* (Rough Rock, AZ: Navajo Resource Center, Rough Rock Demonstration School, 1981), 43–44.

7. Franciscan Fathers, *An Ethnologic Dictionary of the Navajo Language* (Saint Michaels, AZ: Saint Michaels Press, 1910, 1968), 116.

8. John Holiday and Robert S. McPherson, *A Navajo Legacy: The Life and Teachings of John Holiday* (Norman: University of Oklahoma Press, 2005), 212.

9. Frisbie, *Tall Woman*, 174–75.

10. Holiday and McPherson, *A Navajo Legacy*, 266; Franciscan Fathers, *An Ethnologic Dictionary*, 450; Frisbie, *Tall Woman*, 258; Gladys A. Reichard, *Social Life of the Navajo Indians, with Some Attention to Minor Ceremonies* (New York: Columbia University Press, 1928), 134.

11. Frisbie, *Tall Woman*, 258–59.

12. Roessel, *Women in Navajo Society*, 46.

13. Ibid., 47; Reichard, *Social Life of the Navajo*, 134; Frisbie, *Tall Woman*, 258–59; Schwarz, *Molded in the Image of Changing Woman*, 129–32.

14. Newcomb, *Navajo Omens and Taboos*, 28.

15. Franciscan Fathers, *An Ethnologic Dictionary*, 451.

16. Schwarz, *Molded in the Image of Changing Woman*, 140.

17. Reichard, *Social Life of the Navajo*, 96–107.

18. Pliny Earle Goddard, *Navajo Texts*, Anthropological Papers of the American Museum of Natural History, 34, no. 1 (New York: American Museum of Natural History, 1933), 149.

19. Franciscan Fathers, *An Ethnologic Dictionary*, 467–73; Clyde Kluckhohn, W. W. Hill, and Lucy Wales Kluckhohn, *Navaho Material Culture* (Cambridge, MA: Harvard University Press, 1971), 191–201.

20. Aileen O'Bryan, *Navaho Indian Myths* (New York: Dover Publications, 1956, 1993), 73.

21. Schwarz, *Molded in the Image of Changing Woman*, 144.

Chapter Two

1. Charlotte Johnson Frisbie, *Kinaaldá: A Study of the Navaho Girl's Puberty Ceremony* (Salt Lake City: University of Utah Press, 1967, 1993); Maureen Trudelle Schwarz, *Molded in the Image of Changing Woman: Navajo Views on the Human Body and Personhood* (Tucson: University of Arizona Press, 1997); and Schwarz, *Blood and Voice, Navajo Women Ceremonial Practitioners* (Tucson: University of Arizona Press, 2003).

2. Pliny Earle Goddard, *Navajo Texts*, Anthropological Papers of the American Museum of Natural History 34, no. 1 (New York: American Museum of Natural History, 1933), 148.

3. Gary Witherspoon, *Language and Art in the Navajo Universe* (Ann Arbor: University of Michigan Press, 1977), 201.

4. Slim Curly, "Version I," in *Blessingway: With Three Versions of the Myth Recorded and Translated from the Navajo by Father Berard Haile, O.F.M.*, ed. Leland C. Wyman (Tucson: University of Arizona Press, 1970), 172.

5. Charlotte J. Frisbie, ed., with Rose Mitchell, *Tall Woman: The Life Story of Rose Mitchell, A Navajo Woman, c. 1874–1977* (Albuquerque: University of New Mexico Press, 2001), 208.

6. John Holiday and Robert S. McPherson, *A Navajo Legacy: The Life and Teachings of John Holiday* (Norman: University of Oklahoma Press, 2005), 368.

7. Slim Curly, "Blessingway," 239.

8. Frank Mitchell, "Version II," in *Blessingway: With Three Versions of the Myth Recorded and Translated from the Navajo by Father Berard Haile, O.F.M.*, ed. Leland C. Wyman (Tucson: University of Arizona Press, 1970), 385.

9. Ada Black, interview with author, February 2, 1994.

10. Ben Whitehorse, interview with author, January 30, 1991.

11. Florence Begay, interview with author, January 30, 1991.

12. Clyde Kluckhohn, W. W. Hill, and Lucy Wales Kluckhohn, *Navaho Material Culture* (Cambridge, MA: Harvard University Press, 1971), 119.

13. Charlotte J. Frisbie, *Food Sovereignty the Navajo Way, Cooking with Tall Woman* (Albuquerque: University of New Mexico Press, 2018), 92.

14. Aileen O'Bryan, *Navaho Indian Myths* (New York: Dover Publications, 1956, 1993), 37.

15. Franciscan Fathers, *An Ethnologic Dictionary of the Navajo Language* (Saint Michaels, AZ: Saint Michaels Press, 1910, 1968), 222.

16. O'Bryan, *Navaho Indian Myths*, 38; Ernest L. Bulow, *Navajo Taboos* (Gallup, NM: Southwesterner Books, 1982), 58.

Chapter Three

1. The most substantial discussion of the male puberty ceremony is given by Maureen Trudelle Schwarz, *Molded in the Image of Changing Woman: Navajo Views on the Human Body and Personhood* (Tucson: University of Arizona Press, 1997), 156–73.

2. River Junction Curly, "Version III," in *Blessingway: With Three Versions of the Myth Recorded and Translated from the Navajo by Father Berard Haile, O.F.M.*, ed. Leland C. Wyman (Tucson: University of Arizona Press, 1970), 529.

3. Ibid., 535.

4. Stanley A. Fishler, *In the Beginning: A Navaho Creation Myth*, University of Utah Anthropological Papers no. 13 (Salt Lake City: University of Utah Press, 1953), 48–51.

5. W. W. Hill, "Navaho Warfare," Yale University Publications in Anthropology, no. 5 (New Haven, CT: Yale University Press, 1936), 7.

6. W. W. Hill, "The Status of the Hermaphrodite and Transvestite in Navaho Culture," *American Anthropologist*, New Series, 37, no. 2 (April–June 1935): 273; John Holiday and Robert S. McPherson, *A Navajo Legacy: The Life and Teachings of John Holiday* (Norman: University of Oklahoma Press, 2005), 334; Schwarz, *Molded in the Image of Changing Woman*, 251.

7. Elsie Billie, interview with author, March 21, 1990.

8. Hill, "The Status of the Hermaphrodite and Transvestite in Navaho Culture," 273.

9. Franc Johnson Newcomb, *Hosteen Klah: Navaho Medicine Man and Sand Painter* (Norman: University of Oklahoma Press, 1964); see also Will Roscoe, "We'wha and Klah: The American Berdache as Artist and Priest," *American Indian Quarterly* 12, no. 2 (Spring 1988): 127–50.

10. Newcomb, *Hosteen Klah*, 97.

11. Hill, "The Status of the Hermaphrodite and Transvestite in Navaho Culture," 274–75.

12. Sabine Lang, *Men as Women, Women as Men: Changing Gender in Native American Cultures* (Austin: University of Texas Press, 1998), 72–73.

13. Holiday and McPherson, *A Navajo Legacy*, 274.

Chapter Four

1. Pliny Earle Goddard, *Navajo Texts*, Anthropological Papers of the American Museum of Natural History 34, no. 1 (New York: American Museum of Natural History, 1933), 139.

2. Walter Dyk, "Notes and Illustrations of Navajo Sex Behavior," in *Psychoanalysis and Culture, Essays in Honor of Gezá Róheim*, edited by George B. Wilbur and Warner Muensterberger (New York: International Universities Press, 1951), 108–19.

3. Walter Dyk, *Son of Old Man Hat, A Navaho Autobiography* (Lincoln: University of Nebraska Press, 1938, 1967); and Walter and Ruth Dyk, *Left Handed: A Navajo Autobiography* (New York: Columbia University Press, 1980).

4. Dyk, "Notes and Illustrations of Navajo Sex Behavior," 111.

5. Coyote tales lend themselves to many levels of discussion about forbidden behavior. Those stories told on an adult level may examine sexual promiscuity and acts ordinarily not mentioned with younger listeners. See Father Berard Haile, *Navajo Coyote Tales: The Curly Tó Aheedlíinii Version* (Lincoln: University of Nebraska Press, 1984).

6. John Holiday and Robert S. McPherson, *A Navajo Legacy: The Life and Teachings of John Holiday* (Norman: University of Oklahoma Press, 2005), 78.

7. Ibid., 74.

8. Ibid., 72–73. Deer are often associated with promiscuity and sex-related discussions. For further information, see pp. 333–34.

9. Aileen O'Bryan, *Navaho Indian Myths* (New York: Dover Publications, 1956, 1993), 75–77; see also Goddard, *Navajo Texts*, 153–55.

10. See Ruth Roessel, *Women in Navajo Society* (Rough Rock, Arizona: Navajo Resource Center, 1981); Kay Bennett, *Kaibah: Recollection of a Navajo Girlhood* (Self-published, 1975); and Charlotte J. Frisbie, ed., with Rose Mitchell, *Tall Woman: The Life Story of Rose Mitchell, A Navajo Woman, c. 1874–1977* (Albuquerque: University of New Mexico Press, 2001).

Chapter Five

1. William A. Haviland, *Anthropology*, Ninth Edition (New York: Harcourt College Publishers, 2000), 610.

2. Franciscan Fathers, *An Ethnologic Dictionary of the Navajo Language* (Saint Michaels, AZ: Saint Michaels Press, 1910, 1968), 356.

3. Gladys A. Reichard, *Social Life of the Navajo Indians, with Some Attention to Minor Ceremonies* (New York: Columbia University Press, 1928), 16–17.

4. Ibid., 14.

5. Ronald H. Towner, *Defending the Dinétah: Pueblitos in the Ancestral Navajo Homeland* (Salt Lake City: University of Utah Press, 2003), 204.

6. Robert M. Begay, "Exploring Navajo-Anaasází Relationships Using Traditional (Oral) Histories" (master's thesis, Northern Arizona University, Flagstaff, Arizona, May 2003), 67, 70.

7. Clyde Kluckhohn and Dorothea Leighton, *The Navaho* (Cambridge, MA: Harvard University Press, 1946, 1974), 111–13.

8. Franc Johnson Newcomb, *Navajo Omens and Taboos* (Santa Fe: Rydal Press, 1940), 20.

9. Often these two anthropological terms are misused by those who are not clear on their definition. Matrilineal refers to the mother's line and the importance that the society places on female descent. Matriarchal is connected with women ruling in a political sense. During the separation of the sexes, both men and women agreed that war and politics, among other things, were the domain of the male. At present, more and more women are

getting involved in these realms, and according to many traditionalists, this has created a number of contemporary problems.

10. Maureen Trudelle Schwarz, *Molded in the Image of Changing Woman: Navajo Views on the Human Body and Personhood* (Tucson: University of Arizona Press, 1997), 74.

11. Mary Shepardson and Blodwen Hammond, *The Navajo Mountain Community: Social Organization and Kinship Terminology* (Los Angeles: University of California Press, 1970); Louise Lamphere, *To Run After Them: Cultural and Social Bases of Cooperation in a Navajo Community* (Tucson: University of Arizona Press, 1977).

12. Gladys A. Reichard, *Spider Woman: A Story of Navajo Weavers and Chanters* (Albuquerque: University of New Mexico Press, 1934, 1997).

13. Charlotte J. Frisbie and David P. McAllester, *Navajo Blessingway Singer: The Autobiography of Frank Mitchell, 1881–1967* (Tucson: University of Arizona Press, 1978); Frisbie, ed., with Rose Mitchell, *Tall Woman: The Life Story of Rose Mitchell, A Navajo Woman, c. 1874–1977* (Albuquerque: University of New Mexico Press, 2001); Kay Bennett, *Kaibah: Recollection of a Navajo Girlhood* (Self-published, 1975).

14. Karen Toledo, paper on metaphors, January 11, 2008, used with permission, in possession of author.

Chapter Six

1. Martha A. Austin, Kenneth Y. Begishe, Betty Manygoats, Oswald Werner, June Werner, and others, "The Anatomical Atlas of the Navajo with Illustrations," unpublished paper provided by Oswald Werner with permission to cite (Evanston, IL: Northwestern University, 1971), 1–10.

2. Maureen Trudelle Schwarz, *Molded in the Image of Changing Woman: Navajo Views on the Human Body and Personhood* (Tucson: University of Arizona Press, 1997), 81–82.

3. Gladys A. Reichard, *Navaho Religion: A Study in Symbolism* (Princeton, NJ: Princeton University Press, 1950, 1974), 169–70.

4. John Holiday and Robert S. McPherson, *A Navajo Legacy: The Life and Teachings of John Holiday* (Norman: University of Oklahoma Press, 2005), 290–91.

5. Berard Haile, *The Upward Moving and Emergence Way: The Gishin Biye' Version* (Lincoln: University of Nebraska Press, 1981), 6.

6. Ibid., 23–26.

7. Charlotte J. Frisbie, ed., with Rose Mitchell, *Tall Woman: The Life Story of Rose Mitchell, A Navajo Woman, c. 1874–1977* (Albuquerque: University of New Mexico Press, 2001), 183–84.

8. Ibid., 259.

9. Maureen Trudelle Schwarz, *Blood and Voice, Navajo Women Ceremonial Practitioners* (Tucson: University of Arizona Press, 2003), 83, 85–86; Schwarz, *"I Choose Life," Contemporary Medical and Religious Practices in the Navajo World* (Norman: University of Oklahoma Press, 2008), 340.

Chapter Seven

1. Robert A. Trennert, *White Man's Medicine: Government Doctors and the Navajo, 1863–1955* (Albuquerque: University of New Mexico Press, 1998); Alexander H. Leighton and Dorothea C. Leighton, *The Navaho Door: An Introduction to Navaho Life* (Cambridge, MA: Harvard University Press, 1944, 1967).

2. Clyde Kluckhohn and Dorothea Leighton, *The Navaho* (Cambridge, MA: Harvard University Press, 1946, 1974), 192.

3. John Farella, *The Main Stalk, A Synthesis of Navajo Philosophy* (Tucson: University of Arizona Press, 1984).

4. Frank Mitchell, "Version II," in *Blessingway: With Three Versions of the Myth Recorded and Translated from the Navajo by Father Berard Haile, O.F.M.*, ed. Leland C. Wyman (Tucson: University of Arizona Press, 1970), 398.

5. Gary Witherspoon, *Language and Art in the Navajo Universe* (Ann Arbor: University of Michigan Press, 1977), 17–32.

6. Charlotte J. Frisbie and David P. McAllester, *Navajo Blessingway Singer: The Autobiography of Frank Mitchell, 1881–1967* (Tucson: University of Arizona Press, 1978), 155.

7. Charlotte J. Frisbie, ed., with Rose Mitchell, *Tall Woman: The Life Story of Rose Mitchell, A Navajo Woman, c. 1874–1977* (Albuquerque: University of New Mexico Press, 2001), 233.

8. Gladys A. Reichard, *Navaho Religion: A Study of Symbolism* (Princeton, NJ: University of Princeton Press, 1950, 1974), 122.

9. Ibid., 92.

10. Leighton, *The Navaho Door*, 77.

11. Frisbie, *Tall Woman*, 285.

12. Lori Arviso Alvord and Elizabeth Cohen Van Pelt, *The Scalpel and the Silver Bear: The First Navajo Surgeon Combines Western Medicine and Traditional Healing* (New York: Bantam Books, 1999), 114.

13. Ibid., 226; Frisbie and McAllester, *Navajo Blessingway Singer*, 313.

14. Reichard, *Navaho Religion*, 97.

15. John Holiday and Robert S. McPherson, *A Navajo Legacy: The Life and Teachings of John Holiday* (Norman: University of Oklahoma Press, 2005), 310–11.

16. Ibid., 148–49.

17. Maureen Trudelle Schwarz, *"I Choose Life," Contemporary Medical and Religious Practices in the Navajo World* (Norman: University of Oklahoma Press, 2008).

18. Reichard, *Navaho Religion*, 98.

19. Frisbie, *Tall Woman*, 303; Schwarz, *"I Choose Life,"* 83.

20. Frisbie, *Tall Woman*, 234; 260.

21. Ruth Roessel, *Women in Navajo Society* (Rough Rock, AZ: Navajo Resource Center, 1981), 61.

22. Dennis Fransted, "The Secular Uses of Traditional Religion and Knowledge in Modern Navajo Society," in *Navajo Religion and Culture: Selected Views—Papers in Honor of Leland C. Wyman*, edited by David M. Brugge and Charlotte J. Frisbie, Papers in Anthropology no. 17 (Santa Fe: Museum of New Mexico Press, 1982), 212.

Chapter Eight

1. Gladys A. Reichard, *Navaho Religion: A Study of Symbolism* (Princeton, NJ: University of Princeton Press, 1950, 1974), 454.

2. Ibid., 46–47.

3. John Holiday and Robert S. McPherson, *A Navajo Legacy: The Life and Teachings of John Holiday* (Norman: University of Oklahoma Press, 2005), 282.

4. Leland C. Wyman, *Blessingway: With Three Versions of the Myth Recorded and Translated from the Navajo by Father Berard Haile, O.F.M.* (Tucson: University of Arizona Press, 1970), 139.

5. Berard Haile in Wyman, *Blessingway*, 10.

6. Aileen O'Bryan, *Navaho Indian Myths* (New York: Dover Publications, 1956, 1993), 31–32.

7. Maureen Trudelle Schwarz, *Molded in the Image of Changing Woman: Navajo Views on the Human Body and Personhood* (Tucson: University of Arizona Press, 1997), 143.

8. Robert S. McPherson, Jim Dandy, and Sarah E. Burak, *Navajo Tradition, Mormon Life: The Autobiography and Teachings of Jim Dandy* (Salt Lake City: University of Utah Press, 2012), 238.

9. Franc Johnson Newcomb, *Navajo Omens and Taboos* (Santa Fe: Rydal Press, 1940), 75–79.

10. Holiday and McPherson, *A Navajo Legacy*, 371, 382.

11. Ibid., 383.

12. Robert S. McPherson, *The Journey of Navajo Oshley: An Autobiography and Life History* (Logan: Utah State University Press, 2000), 108–9.

13. Berard Haile, *Soul Concepts of the Navajo* (Saint Michaels, AZ: Saint Michaels Press, 1943, 1975).

Chapter Nine

1. Frank Mitchell, "Version II" in *Blessingway: With Three Versions of the Myth Recorded and Translated from the Navajo by Father Berard Haile, O.F.M.*, ed. Leland C. Wyman (Tucson: University of Arizona Press, 1970), 441.

2. Joseph E. Persico, "The Great Swine Flu Epidemic of 1918," *American Heritage* 27 (June 1976): 28.

3. Alfred W. Crosby, *America's Forgotten Pandemic: The Influenza of 1918* (New York: Cambridge University Press, 1989), 228.

4. Benjamin R. Brady and Howard M. Bahr, "The Influenza Epidemic of 1918–1920 among the Navajos: Marginality, Mortality, and the Implications of Some Neglected Eyewitness Accounts," in *American Indian Quarterly* 38, no. 4 (Fall 2014): 484; Persico, "The Great Swine Flu Epidemic," 84.

5. Gladys A. Reichard, *Navaho Religion: A Study of Symbolism* (Princeton, NJ: Princeton University Press, 1963), 19; Ada Black, interview with Bertha Parrish, June 18, 1987.

6. The color red signifies a number of beliefs in traditional Navajo thought. Reichard points out that when it is reversed from its normal role in sandpaintings, it can represent evil associated with lightning or storm. On the other hand, "white apparently differentiates the naturally sacred from the profane—black or red, for instance—which through exorcism and ritual, must be transformed to acquire favorable power." *Navaho Religion*, 182, 187. Thus, the red dawns and sunsets warned of the approach of evil, as opposed to having the white and yellow light associated with the normal beginning and end of day and the directions of east and west respectively.

7. Black, interview, 1–2; Rose Begay, interview with Bertha Parrish, June 17, 1987; Tallis Holiday, interview with author, November 3, 1987; Fred Yazzie, interview with author, November 5, 1987.

8. Scott C. Russell, "The Navajo and the 1918 Pandemic," *Health and Disease in the Prehistoric Southwest* (Tempe: Arizona State University, 1985), 385; Yazzie, interview.

9. Gilmore Graymountain, interview with Marilyn Holiday, April 7, 1992.

10. Franc Johnson Newcomb, *Hosteen Klah, Navaho Medicine Man and Sand Painter* (Norman: University of Oklahoma Press, 1964), 144–48.

11. Ada Black, interview with author, October 11, 1991.

12. Holiday, interview; Yazzie, interview; Begay, interview.

13. Hilda Faunce, *Desert Wife* (Lincoln: University of Nebraska Press, 1928), 301–2.

14. Charlotte J. Frisbie, ed., with Rose Mitchell, *Tall Woman, The Life of Rose Mitchell, A Navajo Woman c. 1874-1977* (Albuquerque: University of New Mexico Press, 2001), 128–29, 133–34.

15. Ibid., 130–34.

16. Ibid., 134–35.

17. David R. Harper and Andrea S. Meyer, *Of Mice, Men, and Microbes: Hantavirus* (New York: Academic Press/Harcourt Brace, 1999), 49–51.

18. CDC Hantavirus, "The First Outbreak," in "Tracking a Mystery Disease: The Detailed Story of Hantavirus Pulmonary Syndrome (HPS)," accessed April 16, 2020,
https://www.cdc.gov/hantavirus/outbreaks/history.html.

19. Ibid.

20. Harper and Meyer, *Of Mice, Men, and Microbes*, 6–8; Pete Herrera, "Vivacious Young Lives Cut Down by Mystery Disease," AP News, June 5, 1993,
https://apnews.com/article/60ebe3d1d7092eb11b978ee448a3fec0;
Paul Brinkley-Rogers, "Mysterious Disease Causing Fear, Frustration in a Navajo Settlement," *Chicago Tribune*, June 2, 1993,
https://www.chicagotribune.com/news/ct-xpm-1993-06-02-9306030382-story.html.

21. Lori Arviso Alvord and Elizabeth Cohen Van Pelt, *The Scalpel and the Silver Bear, The First Navajo Woman Surgeon Combines Western Medicine and Traditional Healing* (New York: Bantam Books, 1999), 122–23.

22. Linda Moon Stumpff, *Hantavirus and the Navajo Nation—A Double-Jeopardy Disease* (Olympia, WA: Evergreen State College, 2010), 4, 10, downloaded on June 2, 2020, from
http://nativecases.evergreen.edu/sites/nativecases.evergreen.edu/files/case-studies/Stumpff%20hantavirus.pdf.

23. Maureen Trudelle Schwarz, *Navajo Lifeways: Contemporary Issues, Ancient Knowledge* (Norman: University of Oklahoma Press, 2001).

24. Ibid., 38.

25. "Tracking a Mystery Disease."

26. Stephanie J. Leuenroth, *Deadly Diseases and Epidemics: Hantavirus Pulmonary Syndrome* (New York: Chelsea House Publishing, 2006), 18.

27. Ibid.; Stumpff, *Hantavirus and the Navajo Nation*, 2.

28. Schwarz, *Navajo Lifeways*, 71.

29. Ibid., 73, 89, 97.

30. Ibid., 88.

31. See Navajo Nation Coronavirus website at https://www.ndoh.navajo-nsn.gov/COVID-19/News-Update for further information.

32. Ibid.

33. Sunnie R. Clahchischilgi, "The Navajo Nation and Coronavirus: Planting Hope Amid the Plague," downloaded on June 4, 2020, from https://www.rollingstone.com/culture/culture-features/navajo-nation-coronavirus-planting-hope-amid-a-plague-1009255/. Navajo Nation Coronavirus website at https://www.ndoh.navajo-nsn.gov/COVID-19/News-Update, accessed August 28, 2020.

34. Perry Robinson, telephone conversation with author, March 27, 2020.

35. Gladys A. Reichard, "Distinctive Features of Navaho Religion," in *Southwestern Journal of Anthropology* 1, no. 2 (Summer 1945): 209.

36. Rima Krisst, "Surviving the Coronavirus Crisis: Diné Perspectives" *Navajo Times* downloaded March 25, 2020, in https://navajotimes.com/coronavirus-updates/surviving-the-coronavirus-crisis-dine-perspectives.

37. Clahchischilgi, "The Navajo Nation and Coronavirus."

38. Barre Toelken, "The Hózhǫ́ Factor: The Logic of Navajo Healing," in Toelken Files, Special Collections, Merrill-Cazier Library, Utah State University, Logan, Utah, 13–14.

39. Ibid., 20.

Index

217